RED
ZONE

ALSO BY APHRODITE JONES

...THE BEHIND-THE-SCENES
STORY OF THE SAN FRANCISCO
DOG MAULING

APHRODITE JONES

RED ZONE

wm | WILLIAM ⟨…⟩ Collins*Publishers*

HarperCollins books may be purchased for educational, business, or sales promotional use. For information please write: Special Markets Department, HarperCollins Publishers Inc., 10 East 53rd Street, New York, NY 10022.

FIRST EDITION

Designed by Nicola Ferguson

Printed on acid-free paper

Library of Congress Cataloging-in-Publication Data
Jones, Aphrodite.
Red zone : the behind-the-scenes story of the San Francisco dog mauling / Aphrodite Jones.—1st ed.
   p.   cm.
ISBN 0-06-053779-5
1. Murder—California—San Francisco—Case studies.
2. Dog attacks—California—San Francisco.
3. Liability for animals—California—San Francisco.
4. Whipple, Diane, 1968–2001. I. Title.
HV6534.S3J66 2003
364.15'23'0979461—dc21   2003048768

03 04 05 06 07 WBC / QW 10 9 8 7 6 5 4 3 2 1

To Diane Alexis Whipple,

whose sacrifice forces us to think about

the relationship of Man and Animal,

and consider our responsibility to animals,

first on a domestic level, then globally

The beast was given a mouth uttering haughty and blasphemous words, and it was allowed to exercise authority for forty-two months. It opened its mouth to utter blasphemies against God, blaspheming his name and his dwelling, that is, those who dwell in heaven. Also it was allowed to make war on the saints and to conquer them. It was given authority over every tribe and people and language and nation, and all the inhabitants of the earth will worship it, everyone whose name has not been written from the foundation of the world in the book of life of the Lamb that was slaughtered.

—REVELATION 13:5–8

RED
ZONE

Esther Birkmaier held her breath as she walked toward the peephole of her heavy wooden door. It was a small peephole that allowed her to look at a person's face on the other side, and she was headed there because she could hear strange wild barking. She had gotten up from her dining room table to see what all the racket was, her heart pounding as she moved her head closer inch by inch.

Ever since she was a kid, Esther was afraid of dogs, especially large dogs, and this barking coming from the other end of the hall was giving her a sick feeling. It sounded frantic, but also eerie, and it reminded her of the terrible incident she had with a dog when she was a child. Esther was a frail seventy-something woman, living alone, and strange noises always bothered her. Usually she had nothing to worry about, but this crazed howling was different. It had an energy attached to it that scared her to death.

As Esther stood straining to see out of her peephole, the barking getting progressively worse, she realized it sounded like there were two dogs out there. But she couldn't see them. She had no vision of the ground directly outside her doorway, so she kept scanning the hallway for any kind of image, hoping to catch some kind of glimpse.

The barking and growling was ferocious. Esther couldn't imagine what was going on. It sounded like grumblings. It sounded like wild beasts. Then all of a sudden she heard a voice cry out:

"Help me . . ."

And even with the barking getting louder and louder and more vicious, Esther heard the voice again:

"Help me . . ."

At that moment Esther's eyes moved toward the other end of the hallway where she could see a body lying on the floor. She could barely make it out, but it appeared to be a woman's body, a woman's body with white clothes, and it was lying on the floor with the top of the head on the threshold of apartment 606. Esther could see the woman's head there and she could see the top part of the body, just about to the waist, but she couldn't see anything more. It appeared the woman was lying facedown, but Esther couldn't be sure. There was a peculiar dark object that covered the rest of the body, and all Esther could identify was lumps of long blond hair.

The dark object that covered the body was not human, at least Esther didn't think so. The dark form seemed to cover the middle part of the woman's body, and Esther kept watching but she wasn't sure what it was she was looking at. Everything looked fuzzy and far away, distorted through the narrow scope of her peephole.

What was weird was that the dark object was very still, the woman's body was very still, yet there was still loud barking coming from the hallway. Esther was shaking, her heart pounding, and she took a step back from the door and tried to compose herself. Then she took a deep breath, went over to her kitchen, and grabbed the phone.

911:	What's your emergency?
ESTHER:	There are dogs barking in my hallway and it's very loud. . . . I don't know if anyone is hurt . . . but.
911:	Well, is it an emergency, ma'am?
ESTHER:	I'm really not sure.
911:	If it's not an emergency, ma'am, you should call your local police department.

Esther tried dialing the local number 911 dispatch had given her, but she had no time to wait for someone to pick up. She was getting increasingly panicked as the barking suddenly moved closer to her front door. The next thing she knew, there were bodies crashing against her apartment, there was banging, such hard banging, that Esther thought the crashing might break her door down.

Without thinking, Esther ran back to her door, the crashing getting more furious, and she took a split second to look out again. This time, she could see nothing but groceries scattered out in the hallway. Esther quickly latched the inside chain to her door, hoping that would hold off the wild pounding, hoping the dogs wouldn't break into her apartment. If the door started to break down, she decided, the chain would at least give her enough time to lock herself into her bathroom.

When Esther grabbed the phone a second time to dial 911, the loud banging in the background was obvious, and now she told police she was sure someone was being attacked. She reported that she heard a woman's shrill voice outside yelling, "Get off! Get off!" and told the dispatcher it was the voice of her longtime neighbor, Marjorie, who owned two very large scary dogs. This time Esther didn't need to say anything more. Police were being sent to the scene right away.

Esther went near her front door one last time, hoping the growling and barking and snarling would stop. But it was endless, it seemed, and it made her heart pound right out of her chest. For Esther, it seemed like an eternity, and police had still not arrived. She was beyond panic, praying that *someone* would get there, when all of a sudden Esther heard a voice giving commands.

"Stop it!" the voice shrieked. "I said stop it!"

And all at once, the barking, the banging, the snarling, all of it just stopped.

There was nothing but dead silence.

It was quiet when Esther went to her window. She just stood there waiting for police. At first, it must have seemed surreal, as though everything was happening in black and white. Esther stayed glued to her window as she watched two policewomen pull up to her building. It would feel like forever, but eventually a half-dozen patrol units would arrive and park downstairs on Pacific.

When Officers Leslie Forrestal and Sidney Laws approached the interior of the building, they had no idea what to expect. Ten-year veterans of the San Francisco Police Department, they were used to responding to violent situations, but this one was tricky, much more dangerous. They had two out-of-control dogs running around on the sixth floor and they were heading to rescue a victim—without the backup of Animal Care and Control.

In the lobby, Forrestal and Laws quickly split up their turf. Forrestal rode the elevator and Laws took the stairs. As it happened, they were traveling at almost the same speed, so when they hit the fifth floor, Forrestal could hear Laws yelling, "Hey, I just saw one dog run past me!"

The building had an old-type elevator that locked into each landing. Officer Forrestal landed on six and had to wait until the mechanism locked before she could open the heavy door. The officer was not prepared for what she saw.

There was a woman lying facedown in the hallway. Her head was just to the right of the elevator, close to the elevator door. She was naked, lying in a large pool of blood, much of it just below her neck. There was blood up and down the hallway . . . there were bloody handprints on the walls . . . there were shreds of bloody clothing and groceries . . . bits of hair and flesh in clumps.

As Forrestal and Laws both witnessed, the victim attempted to raise herself up from her torso, attempted to do a push-up and raise her body a few inches off the floor. The victim had lost almost half of her blood, but she still had enough strength and presence to try to get herself to safety. The victim was trying to crawl toward her open apartment door.

Laws called in a Code 3—emergency mode.

"Just lie still and be calm until the ambulance arrives," Forrestal whispered.

The victim made a motion. There was a slight element of response, and acknowledgment that she could hear.

As Forrestal leaned down, whispering in the victim's ear, the woman ceased her attempt to crawl. The victim was just beginning to relax her body when a heavy wooden door opened directly to Forrestal's left. The officer didn't turn her head to see, she didn't want to take her concentration off the victim, but she could hear a woman's voice asking some kind of question. The voice was Esther's. Now that police arrived, Esther had gathered the courage to open her door and was trying to see what went on.

"Ma'am, please close the door and stay inside," Forrestal ordered, never turning around.

Esther was helpless. All she could do was go back to her window. But now things were different. Esther had seen the mass of blood on the carpet. She couldn't be sure about what had happened in the hall, but in the quick glimpse, she had seen too much.

Through her peephole, Esther had seen the open door across the hall, the door of apartment 606. Now, with a wider view, she realized there were keys stuck in the door and a woman's purse out in the hallway. Esther didn't want to think about it. There were so many bloody handprints. It was so ghastly out there, with a woman lying naked, just shredded to pieces.

Ever more frightened, Esther tried to surmise who the victim was. She thought it had to be one of her neighbors, but the poor woman out there was too bloody and battered to recognize.

Esther stared through her window and watched the action on Pacific Avenue. By then, two vans from Animal Care and Control showed up, a rescue truck from the Fire Department was arriving, then there were more police units blocking off most of the area.

Men and women in uniform began to fill the street. There were CSI teams. Then more paramedics. Suddenly, Pacific Avenue was just a series of big red swirling lights.

Just seconds before the backup units arrived, a haggard woman emerged from down the hall. She was leaving apartment 604, to the right of the elevator. She was wild-looking, with her hair all matted up, damp and stringy, wet with blood. She was Caucasian, maybe in her midforties, and was just covered . . . dark red all over her clothes, her hands, her shoes.

Something about the woman's face struck Forrestal as odd. The blood covering the face looked like a reddish brown mask, a real fright, but beyond that, it seemed like someone had painted the blood on the lady's face—not in blotches, but in evenly spread strokes.

The wild-eyed woman focused only on Forrestal. Ignoring the victim, she began talking in midstream, kind of explaining what took place before the horrible attack. The woman was mumbling and bumbling, uttering things to Forrestal. She said she had just come back from taking her dog out on a walk . . . and the door to her apartment was open . . . and she was putting her dog inside her apartment . . . and her larger dog, the male . . . went to attack the woman at the end of the hall. Somehow, both of her dogs had gotten out in the hallway. Her female dog was tugging at the victim's pants. Her male dog had gone for the victim's throat.

"Where are your dogs now?" Forrestal asked calmly.

"They're in my apartment, locked away."

"Okay. Why don't you just wait here a few minutes," the officer suggested.

"No, I think I'd rather go back. The dogs are secure. I need to go back."

Forrestal was listening but she was also paying attention to the radio traffic. The SFPD crew was on their way up. She could hear teams pounding up the stairway and yelling through the elevator shaft. Her backup couldn't have arrived at a better moment. Forrestal knew they'd have to jump—they needed to keep this crazed dog owner at bay. There was no way they could allow her to open apartment 604. They couldn't chance a renewal of the attack.

Forrestal yelled over to one of the sergeants, and police herded the dog owner in a delicate way, directing the woman to have a seat on the floor. Police didn't want anyone interfering with the trauma scene. Animal Care and Control officers would know best how to secure the dogs inside, police assured, and the ACC officers were headed up the stairs. They were already halfway up, with their come-along poles and tranquilizer guns.

The victim was lying very quiet, waiting. Lying facedown.

As the elevator door opened again on the sixth floor, two medics from the SWAT team, Officers Alec Cardenas and Steve Glickman, were shocked by the sheer brutality she suffered. A large chunk of flesh and muscle tissue was missing from the left side of her neck. She was bleeding profusely from the jugular, blood just gushing out. The men immediately went into overdrive, preparing to save the woman's life, ready to start first aid or any medical help they could.

"You got me!" Cardenas yelled to his partner.

Glickman acknowledged, watching his partner's back.

Cardenas applied direct pressure to the wound, which somewhat stopped the blood flow, but he couldn't press too hard, afraid he might stop her breathing. Then Cardenas bent down and shook the woman's shoulder.

"Ma'am, can you hear me?"

The woman made a purposeful sound.

"I'm Al, I'm here to help you. This is what I'm going to do. I'm going to turn you over, okay?"

The woman made another purposeful sound.

Cardenas called Glickman over to help because he wanted to keep her neck straight. He knew the woman could hear him, and he spoke in medical terminology as a way to assure her that she was getting appropriate help. With a calm voice he told her that he was maintaining a C-spine consideration so he wouldn't interrupt her breathing.

Cardenas held the woman's head and shoulders as best he could—his partner grabbed her around the hips—and they managed to flip her on her back.

The woman made another sound and Cardenas felt for a pulse. The pulse was very shallow, but she was breathing, and there was a pulse.

"I'm just going to try to maintain your breathing, okay?" Cardenas promised. "The ambulance is on the way, and we'll have help here as soon as possible."

Cardenas continued to monitor her, taking her pulse, making sure her chest was rising, checking her breathing. It was the strangest thing, seeing this woman stripped totally naked, seeing all her clothing lying around in shreds, seeing small clumps of hair in among her groceries. Cardenas was mortified, and then suddenly he lost the pulse, he lost the breathing. In a panic, he bent over to administer rescue breathing.

At that very moment Cardenas got hit in the tail by the elevator door. It was the paramedics from the Fire Department, who took over right away and luckily were able to get a pulse back.

The woman was still alive.

As an EMT worked on her, the elevator door opened again and Animal Control Officer Andrea Runge appeared. She was working alone that day and was responding to a call that two large dogs were running loose.

Runge hesitated briefly, trying to assess the situation, but she was devastated. Here was this person ripped apart, stripped nude by animals, just steps in front of her. But it looked like the EMT was handling it, and Runge realized there was nothing she could do to further help. She turned her attention to the police officers talking to a woman at the north end of the hall, for that instant putting the horrible scene out of her mind. Runge had to focus on the dogs. She needed to find out where the dogs were and get them under control.

The lady at the other end of the hallway was crouched down, staring at the police. She wasn't really talking; she wasn't offering much information at all.

"I'm here to get two aggressive dogs," Runge announced. "Who owns the dogs?"

"My husband and I do," the woman answered, continuing to slump.

"Have the dogs ever bitten anyone before?"

"No."

"Have they ever been aggressive before?"

"Not toward humans."

Officer Runge wanted to follow standard procedure. She needed to take the dogs into custody so they could be humanely destroyed at the animal shelter. Runge asked the lady to sign over a form giving the city and county legal custody of the animals, but the crouched woman refused to sign over the female. She would sign over the male, but not the female, and she became emphatic with the Animal Control officer.

"The female had nothing to do with the attack," she insisted. "I can't sign her over because she wasn't involved. All she did was tug at the pants."

Runge handed over a Release and Surrender Form but the woman did not want to bother filling the paperwork out.

"What is the dog's name?" Runge asked, taking it back, filling it out herself.

"Bane."

"And is he registered in San Francisco?"

"I'm not sure. My husband would take care of that."

After a brief pause, the woman signed over her male dog. Bane was surrendered to be destroyed by Animal Control. Apparently, she was afraid of him. She did not want to see him again.

But the lady was still refusing to sign over the female. Runge had no choice but to inform her that they would be taking the female into custody regardless. It was standard procedure. The animal would have to be examined for disposition.

"Would you be willing to take the dogs out to our van?" Runge wanted to know.

The dog owner didn't answer.

"Are you able to take the dogs downstairs?" the officer pressed.

"No. I-I can't do that," the lady stammered. "I can't handle them."

By that time Runge's co-workers had arrived on six. They immediately approached apartment 604, accompanied by a police officer with his gun drawn.

Before it was over, it would take numerous tranquilizer darts, three highly skilled Animal Care and Control officers, and experienced members of SFPD to get those dogs out of that apartment.

CHAPTER TWO

As soon as the victim was transported to San Francisco General, while the dogs were still inside apartment 604, EMT Cardenas walked up to the frazzled lady down the hall to see if she was okay.

"I'm a paramedic with the San Francisco Police," Cardenas said, "and I notice that you have bites all over your arms and hands."

The woman nodded her head at him, her face a bit contorted.

"In a situation like this, you can be so out of it that you don't realize that you're hurt," he explained. "You're not really in touch with your own body, and you don't realize that you might have a nice big wound somewhere."

Cardenas told her that he needed to do a secondary survey assessment. She had a loose sweatshirt on, and the paramedic explained that he needed to determine the bite marks, but because she was covered in blood, he would need her cooperation.

The lady was fine with that. Cardenas wanted her to sit down on the floor and she complied. He said he would do a real quick examination, and he needed her to take off her shirt.

"Do you have a bra on, ma'am?"

"I don't, but I was an EMT," she told him, "so I know exactly what you're doing. I don't have a problem with it."

And, bam, the woman's sweatshirt came off.

Cardenas took a quick medical look and saw that there were no additional bites and that there was nothing bad at all in the way of cuts.

"Okay, thank you very much, ma'am. You can put your shirt back on."

Cardenas thought the woman might be in a bit of a shock. He offered her ambulance services, but she refused. Now that he was down near her apartment, he could hear the dogs barking and growling behind the door. Cardenas didn't like the sound of it, they seemed so aggressive.

"Who owns those dogs, ma'am?" he asked.

"Those are my dogs."

"Well, are you sure you're okay?"

"Yeah. I just have these few bites on my fingers."

"How did that happen, ma'am?"

"I got them when I threw myself down on the victim," she said. "I was trying to get between the dog and the victim."

"You know, you might be a little shocky, and we'd be happy to take you down to SF General and have you checked out," Cardenas offered again.

"No, that's all right. I don't think I have any puncture wounds."

All around 2398 Pacific Avenue there was yellow tape—Police Line Do Not Cross. Up on the sixth floor, an SFPD officer was filling in a crime scene log that included one victim, one suspect, fifteen SFPD officers, two CSI people, three ACC officers, six paramedics, and two neighbors. The scene was gory, with medical devices and debris now also left behind in the mix.

Inspectors Mike Becker and Rich Daniele were on call that afternoon when they got paged by the operations center. Two top detectives with the SFPD General Works Department, Becker and Daniele were seasoned police who handled anything serious, just short of homicide. They dealt with hard-core violent attacks involving shootings and stabbings, things like that. So when they were called by operations and informed of a dog attack in an apartment building in Pacific Heights, a swank neighborhood near the Presidio, one of the most expensive addresses in town, they thought it really bizarre.

First of all, the General Works unit didn't handle dog bites—that was the job of Animal Care and Control, a separate city agency that had SFPD on staff. Pacific Heights was not the kind of neighborhood where dogfights might happen. The type of people in Pacific Heights were primarily yuppies, the kind who had pedicured dogs, the kind who used fancy doggy accessories. Becker and Daniele couldn't understand why a dog bite would call for an investigation by detectives. It was something they probably didn't have to handle, but they wanted to check it out, regardless.

It was the Friday night of what had been a long week. They would go off duty at six, and both had families to go home to. When they received the page at 5:02 P.M., they were on another crime scene. They wrapped that up, jumped in their car, and made their way across town in rush-hour traffic.

As they arrived on the scene and saw the ambulance and fire trucks, they realized this was serious. Immediately, the inspectors were on it—getting as much information as possible from the uniformed patrol officers out on the street.

Becker and Daniele rode the elevator up to Six, where they met with Crime Scene Investigators who were in the process of getting everything locked down. The area was cordoned off, the hallway was a mess, the floor just covered with blood. There were grocery bags down one end of the hall—and a woman with a bloody face staring at a few uniformed officers down the other. Becker didn't waste too much time with CSI. He needed to befriend this woman. He wanted her statement, and he wanted it on tape.

"Ma'am, I'm Inspector Michael Becker with the San Francisco Police, and I wonder if you'd like to talk to me?"

"Well, I already gave the other officers everything they need," she said, her voice giving away her annoyance.

"I understand you spoke with the officers and you gave them your name, your last name and first name. Is it Marjorie, is that right?"

"Yes, it is."

"And your last name is Knoller, I believe?"

"Yeah. You know, I'm really sorry. I just don't feel like talking to anyone right now," Knoller said coldly. "Like I said, I've already given my information to an officer here."

Becker was fully aware of that. He knew the dog owner was calling it an accident. He had been briefed by law enforcement as to the possible culpability of the dog owner and had placed a call to his lieutenant, who was on the way down. There had never been a precedent for this type of case in San Francisco. There had never been an adult seriously mauled by a dog that Becker was aware of. He was told that there was a strong chance that the victim wouldn't make it, but even if the victim did survive, uniformed police believed that serious charges should be brought against the dog owners. Over the radio, Becker had been told by his lieutenant to handle it. It was now officially Becker and Daniele's case.

Initially, it wasn't being treated as a homicide case—there was no evidence of malice, the victim was still alive, and there was this strange fact that the incident was caused by an animal, not a human. It was an odd situation.

Becker later recalled, "When I first saw Knoller at the scene, she told me twice she didn't want to talk to me. She was angry with the uniforms . . . that's what she was mad about. She was just mad that she was being treated as a suspect already, and she felt put out by that."

Becker had a way about him. He talked to Knoller in a very compassionate manner, addressing the cuts to her hands, getting her to feel sorry for herself. Becker noticed that Knoller had a contusion over her right eye. He wanted to know if she was all right. He walked her down the hall, away from the other officers, and began to slowly calm her nerves.

Becker was hoping he'd be able to coax Knoller into her apartment, telling her she should put ice on her eye, playing to her own sense of victimization. Becker was able to sweet-talk Knoller a little bit, convincing her that he was on her side and that he was on a routine check in the neighborhood. Becker said that he and his partner considered this a tragic accident. Neither inspector ever referred to the incident as a crime. Not at all.

Becker and Daniele made a great impression on Knoller. Both of them were attractive and, despite their starched white shirts, jackets, and ties, they seemed easygoing, cool, and calm. They were likable, they were the kind of guys who were hard to say no to. Becker was soft-spoken; Daniele came across as sympathetic. They didn't seem like hard-core police. They were more like big brothers who were there to serve and protect.

The inspectors knew it would only be a matter of time before they would break Knoller's wall down. And they were close, they were just at the point of getting Marjorie into her apartment, when all of a sudden, the elevator door opened and Knoller's husband, Robert Noel, appeared.

Robert Noel had no idea what was going on when he returned home late Friday afternoon. When he turned onto Pacific Avenue, he was confronted with the SWAT teams, police cars, his whole building was teeming with cops. Noel couldn't get down his own street, but he got close enough to notice Animal Care and Control vans. Immediately, he presumed the worst—someone from a government agency had come to cause more problems with his dogs.

Despite the commotion, Robert was able to pull over just shy of his building, unnoticed. He was watching to see what was going to develop. His whole ride home, he had a strange feeling something was wrong. He had been trying to reach Marjorie from his cell, but the phone just kept ringing off the hook, which made absolutely no sense. Marjorie wasn't supposed to be going anywhere. She was working at their office in the apartment.

Suddenly, Robert saw his prized guard dog, Bane, being led out by men and women in uniforms. That was when he decided it was time to get inside his building. He was clever enough to find a way to navigate around the blocked-off street without being detected, and he entered the building in stealth, using the back-door garage.

Robert hid in the back stairwell, just a few feet from the action in the lobby, listening to law enforcement on their radios. He was trying to assess the situation. For years, he and his wife had been the victims of secret surveillance, they had been hassled by law enforcement, and he distrusted cops. He and his wife were both defense attorneys who made a career of fighting the corrupt justice system—and because Robert was so brazen, he and Bane had already been the victims of a dog attack that he blamed on the California Department of Corrections.

Now, standing perfectly still in his back staircase, Robert waited in the shadows to see what kind of information he could pick up. Robert had reason to feel paranoid about law enforcement. He and his wife had been raided numerous times. And in recent months, he had evidence that he and his clients were being followed by the Special Service Unit of the Department of Corrections. Noel didn't really care that his clients were being monitored, but now someone was fucking with his dogs. He wanted to listen as long as possible so he could stand a better chance to fight whoever it was in court.

When Robert heard a dog growling, along with a team of footsteps that came rushing down the stairwell, he poked his head out from the garage in time to see Hera being led away by police. It confirmed his theory that law enforcement was there to cause him problems, to play more games, to harass him with trumped-up violations against himself, his wife, and his clients.

Robert was steaming. He was waiting to hear what would happen next, and just then, he overheard a brief conversation.

"What do you think happened to that woman?" a voice asked.

"Do you think that woman is dead?" another asked.

"Who knows?" someone responded. "To me, she looked pretty bad."

Robert's heart jumped. He was sure it was Marjorie.

A chill went up his spine.

He waited until the lobby cleared a bit more, he didn't want to chance being detected by the cops, then he heard the elevator mechanism stop at the lobby. Quietly, Robert Noel found the opportunity to sneak upstairs and see things for himself.

When he arrived on his own floor, he couldn't believe his eyes.

All the gore. It was overwhelming. It was out of a horror movie.

"It was like walking into a slaughterhouse," he would later comment. "The crime scene photos didn't do it justice. There was a spray of blood everywhere."

15

Robert glanced past the CSI units, the bloody walls, and the cops with guns. . . . Looking down toward his apartment, he was incredibly relieved to see Marjorie. She was by their front door talking to two plainclothes guys . . . but then her strange appearance started to register with him.

What the fuck? was all Robert kept thinking.

"Marjorie was glistening," he recalled. "She was covered with blood. It was like the scene from *Carrie* where Sissy Spacek has a bucket of blood thrown on her. Her hair was dark with blood, her face was soaked, her hands were covered, she was just glistening deep red."

Robert went over to give his wife a hug. He didn't know what else to do. He could see she was in shock and he wanted to comfort her. He had been in Martinez that day, working on a court case. On his way back, he was delayed a few hours because of a flat tire. He felt awful about that. He should have been home hours before.

"Don't touch me!" Marjorie yelped. And Robert complied. He really had no idea what could have happened to her. His wife looked like she had been run over by a truck.

Becker and Daniele introduced themselves, explaining that there had been an accident, showing Robert the contusion to Marjorie's eye and the cuts to her hands. Becker wanted to take pictures, and Robert thought that was a good idea. Becker had one of the Crime Scene Investigators come over to take a few quick snapshots of the black eye. Becker also suggested that Noel check his wife over for puncture wounds.

Obviously, his wife had been in some kind of struggle, and Noel was anxious to hear about it, so he led the inspectors inside his apartment, where they all could have a closer look at Marjorie's injuries.

Once inside, Marjorie remained pretty calm and quiet. She looked at her eye in the mirror and allowed Robert to take a closer look at her injuries. The inspectors were surprised by Knoller's cool, calm demeanor.

As she spoke, Marjorie was matter-of-fact about the altercation in the hall. She said she would allow the inspectors to turn on a recorder, though she insisted she didn't have much to say. Robert just sat quietly and listened, having no idea what Marjorie would tell them.

It seemed clear to him, however, regarding the attack, that his wife was somehow a victim. He was pretty confident about that. And even under these dramatic circumstances, he was glad to see that she wasn't breaking down with the police. Marjorie was handling herself well, and Robert expected nothing different from her. His wife was a very strong woman.

"In the thirteen years I've known Marjorie, she has cried very rarely," Robert reflected. "She's not one to emote. She's the type to hold everything in."

"I'm Inspector Becker of the SFPD, with me is Inspector Daniele. The date is January 26, 2001. The time is about ten minutes to six in the evening. I'm here at 2398 Pacific Avenue, apartment 604, speaking with Marjorie Knoller. Would you please spell your last name for me?"

"K-n-o-l-l-e-r."

"Okay. Now, taking you back to about 3:45 in the afternoon, would you just tell me what happened to the best of your ability?"

"I had opened the apartment door. I was coming back from a walk. I had the dog restrained, on lead. And the female dog, who lives here as well, barked. And then he saw the woman at the end of the hallway and reacted to her negatively."

Becker and Daniele sat at the kitchen table, listening intently. Noel stood in the corner of the room, quiet, like a giant fly on the wall.

"And I was trying to get him back into the apartment," Knoller continued, "but he is a rather strong dog."

"About how big is he?" Becker asked.

"About 125 pounds. Solid muscle."

"And what kind of dog?"

"He is a Perro de Presa Canario," she said, using the Spanish pronunciation. "They're members of the mastiff family and they come from the Canary Islands. A very rare breed of dog."

"And his name is?"

"Bane."

"Just to get an idea," Becker asked, "how far is your doorway to where . . . all the way down where she was?"

"I can't estimate."

"But you were holding on to a lead and it's a six-foot lead—"

"Yes. And I was holding on to it and the harness as well, and I was trying to restrain him. As I was going down the hallway, then there was a point in time where I could no longer hold him. And that's when he jumped on the female."

"And the female is your neighbor down the hallway?" Becker asked.

"Yeah. Right in front of her door."

"And then he commenced to attack?"

"I'm not sure what he did," Knoller stammered. "You know . . . in terms of . . . his reaction, I'm not sure what he did. But once . . . she's in the apartment . . . I believe that's when he started to try to bite her."

"And was she screaming in reaction at the time?"

"Actually, I was the one who screamed."

"Okay. And you were yelling at your dog, Bane, trying to get him to come back?"

"Well, I was trying to get him to respond to me."

"Right . . ."

"To control him," Knoller said.

"Okay, to get him to listen to you. Did the woman's door open at her apartment?"

"Yes. We were in her apartment originally. When he jumped on her, she had opened her door and I tried to get her into her apartment, and I believe that's when she was on the floor. I believe that's when the attack had started. I don't know . . ."

Just then a cell phone started ringing and Daniele answered in order not to disturb Becker, but everyone in the room could hear the frenzy of radio police traffic coming through. It was a bad time for a phone to interrupt because Knoller could change her mind about talking at any point, and Daniele could see that Noel was studying her every word, ready to give her the cut-off signal at the first hint of culpability.

However, Becker didn't let the interruption stop him, not for a second.

While Daniele took care of his police business quickly, slightly moving away from the table, Becker stayed right on Knoller, keeping calm, and more important, keeping Knoller calm. It was as if Becker kept the conversation going in an isolated capsule, holding everything else in the world back.

So Knoller continued:

"I don't know exactly what happened in the hallway, to the victim. I was trying to get her into the apartment and get him off her and out of the apartment."

"Okay. Now, the victim is on the ground, and the dog is over her, and you stated earlier that you put your body between your dog and the victim, right?"

"Correct."

"Attempting to stop the dog from biting the person?"

"Correct."

"Okay. And at some point, you were successful?"

"Yes. Right. And each time as he tried to get to her, I got him off her, as best I could," Knoller stated. "Every time I moved, or she tried to move away from me, he would renew his attack on her. But as long as I was between him and her, he wouldn't do anything."

"Okay. And, if she started to try to get up and move away, he would start the attack?"

"Right. Anytime she tried moving away from me, my physical body being on top of hers, she would renew the attack. . . ."

Becker and Daniele sat very quiet. Knoller had said "she." They both caught it. Either Knoller was implying that the victim was at fault, or Knoller slipped, and was perhaps referring to the female dog involved, Hera. Becker and Daniele just let her ramble to see what would come up.

". . . my female, the female dog, was also out in the hallway, I believe, pulling at her clothing, on the bottom of her leg. The clothing . . ."

"Okay. Now, was the victim brought down the hallway by the dog?"

"Yes," Knoller said, pausing. "Well, actually, not by the dog. By trying to get her into a safe area, which I looked at as the elevator. She was trying to crawl toward the elevator so that . . . we could open the door and get her in there."

"Okay."

"Each time that she would move her body away from my body, he would renew his attack on her."

"Okay. And you don't know why, though?"

"I have no idea what precipitated it. No. I've never seen this kind of behavior with him . . . uh . . . he's very friendly and open with people," she stammered. "I'm generally not the one who has walked him . . . um . . . Mr. Noel is usually the one."

Knoller was getting edgy. She was looking at her husband for a sign and Noel could see his wife was a bit uncomfortable. She had only agreed to talk for a few moments on tape, to make a brief, brief statement. She wanted to talk about her wounds, for the record. That was really what she was interested in. She had agreed to talk, for the most part, because she wanted it known that she made a very heroic attempt to save the victim.

Now she was eyeballing the clock.

She wanted the police to get out. She was clamming.

Becker took the cue. He would wind things down.

"And you had Bane and the female since September of last year?"

"No. We had Bane since September of 2000 and the female has been living with us here since May."

"Okay. The female's been here since May."

"Correct."

"All right. And no problems between the two?"

"No."

"Okay. And, just about the victim, a couple of questions. Do you remember where she was attacked at?"

"Um . . . initially what I remember . . . the neck and her head."

"Okay. And the other dog was just pulling at the clothing?"

Knoller paused.

"The female dog?"

"Yeah."

Becker wanted to know if there was anything else Marjorie Knoller could tell him that he hadn't asked about. Knoller said there was nothing else, other than the injuries she received. Before the interview was concluded, the inspector asked Knoller if she was making her statement voluntarily, if she agreed that no one was forcing her or promising her anything. Knoller agreed.

The inspector finished by making a note of each of Knoller's injuries on tape, recording every little detail: a black-and-blue mark over her right eye; a cut on her right thumb; a bruise on her right forearm; a cut on her left index finger.

That was the extent of Marjorie Knoller's injuries.

The inspector wanted to make double-sure, so he asked her about the examination she had by an EMT on the scene, and Knoller said the EMT had checked her body and there were no other bruises.

"Okay," Becker added, "none that you know of."

"Right."

Back out in the hallway with the Crime Scene Investigators, Becker and Daniele studied the handprints and the blood-soaked carpet. They looked at the violent scene with the eyes of law enforcement, but it was hard not to feel devastated for the victim. Here was someone trying to get into her own home, within the safety of her locked apartment building, someone just minding her own business, trying to get home on a Friday afternoon with her hands full of groceries. And to be attacked like that . . . at her own threshold.

It looked as if she'd been devoured by wild animals.

"We talked pretty much to ourselves about what this poor woman must have been thinking when she was getting attacked," Daniele confided. "That was in the back of my head. I could just feel for this woman—and imagine the pain. I could just imagine her thinking, *When is it going to stop?*"

Becker reflected, "To see it in real life, something that live, that grotesque, and that demoralizing . . . for a person to go through that . . . it's hard to understand how something like that could happen."

These two police veterans, with their decades of experience, had never seen anything as barbaric as this, yet Knoller was acting cold and callous about it all. She said she had no idea what the victim's name was. She had never once asked about the condition of the victim, not to the paramedics, not to the uniformed police, not to a soul. To Knoller, it was as if the victim didn't exist. All she cared about was her dogs, her bruises, and her legal standing.

What struck them even more about Marjorie Knoller was that she wasn't shaking. She wasn't really shaken up at all. Becker and Daniele were taken aback by how nonchalant she was. Here she was in her tiny one-bedroom apartment, probably no more than eight hundred square feet, with blood on the walls, with a stench of urine and feces lingering, and she was acting as if everything was just fine. She had done her part, she had tried to help, but she couldn't stop this terrible accident.

Out on Pacific, amid the last of the CSI and patrol units, Becker and Daniele reported a summary of Knoller's interview to their lieutenant, Henry Hunter, who had just arrived. Becker and Daniele made a few preliminary observations, telling Hunter they had tried to interrogate Knoller, but she was hostile, and they had to walk on eggshells. They explained that there was no known cause for the attack. Off the record, Becker had asked whether anything had happened between the two women, like maybe they had a fight, but Knoller was insistent that nothing of that sort transpired.

Becker thought Knoller was being methodical, taking her time about answering his questions, thinking out what her best answers would be. Daniele had a different perspective. He thought Knoller was acting in a way that indicated she might have felt guilty inside. Either way, it was a tough call, in terms of charging her.

Becker had done a physical overview of Knoller. He studied her clothing and saw everything she had on was intact, except for one three-inch rip on her sleeve. That wasn't enough to be considered evidence, so he didn't bother to ask for it. With what little they knew early Friday evening, there were no criminal charges to be filed—at all.

Hunter listened to the facts of the case, and told his inspectors to find out what they could about the victim—thirty-three-year-old Diane Whipple, who was undergoing surgery at San Francisco General. Everyone was hoping she would pull through.

Hunter wanted his men to get over to SF General to see what they could find out.

At the hospital, Becker and Daniele met Diane Whipple's roommate, Sharon Smith, who was in the ICU waiting room. Whipple was still in surgery, and Smith was too upset to talk. She gave some very minor personal data about Diane Whipple to Daniele, and shortly after that, she asked Diane's treating doctor to tell the inspectors that she did not want to talk. Becker and Daniele handed Whipple's keys to Smith, but she was on her cell phone with someone and barely acknowledged them.

The inspectors left their names and numbers with a social worker, asking that the information be passed along to Smith, and they headed back to their office to start their investigation from scratch. First order of business would be to interview the elderly neighbor who twice dialed 911.

On their way back to the station at the Hall of Justice, Becker and Daniele speculated about their prime suspect. Knoller had only the slightest of cuts, nothing that even needed a bandage, yet she was soaked in blood. She was claiming that she was party to the attack, but her physical status didn't reflect it.

"Wasn't it funny that Knoller left all that dried blood on her face?" Daniele wondered.

"Yeah. It was completely dry. As if she wanted us to see it. I don't know that she purposely wiped it on her face," Becker surmised. "I mean it might have gotten there accidentally."

"It might have. It probably happened when she was trying to get her dogs back into her apartment. That's how she got soaked."

"Yeah, that makes sense," Becker agreed. "She got covered when she was separating them, because CSI said the one dog was dripping blood."

"Did she ever call 911?" Daniele was curious.

"Not that we know of. We haven't heard any record of that."

CHAPTER THREE

Diane Whipple had left for work the usual time, 5:30 A.M. on January 26. The head coach of the women's lacrosse team at St. Mary's College, Whipple was extremely dedicated to her job. She would leave extra early to beat the traffic of the morning commute. She loved her players, she admired her fellow athletic directors, and she started each day filled with enthusiasm. She was a beautiful woman, an avid athlete, a former member of the U.S. lacrosse team, and a two-time member of the World Cup lacrosse team. She was, by every account, an all-American girl.

Raised on New York's Long Island, she did her undergraduate work at Penn State, where her athleticism won her the honor of being chosen NCAA's Female Athlete of the Year. After Penn State, Diane moved to San Diego, where she trained to make the 1996 U.S. Olympic team. She didn't qualify, but she came close, and just about that time, she fell in love with Sharon Smith, an attractive brunette who was training to become a Charles Schwab branch manager in San Francisco.

Diane and Sharon were introduced by a mutual friend. They had their first encounter in Los Angeles—it was not set up, just a bunch of girls getting together—but when Sharon walked into the room, Diane was love-struck. Diane actually grabbed her buddy and whispered, "*That* is going to be mine."

As it turned out, Diane and Sharon had a lot in common—they were into the same sports, they shared the same set of values—and they became close right away. Neither played hard to get, they were a perfect match and both traveled the distance to meet halfway in Los Angeles, Diane driving up from San Diego, Sharon flying down from San Fran. They had the kind of love story sappy romance movies are made of. The timing was right, and the two found a balance between them. Sharon was the "serious" person. Diane was the fun-loving "goofy" spirit.

The women moved in together just months after they met, Diane relocating to San Francisco to be with Sharon, and they quickly became inseparable. Sharon liked calling Diane by her middle name, Alexis, which was part of their own little love connection. Diane adored Sharon and discussed the idea of having children. They traveled to Europe and the Caribbean, they planned to buy a house—they did all the things couples do. Through good times and bad, they had lived together for seven years.

On that particular January day, in the winter of 2001, for some reason, Diane called Sharon at Charles Schwab and asked that her partner come home early. Diane was headed on her way home, she said. She wanted to make a taco dinner, then head out to a seven o'clock movie.

At Diane's request, Sharon left work at about 4:45 that afternoon and worked her way through traffic to Pacific Heights. She reached home about forty-five minutes later, but had to drive past her building, circumventing all the police cars, media vans, and fire trucks.

Sharon parked her car on the street, unable to get to her parking spot, and when she walked up to the crime-scene yellow tape—Police Line Do Not Cross—she was met by her building manager. The manager told Sharon that Diane had been attacked by the dogs on the sixth floor, that she'd been rushed off in an ambulance to the hospital. Sharon listened with knots in her stomach. She knew Diane had become deathly afraid of those dogs. Diane was so afraid, in fact, that she was almost phobic about them.

25

Sharon got to the hospital in time to discover that Diane was alive but in "very critical" condition. Surgeons were working on her neck. They spent almost two hours repairing the veins and arteries, but some of the wounds were so deep, doctors had to insert a tube into Diane's throat to support her trachea. The prognosis didn't look good.

Diane remained alive after surgery, just long enough for Sharon to go up and see her. Sharon believed that her lover hung in there just so she could hold her one more time, so she could say good-bye in person.

Diane Alexis Whipple died 70 minutes after she left the operating table. When she had arrived, she was in full cardiac arrest. Surgeons and doctors did all they could to save her, but it was not meant to be.

Reporters had no idea what kind of dogs mauled Whipple, so early media accounts referred to the "killer dogs" as bullmastiffs. No one was quite sure what breed the dogs were. Some people thought they were pit bulls. Some news coverage called them "Canary" dogs. It would be a few days before the words "Presa Canario" would hit the air waves.

As news of Diane Whipple's death spread, calls flooded in from all over the country. To her lacrosse players, teammates, and coaches, Diane was a mentor, a role model, an inspiration in every sense of the word. She was such a positive force in her players' lives, it was no wonder that her team at St. Mary's was torn up and heartbroken. Those closest to Diane were filled with anger, confusion, numbness, and disbelief. Her partner and close friends were unable to be comforted. Not even the priests at St. Mary's could understand how such a vibrant young woman could be ripped from the world so violently.

A few days later more than six hundred people filled the St. Mary's chapel to share their memories of Diane Alexis Whipple. It was a campus memorial, and even though it was a private ceremony, there was such a heavy overflow crowd that many people had to stand outside and listen.

"She believed there was no evil," Sharon Smith told mourners, "and although her time with us was short, for some reason we don't know, we are blessed that God gave her to us for thirty-three years."

During the mass, the entire chapel building shook because of a small, but jolting tremor. Some people nervously chuckled. Others believed it was Diane *declaring her presence.*

THE LEGAL WILL OF DIANE ALEXIS WHIPPLE:
EXHIBIT A

I, Diane Alexis Whipple, do hereby give
all my assets to Sharon Kay Smith, born 8/6/65,
except my Braided 18k bracelet,
which goes to Emily Whipple to continue the family tradition.

To my grandmother, my All-American certificates, wins,
and High School College Diplomas, and PSU rings.
To Wayne, my digalite satellite system. To Bug, all my CDs
especially Rocklobsters B-52.
To Sharon, I leave my cat, Bootie Kay Whipple Cutie,
Stinky Cat Shadow, and Porky Pig Mocha Smoka Bean.

My last wish and testament is to cremate me and
spread my ashes on my PSU Lady Lax field at the center circle,
my Manhasset Lax field, in the Ocean, and on the front step
of my old Manhasset home. Oh, and do not forget to keep me
(what's left, that is) on your fireplace in an urn.
And promise me you will take me *off* Life Support
if I'm on it for more than *1 week*.

My last and final wish is for Sharon Kay Smith
to find out the truth about _____
and have _____ sign a notary that she is a lesbian
and Read this to me while I sit on your mantelpiece
in my green marble urn!

Oh, and remember to think about me and
say I Love You every hour on the hour
for the rest of your life.
That's all for now.

Signed,
Diane Alexis Whipple
"And I
love you"

At nine in the morning on Saturday, January 27, the chief medical examiner of San Francisco, Dr. Boyd Stephens, along with Assistant Medical Examiner Venus Azar, filed the Necropsy Report on Diane Alexis Whipple.

Dr. Stephens telephoned Diane's mother, Penny Whipple-Kelly, and told her that the Necropsy Report would be sealed by the San Francisco police. She was further informed that her daughter's death was not being treated as an accident. Penny Whipple-Kelly understood that while there would be some delay in the release of the death certificate, that would not prevent her from holding a memorial service. She and her family would eventually hold such a service for Diane Alexis on Long Island.

In all, the medical examiners counted seventy-seven lacerations, bites, contusions, and abrasions, covering virtually every part of Whipple's body, including abrasions consistent with canine bite marks on the victim's *upper thighs*, left breast, and *upper buttocks*.

The body of the white female, measuring five feet five inches, weighing 135 pounds, with gray eyes and brown hair, had blood-soaked gauze around the neck, sutured plastic catheters inserted into the veins, and blood-soaked gauze around the left wrist.

There were gaping wounds.

There was a stapled 5½ inch laceration on the lower neck.

There were scratches all up and down the neck.

There was a 2¼-inch laceration at the jaw.

There was a 1½-inch laceration on the neck that extended into the *muscles*.

The left external jugular vein had been surgically bound.

There was a surgical clip in the carotid artery.

The upper larynx had been crushed.

The cause of death was determined to be "loss of blood from multiple traumatic injuries (dog bite wounds)."

One troubling problem with the findings: the wounds were so multiple and so deep that it was impossible to determine whether they were the bite marks from one particular dog—or two.

CHAPTER FOUR

Throughout the weekend after Diane Whipple's death, Animal Care and Control was flooded with calls from the media and the San Francisco public. As the news was reporting up-to-the-minute accounts about the mauling, panicked people were calling about scary dogs around the clock.

Captain Vicky Guldbech, who had been in Los Angeles that weekend, returned to work on Monday with a heavy heart. "When I got the call in L.A., there were so many emotions going on," Guldbech confided. "I didn't know what to feel. I didn't know *how* to feel. A person was dead because of a dog. This is what I do for a living—I work to prevent this kind of thing."

Guldbech had already seen the news accounts. She was acutely aware of the public hysteria and of the joint investigation by the police and the San Francisco DA. She knew the case would be one of the largest she would come up against. As the ACC person designated to speak to the press, Guldbech was bracing herself for whatever media throng would be awaiting her. To herself, she chanted prayers, looking for answers and for the strength to face the day.

"I can't exactly remember how many cameras were there as I drove in," she later said, "but I do remember, vividly, that when I went to read a press release in the garage of our building, there were cameras as far to the right of me as I could see, and cameras as far to the left."

Guldbech had experience doing press conferences. She had recently been in the spotlight regarding a professional dog-fighting ring, so she was used to answering questions and seeing her face on the nightly news from time to time. But this was incredible. So many journalists were present that Guldbech was given a box to stand on so camerapeople could get a good view of her. She was standing on a crate, it was a freezing winter day, and she was not only cold and shaking, she was extremely nervous. Her stomach was growling, her whole system was upside down.

Guldbech had to get a grip. She was being bombarded by requests from local TV news stations, there was a horde of newspaper reporters and photographers with flashbulbs going off, and then, to make matters worse, the national media was present—FOX and CNN were the first on the trail of what would soon become a national media bonanza.

Guldbech was filled with concerns and emotions as she read her short press release. In answering questions, having no script, she spoke off the cuff, but these reporters were intense. They wanted answers, and they wanted answers *now*. What did ACC know about Noel and Knoller? What information did they have about Presa Canario attack dogs? What fatal mauling statistics did they have regarding pit bulls and Rottweilers? Would the Presa Canario breed be banned from the city? Were they trained to kill? Why were the owners raising this rare breed?

Guldbech was unprepared for all that. She had no idea who Noel and Knoller were, let alone the reason they were housing this kind of dog. Breeding fighting dogs in Pacific Heights seemed impossible. Breeding dogs trained to kill, however, was not out of the question. But Guldbech couldn't really comment. With a criminal investigation under way, she could say nothing that would jeopardize the case. She told reporters there simply was not enough information yet to provide a clear picture.

Guldbech was there primarily, she reminded the press, to assure the public that guard dogs were not necessarily ill suited for urban living. The ACC officer understood the public outcry over the Whipple dog mauling; she felt that was warranted, but she and her colleagues hoped people could go on with their daily lives. Guldbech wanted San Francisco residents, and especially Pacific Heights residents, to stop living in fear.

She confirmed that the male dog, Bane, had been destroyed at the animal shelter on the night of Whipple's death. The female, Hera, remained in ACC custody, and her fate would be determined by a "vicious and dangerous dog hearing" to be held by ACC officials in an open courtroom at San Francisco City Hall. The public was welcome to attend.

That night, after Guldbech's news conference hit the airwaves, weird calls started pouring in. Some were the threatening voices of activists. Some were crackpots. Others were angry citizens. There was a stream of voices waiting for her on her office answering machine:

"You kill that dog, and you'll die."

"Don't kill Hera. I'll pay for her rehabilitation. Let me have her."

"Hold those damn pet owners accountable!"

"Why should this dog be entitled to one free bite? Kill Hera!"

"Please do not punish the dog. Don't put her down."

"Save Hera!"

"Give Hera a chance. Please don't let Hera lose her life."

"Ban those killer dogs from the state of California."

"Does someone *else* have to die before you people do something?"

The mauling had become fodder for daily news tidbits. It was a bizarre "coming out party" for the Presa Canario breed, opening people's eyes about the genetic makeup of the dogs, their character and traits. The media reported that Presas were territorial and fierce. Presa Canarios were used for dog fighting; they had a history of violence and had been banned in the Canary Islands back in the 1960s. They were like pit bulls on steroids. They were allegedly used by drug lords to guard drug labs, and the few that were in the United States were trained to kill.

The media had a field day, reporting every new frightening detail about the "killer dogs." But at the same time, the news was a cause for concern for animal activists worldwide, for dog owners across the nation, and for an increasingly fearful Bay Area public. The media was reporting that the Presa Canario was inherently "people aggressive," and would fight to the death, calling Bane and Hera the "dogs of death."

Presa Canario chat rooms sprang up on the Internet—dog trainers felt they needed to educate people about the good qualities of the Presa.

Presa owners wanted to set the record straight about their lovable guard dogs, but their comments weren't making the news. Presa owners all over America felt their dogs didn't deserve that kind of negative publicity. To them, Presa Canarios were lovable, gentle, smart animals. Comparing American Presas with the fighting Presas of the Canary Islands was just absurd. But their isolated voices were never really heard. All the media seemed interested in was casting an image of "killer" animals. "Killer dogs" grabbed viewers' attention.

It wasn't long before large-dog owners in San Francisco felt they were being wronged. Anyone with a pit bull, a mastiff, or a Rottweiler was being given the evil eye on the streets; people were literally running away from them and their dogs. The mauling was creating problems for everyone. People were on edge. People were afraid of any kind of large dog. Things were getting nuts.

Animal experts were consulted by media to give their theories about what exactly went wrong with these particular "killer dogs." Most experts believed Bane and Hera had been raised improperly. They blamed the dog owners, speculating that the dogs had been allowed to take control of the Noel/Knoller household. They speculated that these dog owners hadn't set up proper boundaries for their animals. Somehow, it seemed the animals had become their owners' masters. Experts guessed that Noel and Knoller's relationship with their dogs was *twisted*.

Dog trainers surmised that when Bane went after Whipple, especially when he had her by the jugular, he entered the "red zone." It was a non-scientific term being used to describe a dog in the height of attack mode. A large dog in that kind of zone could be stopped by nothing. Once the killer instinct took over, the animal was beyond human control.

Angry Californians were also calling the District Attorney's office, demanding that DA Terence Hallinan throw the book at the couple who owned Bane and Hera. Hallinan, a legendary prosecutor and a controversial figure in San Francisco, wanted to assure the public that justice would prevail, but he could not address the flood of individual calls, nor the media requests, until the police completed their investigation.

Fred Gardner, the spokesman for Hallinan's office, told media that the DA was doing everything possible to move the process along. Hallinan had assigned two of the office's own investigators, Carlos Sanchez and Dave Parenti, to assist Becker and Daniele at SFPD. The two teams of seasoned law enforcement officials were working in tandem to determine the history of the dogs and their propensity for violence.

Reports were surfacing in newspapers with Whipple's neighbors referring to Bane as "the Beast," and "the Dog of Death." Neighbors who lived down the hall from Diane Whipple told the media that they regretted not having reported their fears before the attack, admitting they felt intimidated by the large, unfriendly dogs.

Other Pacific Heights residents were coming forward to report they had problems being near the unusually fierce dogs. Dog walkers in that neighborhood admitted they were uneasy about the size and character of the canines, who would lunge and growl at other dogs for no reason. "The male owner [Noel] would physically restrain the dog and pull him to the other side of the street to get away from my dog," one dog walker confided early on.

As footage of the dogs and their owners kept flashing on the TV news, more and more people were calling the police. Having recognized the photos of the massive dogs and their odd-looking owners, they had stories to tell. DA Hallinan was keeping close track of the calls flooding into SFPD. A number of Whipple's neighbors were now recounting frightening incidents.

There were significant allegations that Banc and Hera had been initiating aggression toward other dogs. Though no actual complaints had ever been filed, one Pacific Heights resident provided Hallinan's office with a veterinary medical record to back up an account of Knoller's dog viciously attacking a Shetland sheepdog.

With the public pressure mounting, Hallinan wanted to bring felony charges against the dog owners, but he couldn't be too hasty. At the crux of the matter was whether or not the dog owners knew about the dogs' ability to kill. There was absolutely no proof of that.

Hallinan was considering involuntary manslaughter charges when an odd piece of information came in from his own investigators. There was a report that Bane and Hera were the property of two white supremacist inmates housed in Pelican Bay State Prison and that the two attorneys, Noel and Knoller, were not the legal owners of the animals.

Hallinan immediately sent Sanchez and Parenti up to Pelican Bay to check it out. Becker and Daniele were also on it, having meetings in Sacramento with Devan Hawkes, an agent with the Special Service Unit of the California Department of Corrections, who had been tracking an inmate-run Presa Canario dog-breeding ring.

Of course, this new information made things even more thorny for the DA. If Noel and Knoller weren't the legitimate owners—if the Presas belonged to inmates or the families of inmates, and Noel and Knoller could prove they were only temporary caretakers—that would make it all the more difficult to indict and convict them.

For a city named after Saint Francis, the patron saint of animals, for a city that loved animals as much as people, the idea that these Presa Canario dogs might belong to white supremacist inmates would be explosive. San Francisco was a dog lover's paradise. It was a place where dogs were held in high esteem. But if the dogs who killed Diane Whipple were part of a dirty dog-breeding scheme—and it was happening right under their noses in one of the most treasured parts of their town—that would turn an already anxious public into an angry, stomping mass.

Hallinan was very careful to walk a fine line. The district attorney already had shows like *Dateline* and *PrimeTime Live* calling, and, being a great believer in the power of the press, he wanted to appear cooperative. But in reality, Hallinan was keeping the media in the dark. He wasn't about to divulge law enforcement tactics or recent findings.

Instead, he allowed his general litigation prosecutor, Kimberly Guilfoyle, who was initially handling the Whipple mauling as a dog-bite case, to address media requests. Guilfoyle was good with that. An extreme beauty, the media fawned over her, eager to hear every detail she could reveal. In the first days after Whipple's death, Guilfoyle was given Hallinan's blessing to appear on *Good Morning America, Geraldo Live!, Inside Edition*, and *Extra*. Hallinan wanted the media involved. He knew media attention could help bring witnesses out of the woodwork.

If Hallinan was overly passionate about the Diane Whipple case, he had good reason to be. He had gay activists up in arms, he had animal activists up in arms, he had dog owners worried about new leash laws, and he had frightened people making complaints about large dogs all hours of the day and night.

All hell was breaking loose, and Hallinan needed to find a way to avenge Diane Whipple's senseless killing. But until his office knew all the facts, his hands were tied. He let Guilfoyle supply the media with cosmetic information. But the real info would ultimately be sealed by a judge. In the interim, the angry public would have to sit tight.

With public pressure mounting day by day, the Whipple mauling was turning into a homicide investigation, and Hallinan went to his right-hand man, Chief Assistant District Attorney Paul Cummins, to decide which of their top homicide prosecutors should take over. They looked at ADA Jim Hammer, who had over a decade of experience in the criminal justice system. Hammer was a tough guy with an impressive track record as a prosecutor. He was intense, but he also had an inner sensitivity and was good with a jury.

The Whipple mauling had originally been reported as a "freak accident." Hammer had read about it while he was on vacation in Mexico. The prosecutor recalled thinking it was crazy that someone in San Francisco would be killed by her neighbor's dog. At the time, murder was not on his mind, so never in his wildest dreams did he expect the Whipple case to fall into his lap.

Before Hallinan had a chance to get to Hammer, a weird thing happened. About a week after the mauling, he was awakened at home by a team of news cameras flashing lights in his front yard. It turned out Robert Noel had faxed an eighteen-page letter to the newsroom at San Francisco's Channel 4; the letter had been faxed to the DA's office as well, but it must have arrived there after office hours. Hallinan knew nothing about it.

"The method of delivery was very dramatic," Hallinan recalled. "We got it the next morning, when we came in, but here was a news crew in front of my house at about ten o'clock at night."

"Would you be willing to comment on this letter, sir?" the reporter asked, shoving the eighteen-page missive at him.

"Well, give it to me," Hallinan said, "let me look at it."

With the camera lights blinding him, the DA flipped through the single-spaced document, which was addressed to him personally. There was a wealth of information there, mostly Noel's defense theory, but also there were sections that bashed Hallinan and his office.

"I'm not going to comment on this thing," he told the reporter, angry that he'd be disturbed in the night. Hallinan handed the thing back and slammed his front door.

The next day, the letter, written on Noel & Knoller stationery, was waiting on his desk.

Noel was asking Hallinan to have a discussion with him. He wanted to give Hallinan the truth about Hera and Bane. The letter expressed Noel's rage regarding the DA's refusal to meet with him. Days earlier, Hallinan had placed "unacceptable" conditions on their meeting: the DA requested Noel and Knoller hire an attorney and that they refrain from talking to the media.

To Robert Noel, those conditions were ludicrous. For one thing, the media was already all over the case, Hallinan had issued statements through his spokespersons. Regarding the hiring of counsel, Noel was insulted that Hallinan didn't expect him to represent himself and his wife. The letter explained the full details regarding Bane and Hera: the dogs belonged to inmates Paul Schneider and Dale Bretches, two members of the Aryan Brotherhood, a fact about which Hallinan was already aware. Noel assured the DA that neither his wife, himself, nor his clients, Schneider and Bretches, had committed any crime. Citing the Department of Corrections report that confirmed their operation of a "dog breeding business," Noel offered proof that "there was no illegal activity by either us or any other person in connection with the dogs."

The letter was abusive at times, and friendly at others. It seemed to have been written in waves. Some sections attacked Hallinan; other sections praised the Presa Canarios; some sections blamed other people's dogs for attacks on Bane and Hera. Noel just rambled. There were a lot of new leads to go on, as well as shocking stories about dogfights. Hallinan forwarded a copy of the letter to SFPD and they began contacting every person Noel named.

Apart from the leads, the letter was disturbing to Hallinan on multiple levels. For one, it insulted him on a base level, calling him "half-cocked" and "calculated." But much worse than that, it hinted at blaming the victim, Diane Whipple, for provoking the attack somehow, possibly with her perfume or use of "steroids."

"I kind of said to myself, wait a minute, Terence, you've got to calm down here," Hallinan confided. "You can't get into a fight with this guy. He's trying to get you into a fight and it would be the one way you can blow this case."

But in terms of how the letter would affect the case, Hallinan was right to be aggravated, because Robert Noel had revealed secret adoption proceedings held at Pelican Bay State Prison. Hallinan didn't want that information divulged to the media under any circumstances—in fact, there was a gag order being put in place. But now Noel had opened Pandora's box, which would make for more panic and more anger in the city.

Moreover, the public would be thrown by the prejudicial nature of this information, which would make it difficult to get an impartial jury in San Francisco. In Noel's mind, he was throwing out a red herring, deflecting the issue of his and Knoller's responsibility for the actions of their dogs. He had no idea the kind of turmoil he would eventually stir up. He was just looking to blame inmates, third parties, and anyone else he could think of.

The papers and TV news channels had a field day reporting that on January 29, three days after the fatal mauling, Robert Noel and Marjorie Knoller had driven more than eight hours to Pelican Bay, where they legally adopted inmate Paul John Schneider, officially making the thirty-nine-year-old convict their "son." People in the Bay Area were stunned. No one could conceive of it. These were two Pacific Heights attorneys who at one time were fringe members of the San Francisco socialite set, partying with Ann and Gordon Getty—and now they were "parents" to a man who was considered one of the most dangerous felons in the California penal system.

The press reported as much of Noel's letter as made sense—the extraneous names and conspiracy theories he tossed around were left out. The revelation that mattered to the media was that Robert Noel had outlined a "dog breeding ring" involving eight Presa Canarios. He divulged that these dogs, including Bane and Hera, were purchased using $20,000 in cash from Schneider. Noel also revealed that he and Knoller had become part of a convoluted scheme involving Paul Schneider and a third party, Janet Coumbs, whom Schneider used to raise the dogs up in a far-away place nobody ever heard of called Hayfork.

In Robert Noel's way of thinking, the letter was written to serve multiple purposes:

It was an attempt to intimidate the District Attorney.

It was an effort to attack the "corrupt" California Department of Corrections.

It was a chance to explain Marjorie Knoller's innocence.

It was a bid to vindicate Bane and Hera.

And it was an effort to lay blame on Diane Alexis Whipple.

CHAPTER FIVE

By some accounts, Paul John Schneider was considered the "Hannibal Lecter" of Pelican Bay. When the feds charged Schneider under RICO for masterminding the murders of enemies of the Aryan Brotherhood, Schneider found it amusing. He was indicted, along with seven others, on federal charges that he ordered the killings of two dozen people. Those federal charges were filed, and a RICO trial awaited him in the months after Whipple's mauling.

Schneider was also charged with conspiracy to commit the 1995 murder of a sheriff's deputy in Sonoma County, who was shot in the head execution style by one of Schneider's Brotherhood members. Schneider had taken pleasure in hearing that Bob Scully, an Aryan buddy just fresh out of Pelican Bay on parole, had forced Deputy Frank Trejo to bend down on the ground, begging for his life on his knees. Schneider took even greater pleasure, however, when Bob Scully was later tried and convicted of the deputy's murder, and sent to San Quentin's death row.

Schneider had earned his way into the Aryan Brotherhood the hard way—by stabbing correctional officer C. Kropp in the neck at New Folsom State Prison. That was back in 1987. An unusually cruel and cunning man, Schneider was considered the worst of the worst. Even in the brutal prison environment, he was feared. Correctional officers knew him to be a flight risk. Back in his early prison days, like Houdini, Schneider managed to escape from a maximum-security prison in Oregon. Schneider was slippery. He was a constant threat to everyone who came near him.

When the super-max Pelican Bay State Prison opened in 1989, Schneider was moved there immediately. Schneider would thrive inside the no-man's-land of Pelican Bay, considered the modern-day Alcatraz, fighting authority at every possible turn. Schneider was serving time for a number of Brinks heists, but it wasn't long before he was indicted and given a life sentence, without parole, for the attempted murder of correctional officer C. Kropp at New Folsom. Then in 1990 Schneider was further charged when he stabbed an attorney at a Sacramento courthouse. Schneider had managed, wearing shackles and wrist cuffs, to sneak a handmade knife into court. In the back of the courtroom, Schneider stabbed the attorney through the leg and the wounds were found to contain fecal matter. Schneider's handmade weapon, called a "shiv" in prison lingo, was so cleverly crafted that it came complete with artwork— inscribed with the word "Bane."

Schneider was good at making bad things happen. He was versed in crafting and hiding weapons—usually he would hide them in his rectum, but occasionally he'd hide a small piece of metal in a large open wound he had in his right leg. His bad leg was a sore spot for Schneider—apparently he had trouble getting medical attention from the Department of Corrections—so the wound remained infected, and it oozed, on and off, for over ten years.

If Schneider lived to create death, ruin, and destruction, even from behind the walls of the tightest housing unit at Pelican Bay, many of the women he seduced didn't realize it. Housed in the Security Housing Unit (SHU), in twenty-four-hour-a-day lockdown, Schneider was still able to conduct business. A tall, blond, muscle-bound man, Schneider had a way with women. From his cage at Pelican Bay, he wrote love letters and drew artwork. He had more than one lady fall in love with him. Women were easy prey. And Schneider learned that ladies could come in handy.

As it happened, Schneider developed a special relationship with a woman named Brenda Moore. Soon after another Pelican Bay inmate put them in touch, Brenda became so smitten with Paul that she left her home near Sacramento and moved up to remote Crescent City, just to be near Pelican Bay. Prison officials would later find maps, drawings, and photos to prove that Moore was helping Schneider plan an escape.

In the meantime, during his decade in the SHU, Schneider managed to become one of the key members of the notorious Aryan Brotherhood prison gang.

Schneider was adept at using street gang members on the outside to do business with members of prison gangs on the inside. Schneider knew all about control. He had the Aryan Brotherhood affording him more and more power. And, by successfully doing business with other prison gangs, primarily the Mexican Mafia, *La Eme*, he was able to get cash, drugs, electronic equipment, alcohol, whatever he needed.

Schneider kept up his lethal reputation by wreaking havoc now and then in the prison showers. He fashioned knives out of air-conditioning vents, and supplied Brotherhood members with weapons hidden in stairwells and wall cracks. He was smart enough to never get caught. The man knew how to beat the system. He was a genius in the ways of deception, and he had at least one prison guard eating out of his hands. That man was Correctional Officer Jose Garcia, who would later be sent to prison himself for helping Schneider set up attacks on other inmates. Before Garcia was led away in shackles, the unorthodox prison guard admitted to Pelican Bay officials that he had considered giving Schneider a correctional officer's uniform.

Schneider was that good.

Schneider worked it.

And Schneider had more than just one prison guard doing his bidding. He had numerous lawyers handling his "business" as well. And among them were Marjorie Knoller and Robert Noel.

After the news of the adoption became public, Noel, Knoller, and Schneider each granted interviews to the *San Francisco Chronicle*.

"Mr. Schneider is definitely a man of more character and integrity than most people you're going to find in the California Department of Corrections," Noel professed. "He's a stand-up guy. He won't lie for prosecutors. He's not a snitch."

"By adopting Paul," Knoller explained, "we now have a legal say in his medical treatment. If something bad happens to him in prison, we can sue. He's a very intelligent, articulate individual. He's special. He's our kid, and we love him."

"I just love them both like they are my parents," Schneider told the paper. "I can completely trust them. I know they care deeply and there's no ulterior motive."

But Noel and Knoller clearly hadn't adopted Schneider just to give him "protection." They had become involved with him, first as attorneys, then on a business level, and finally as his would-be lovers. Pelican Bay officials would later discover hoards of erotic letters and hundreds of pictures Noel and Knoller sent Schneider of the dogs—among them were numerous photos of Knoller in the nude, photos of Knoller ready to perform sex acts, and photos and drawings that hinted at bestiality.

"I flashed my breasts in some pictures," Knoller admitted. "Bob might have sent one of those to Paul. There was nothing to do with dogs."

"Paul has an inner life he shares with us," Knoller would also confide to a *Rolling Stone* reporter, "and threesomes are a pretty standard erotic fantasy. It's a tradition to write erotic letters to inmates. It helps them.

"Paul was writing a novel, an erotic medieval fantasy. We wrote chapters back and forth. We were all characters in it."

"We were a part of keeping something in Paul alive," Noel told *Rolling Stone*. "Bane punched a hole through that cement box Paul lives in and gave him a window on the world. We wanted to help keep that window open."

The threesome also made comments to the press about their innocence, calling the mauling incident a "tragedy" and an "accident."

"It was definitely wrong," Schneider said of Bane, "but in his little dog brain, for some reason, he felt he was doing something right."

"Did I know the dogs were going to be used for fighting? They were never going to be used for fighting," Noel told columnists. "They were going to be bred and sold. Do the dogs have lawyers? Yes. *We* are their lawyers."

But Department of Corrections special agents weren't buying Noel and Knoller's story.

"You'd just as soon adopt a rattlesnake and put it in your bed," one corrections official was quoted as saying.

Corrections authorities would tell media that they suspected Schneider and his cellmate, Bretches, were using Noel and Knoller in what they described as an "elaborate prison scheme to supply vicious canines for dog-fighting rings and methamphetamine labs."

"That's what we suspect," said Stephen Green, an official with the California Youth and Adult Correctional Agency. "In meth labs, and perhaps beyond," Green told reporters, "they [Schneider and Bretches] may have some links with some of the Hispanic gangs."

Law enforcement sources at the California Department of Corrections had been tracking Schneider and Bretches's mail and they were convinced the two cellmates were breeding dogs to be used as weapons. Dale Bretches, also a member of the Aryan Brotherhood, was a convicted murderer serving life without parole. Correctional officers considered the two inmates partners, referring to Paul and Dale as criminal "soul mates."

"They used code names to disguise what they were up to," Special Agent Devan Hawkes later revealed. "They were involved in all kinds of underground activities."

On Monday, January 29, just days after Whipple's demise, California Department of Corrections officials met with the SFPD and investigators from the district attorney's office. The picture they painted was demonic. Prison officials suspected Schneider and Bretches were already selling the Presa Canario dogs to guard methamphetamine labs, or so-called super-labs, controlled by Mexican nationals, and that members of a known Mexican drug cartel were already in possession of Bane's offspring. This last bit of news dumbfounded SFPD Detectives Becker and Daniele.

They would become even more shocked, however, with the findings of District Attorney Investigators Sanchez and Parenti, who were up at Pelican Bay sorting through the boxes of lewd photos and letters about the dogs, along with Schneider's plans of a lethal dog-breeding scheme. The volumes of materials had been seized by Pelican Bay officials from Schneider and Bretches's cell immediately after Whipple was killed.

Media reports were surfacing about how Schneider and Bretches went about purchasing the dogs. Apparently, Bretches had bombarded a Canadian Presa Canario dog breeder with requests to buy the animals. But Angelika Morwald, owner of WereWolf Kennels in Ontario, later told the media she was hesitant to sell any of her dogs to him.

Bretches's initial inquiries about the Presas were filtered, readdressed through one of his family members so his letters wouldn't arrive marked as "Official Prison" mail. Bretches asked Morwald questions related to the power and size of the animals; it was clear the man intended to purchase massive, muscular dogs of some sort, but something about Bretches's style made the dog breeder nervous. As soon as he revealed he was an inmate, Morwald refused to do business with him. She had been leery of him all along.

"I was getting the feeling that something didn't jibe," the WereWolf proprietor told reporters. "It didn't seem kosher. He was too persistent."

The dog breeder especially didn't like the idea that Bretches wanted to buy breeding rights. Morwald didn't sell dogs with breeding rights, she explained to him, asking Bretches to look for Presas elsewhere. Nonetheless, the inmate continued to write, boasting that he already owned a few Presa Canarios, hounding the breeder with letters asking why she wouldn't return his calls or postcards.

When things didn't work out with WereWolf, Bretches and Schneider used associates to contact Presa Canario breeders in Ohio and Illinois, just to scope things out. Having indirect access to the Internet, they wanted to cover all possible ground; they researched breeders as far away as the Canary Islands and South America and were determined to purchase those dogs, whatever it took. They couldn't afford to get into another snarl with a breeder. Their experience with WereWolf taught them that they needed a beard, someone who could cloak their identities completely. Ideally it would be a woman, a gullible person, a trusting type whom Schneider could win over. After a few veiled threats to Dale Bretches's "girlfriend," Janet Capes, they came up with a great prospect. Capes knew a Christian lady, a plain woman who lived up the road from her in Hayfork.

Capes was familiar with Bretches and Schneider's threatening ways.

Department of Corrections officials believed that Capes had been used in an earlier scheme to help Bretches and Schneider print what looked like "Department of Justice" stationery, through which drugs were smuggled into Pelican Bay. Capes had been threatened, officials believed, and they suspected she was forced to destroy a $5,000 printing press. Janet Capes has never been charged for these crimes, and now Bretches was hinting at blackmail if she didn't help him out with his dog scam.

Hayfork, nestled up in the mountains of Trinity County, was an isolated place where everybody knew everybody. In this small rural town, since a lot of folks kept livestock on their land, Bretches figured it would be easy for Capes to find someone who could raise big dogs, and possibly split the profits on the sales of the pups.

Capes decided on Janet Coumbs, a reclusive Bible thumper who lived on a four-acre parcel, where she spent most of her time tending to livestock, along with her young daughter, Daisy. Coumbs was naïve; she led a sheltered life. The woman had hardly ever been out of Hayfork, but Capes thought she could coax Coumbs into visiting Schneider. Coumbs had no real boyfriends, she was desperate for a man. To Bretches, it sounded like a perfect fit.

On a bright Sunday morning in June 1997, Capes visited with Janet Coumbs after church. She knew Coumbs liked being thought of as a "good Christian woman" and she played on that, complimenting Janet on all her good Christian deeds.

"Hey, why don't you come with me the next time I go up to the prison to visit?" Capes asked, as they sipped coffee in the back hall.

"Why would I want to do a thing like that?" Coumbs wondered. "I don't know a soul in prison."

"Well, you'd do it because it's your Christian duty. That's why I go. Didn't you know that? Don't you know about ministries for prisoners?"

"No. I never heard of anything like that."

"Well, if you read your Bible, you'll see it tells you right in there," Capes said. "It's our duty to visit the sick, the impoverished, the imprisoned."

Capes opened up the Holy Book and pointed to the scripture. Coumbs looked at it while Capes kept trying to shame her into visiting Pelican Bay.

"I don't see why I would want to," Coumbs argued, "I hardly have

45

enough time to take care of my farm. And Crescent City? That's too far a drive."

"I'll tell you what," Capes suggested, "the reason I'm asking is cause my boyfriend Dale has a friend, Paul, who hasn't seen a visitor in four years. The man needs something to believe in, Janet. He ain't got nobody, and you might really be helping someone."

"Really?"

"Yeah. Cause the poor guy is so lonely. He's stuck in there twenty-four hours a day, with nothin' to look forward to. He doesn't ever get to see the light of day."

"Well, what did he do to get himself in there?"

"He just robbed some convenience store," Capes lied. "And I thought you and me and Daisy could go up there, take a ride sometime."

Janet Coumbs started to hesitate. She was beginning to give in.

"Cause, you know," Capes said, "just think what it would be like to just stare at concrete walls all day. Sittin' there all alone."

"What about his family? Don't they visit?"

"Paul don't have no family," Capes told her, making Coumbs feel guilty for asking. "Do you think you might at least write to him, if I give you his address? Just send him a little hope?"

And so the letters began. . . .

Just days after Capes laid on the Christian guilt trip, Janet Coumbs sent Paul a note telling him about herself, mentioning that her nickname was "Calamity." Paul wrote back instantly, telling her the nickname suited him just fine. Apart from his note, he said he was shooting off a postcard to her with a drawing of a Bengal tiger he had done. That tiger drawing would be the first of many little gifts Janet would receive. Paul said he liked drawing animals, explaining that he spent a lot of laborious hours with the guidance of Dale, trying to refine his art. This surprised Coumbs. She never expected a convict to be so sensitive.

Janet loved the artwork. The tiger was so intricate, so beautifully done. No guy had ever sent her anything like that before. Overweight and suffering from low self-esteem, Janet wasn't used to any kind of male attention. So of course she was impressed when Paul wrote her so often, returning her letters so quickly. When she sent him a note to compliment his talent, she included a few snapshots of her farm, as a thank-you. She wanted him to see all the animals she lived with.

Paul wrote back in a more detailed, more intimate way. At first, Paul wanted to have fun with Janet. He played a game and told her he was a big fat guy, with green teeth and straggly hair. Janet was believing every word she read, until Paul got serious and offered up his true physical data: he was six feet two, age thirty-five, weighed 227 pounds, with blondish hair and gray eyes. He said some people thought he was handsome, but he hardly got to look at himself in the mirror.

He quickly moved through his personal history, starting with where he grew up (near Laguna Beach down in Orange County) and explaining he graduated from high school a year early, got married and divorced before he turned seventeen, then went into the Air Force the day he turned eighteen. He had lived a fast life.

In the Air Force, Schneider said, he was a "boomer"—a boom operator in flight. He claimed he also managed to go to Spokane Falls Community College during that time, where he picked up an associate's degree in drafting. Paul had planned to get a B.A. in architecture, but then got commissioned as an officer in the Air Force. He wound up with a pilot's license, which he could no longer enjoy.

He claimed that from the age of nine, he had been flying his father's private Cessna 172s and 210s. He said he liked flying and had a good life at Fairchild Air Force Base outside Spokane. But then he got impatient, he missed Southern California, so instead of reenlisting, he decided to return home, where he married a "typical California girl," Mindy.

"This was the start of my life of crime," Paul wrote. "Mindy got fired by this bozo who owned 13 Shakeys' Pizzas, cause she wasn't receptive to his little sexual advances, so instead of doing any physical harm to the guy, I decided I'd teach him a lesson, and I proceeded to rob all 13 of his Shakeys' stores. . . . Did all 13 in 11 days."

The easy money got him hooked, Paul admitted. It was a rush to get away with something like that. He said the idea of the heists got him so excited, he wouldn't sleep for days. Paul would lie awake every night, figuring out his next moves. He claimed it wasn't the money that was so important—it was really the planning and the challenge. So after a while, still keeping his regular jobs, Paul decided to try his hand at a few armored-car robberies, and he was able to pull off five of them before he got caught and sent to prison.

The last robbery, he said, ended with four shots fired "by the guards and by myself."

It was funny, the way Paul explained it, that at first he thought he "got away" with everything. He took his $78,000 from the last heist, moved back to Washington, married his next and "final" wife, Kim, and bought a house, along with a second lot on Spokane Lake. Paul said he had it all—bought Kim a BMW, bought himself a new dog—and he settled down to enjoy life.

But his life of domestic bliss was not meant to be. It all came to a crashing halt because he lent money to a friend who was dealing cocaine. Somehow, because he lent the friend cash, when the friend got busted, the friend told police that Paul had supplied the coke money with cash he'd stolen down in Orange County.

"One thing led to another," he explained, and next thing Paul knew, he got thrown in prison.

Schneider was good at making the chain of events seem so innocent. He made it all sound almost reasonable, telling Janet that his little crime spree was nothing compared to the unjust treatment he suffered at the hands of the corrupt California penal system. Schneider was wonderful at presenting himself as the victim. A fairly adept writer, he was good at being self-deprecating; he knew just how to ingratiate himself.

Paul's letters were engaging. He would make jokes, then get serious; he would express all kinds of emotions back and forth, always making himself out to be the poor schmuck who just happened to get caught when he was too young and stupid to know better.

Paul's letters went on to talk about how frustrating being in prison was, about how lucky Janet was to have all that property, with a pond, and all those animals running around. He said he envied her good lifestyle. He loved seeing her animal photos. Did she want them back? Either way, he wanted to see more, and he was planning to write to Daisy, to see what kind of drawing she might like.

"Sounds like you've got a pretty big unselfish heart," Paul wrote, becoming overly familiar quickly. He really liked that about her, he said, and he also liked the fact that Janet was part Native American, because it made her mystically connected to animals, to the Earth. He wondered if Janet knew anything about the ancient druids. Would she like to know? He could tell her all about them. Druids were nature worshipers, just like her.

It didn't take long for Janet Coumbs to become convinced that Paul was an honest, affable guy. She started feeling sorry for him, especially when he described his ailments: his bad leg, his bad back, his open wound. He hinted at how much pain he was in, and she felt bad that the prison refused to give him proper medical attention.

Paul baited Janet with a discourse on religion, confiding that he was not at all religious, though he could understand *her* being into her religion; as for himself, having attended Catholic school for years, having been through his first communion and confirmation, he understood that organized religion could be a good thing. But he challenged Janet, telling her he didn't believe in it anymore. It wasn't that he felt negative about religion—he just didn't feel there was any place for it in prison.

For Janet, that was "the call" she needed. Here was a man reaching out to her, a man she could possibly "save." And there was something so alluring about having a man pour his heart out, about Paul being so open and honest, at such great length—she was just amazed. He really had her going.

As Paul ended his first "intimate" letter, he threw in a few lines about buying a dog for Janet Capes as a "gift," mostly for protection, or possibly for breeding or showing. Paul said Capes was going to supply him pictures of "their" dog, so he could have drawing reference materials. Apparently, he planned to buy Capes a large dog because that's what he liked—Saint Bernards, Alaskan malamutes, bullmastiffs, and mastiffs.

Janet had never even heard of a mastiff. She later went to the library to look the breed up.

"So you've got all those animals around and no dogs??!" Paul wrote in his sign-off, half joking. "Sounds mighty suspicious!!"

Paul hoped to hear from her real soon. He made sure to tell "Calamity" how much he appreciated her taking a chance on him, about sharing some insight into her life. He wanted her to know how special she was, that there had been exactly *two* women he had ever written to from prison before . . . and he hadn't had much luck at turning them into girlfriends.

"I'm anxious to know your life and get away from this prison stuff," he told Janet, throwing the ball in her court. "Cause it seems so hard to get folks to look past the prison walls and see you as an individual. . . . Sometimes, it don't seem worth the effort."

In one of his letters, Paul drew the outline of his hand. It was large enough to fill the entire eight-by-ten page, and he drew it to give Janet an idea of his size, telling her that not only did he have large hands, he had strong tough hands. From the description he gave of himself, Paul was a strapping guy, with a mustache and goatee, who once drove race cars, walked the streets in jeans and cowboy boots, and liked to wear Lagerfeld, "the good kind, not the watered down version."

But prison had changed him. He said that his neck was covered with tattoos of lizards and spiders, that he had snakes tattooed on his face—only kidding—though he did have few tattoos—one on his stomach, a small one, written in Old English letters; another one *"Weiss Krieger"* which he said meant "White Warrior"; and a couple of tattoos with the letters AB and 666 inside a shamrock, which "sounded like a good idea at the time."

As he continued to get to know Janet better, he began filling her ears with funny stories and suggestive compliments. Paul would be sure to ask about her health, specifically Janet's knees, which gave her trouble; he would send his regards to Daisy and to Janet Capes; but mostly he was concerned about her "critters," who Janet said were being attacked by wild mountain lions. Paul thought a few big dogs might help take care of that problem . . . but Janet wasn't so keen on that.

At first, Paul just wanted to have a friendship with Janet. He wanted her to feel uninhibited and relaxed with him. He wanted her to be able to say anything to him without feeling on guard. He wanted her to look at him as a new friend, and take her time, so they could really get to know each other. He didn't think she should worry about what anybody else thought. He joked about the burgeoning friendship, often reminding her to lighten up, and "smell the henhouse!"

He wanted Janet to stop worrying so much about things like money and her broken-down truck. Everything would work out for her in time, Paul assured her—she'd find a way to pay her bills at the farm, but meanwhile she needed to just take a breath and enjoy life.

"Make it a point to take a break occasionally, woman, set aside an afternoon now and then for yourself," he advised. "Go sightseeing, walk through the redwoods, go smell the salty air blowing off the beaches."

Paul liked being Janet's advisor. He felt she worked too hard, that she was too concerned with life's responsibilities. She was trying hard to make ends meet, but her animals weren't producing enough income, the Tupperware business she had wasn't going well, so Paul threw out a few suggestions for her. Perhaps Tupperware was a good way to show her friends his art? That way she could sell the two things at the same time. If she could find a way to afford to make laser copies, or even color Xeroxes, he could start sending her more of his drawings. He thought his artwork would sell for good money—he'd already sold a few pieces on the Internet—and he would be willing to let her do that. If Janet started getting orders for his artwork, she could take half the money. Would she be interested? Paul wanted her to consider it.

When Janet received the proposition, she was touched. She became more serious about getting to know Paul, especially if they were going to try to do some kind of business together. Really, she knew little about him, so she wrote with a bunch of questions, and he answered her in detail, explaining what prison life was like.

Paul said the "mainline" was a place just like in the movies, where everyone went to chow in the mess hall together, where everyone went to work, where inmates spent their days out in the yard together. The mainline folks had a lot available to them, things like weights and basketball and sunshine.

He explained that if he wanted to go to the "mainline," where he'd have regular privileges, he could do that. But he chose not to, because that would entail being a "snitch," and he was too much of a man of honor to make up lies about other people just to help his own hide. Paul claimed that was what most inmates did—they just lied and ratted on people to get "insider" favors.

But where he lived, in the "hole" or SHU, there were no perks what-

51

soever. He and the other guys were forced to eat in their cells, the guards would bring them a breakfast tray along with a sack lunch at seven in the morning, and then a dinner tray would be delivered again at six at night. He was fed through a slit in the door.

Whatever "privileges" he had were few. Basically, he was allowed to shower, go to the law library, and visit what he called the "dog run," which was a larger bare concrete cell with a thickly coated "sky light" that allowed him to catch a glimmer of the outside. It was a cubicle, a place that was supposed to be an "outing," but really all it was was an empty cell, and, because of the thick coating on the ceiling, all he could ever see was gray.

Hearing that was very upsetting to Janet. She didn't think it was healthy for Paul to be deprived of sunlight. She felt that kind of treatment was harsh and inhumane. She didn't think it was right, but Paul told her that the prison had already been sued about the issue, that an inmate filed a suit to fight for windows years before and lost, so there was nothing more anyone could do.

As far as the guards went, Paul explained they were just like everyone else in the world. Some were friendly, some were aloof, it all depended on the person. Some were talkative, others were quiet. But none of them were overly friendly, since they could get in trouble for being "too nice." Guards were not allowed to engage in what they called "over familiarity" with the prisoners.

Of course Paul didn't want Janet to feel sorry for him. Not at all. Always the macho guy, Paul insisted he had a pretty decent time in his cell, listening to the radio all day, mostly rock or country music, keeping himself busy with his art and his writing, and breaking up the day with his own special workouts, using the bunk beds as bars, using the floor, whatever else he could, to keep himself in shape.

When Janet wrote again, wanting to know how many other people Paul was in communication with, he mentioned that he corresponded regularly with a woman named Brenda Storey and her husband, Russ, the parents of his "ex-cellie." He sent drawings to the older couple and wrote notes back and forth. Brenda and Russ were good folks who really cared about him, and Paul appreciated them.

Other than that, there was his sister Tammy and there were some attorneys down in "Frisco" whom he wrote to semiregularly—they were people he and Dale were "doing business" with—and that was about it.

Paul was glad that Janet was finally asking him questions. He knew it was a way for them to get close. He told her how much he enjoyed her letters. He thought they were well written. He could tell that she was smart, funny, and had a good personality. And he wanted more. He hoped she would let him call her sometime, so he could hear her voice.

Regarding his crimes, Paul wanted to be honest. He told Janet he didn't feel any remorse about them whatsoever, because for one thing, he'd never stolen anything from an individual's car, home, or person. And as to stealing from armored Brinks trucks, he wasn't going to lie to her about that. He didn't regret what he did one bit. He took money from companies like Alpha Beta and Kmart, big corporations that were covered by insurance. If he had taken something from a person who worked hard for it, then he'd feel differently. But from a big corporation? He had no love for them.

When Janet wrote to say she was considering coming to visit him, Paul acted completely surprised. He wasn't sure if he could handle that. Not having seen a woman in so many years, it would be shocking.

"I'm really out of touch with society, with women, non-prisoner style mentality," Paul wrote to her, explaining that the idea made him a bit nervous. "I'm used to talking almost exclusively to men."

Paul wanted her to know that if she did decide to show up, she wouldn't be treated badly by the prison system. The atmosphere was more like a giant warehouse than anything; the guards would treat her fine. He certainly didn't want to deter her from coming, but he wasn't sure she would like it. He wanted her to know what to expect. Pelican Bay was a barren land, a sterile-looking place, and they'd have to talk from behind glass, via phone. They would never be permitted to have contact and he would be brought out in a private booth away from the other inmates.

Paul claimed he'd been visited by only one woman in twelve years, so if Janet felt nervous about it, she should just imagine how *he* felt about it. Paul told her that he would be the one who would feel out of his element.

In fact, he was so uncomfortable with the idea, he wasn't sure if he wanted her to see such a sorry sight. He hadn't had sun in years, he was white as a ghost, and he would be wearing a crazy-looking yellow jumpsuit, which made him look even more awful.

He wasn't sure if she should see him that way.

"It's a big deal to me," he wrote. "I'd be nervous as a chicken in a fox den."

After their correspondence about the visitation, Paul heard nothing from Janet, not a word. A month went by without him getting any return mail, and he began to worry that he said something to offend her. But then, just as he was starting to lose hope, out of the blue, Janet wrote to tell him that Daisy was begging to get a big dog, and she was thinking about it.

Paul was just ecstatic.

"A dog! Get out! Sounds like there's some smarts in her blood," Paul told his buddy. "Keep me up to date if you do get one, cause I'd like some pictures. I just might make you a portrait!"

CHAPTER SIX

Paul had a strange love-hate relationship with his sister Tammy. She still wrote to him, but he was outraged that she refused to come visit him at Pelican Bay. The two of them had been so close growing up, and for years, she hadn't given up on him the way his other sister, Kim, had. But now, with so much time having gone by, it seemed Tammy had become more distant.

Because of their strong attachment as kids, because Tammy understood the reasons behind Paul's anger, in his early days behind bars, Tammy would try to provide him with a sense of family, a sense of love. But even then, it was a tall order for her. Paul was changing, becoming hardened; he was no longer the sweet boy she'd grown up with.

Paul and Tammy were best buds as kids, perhaps because they were close in age, perhaps because Tammy was the prettiest one in the family. But mostly it was because Paul and Tammy shared a common threat: violent abuse from their stepfather.

As the eldest of the children and the only boy, Paul felt a need to stand up to his stepdad on behalf of himself and his sister. He didn't like the man's abusive ways and hated the fact that he and Tammy were subjected to this "military-style" angry man. The house where they grew up was run, not by their mom, but by their retired Air Force stepdad, and it was a hell house for them. Of course, their mother didn't seem to notice.

Tammy would later tell *Rolling Stone* that her childhood memories of military discipline bordered on sadism. "Our house was a prison, and our stepdad was the warden," she told the journalist, refusing to reveal her stepfather's name. "That man used to beat the shit out of Paul."

Tammy and Paul bonded out of a need to protect and nurture each other. While baby Kim didn't suffer the same fate, Tammy alleged that she and Paul were both abused with beatings, and that she was abused in other ways as well.

According to *Rolling Stone*, their stepfather would enjoy punishing the children for no apparent reason, waking the kids up in the middle of the night to scrub bathroom floors with toothbrushes, mocking them whenever he felt the whim.

Luckily, Tammy grew up to be an attractive woman and was happily married to a firefighter. She still had the emotional scars from childhood, but she was living a good life. She felt protected and loved by her husband, Greg. The two of them had a solid marriage, and that made up for a lot of the bad memories.

But Tammy knew her brother wasn't quite as fortunate. Her brother's life seemed to be riddled with problems. Paul had married young to escape his stepdad, but was quickly divorced by the girl; she dumped him the minute he enlisted in the Air Force. Paul had been kicked out of the Air Force for writing bad checks, and when he moved back to Cerritos, the town where they grew up, the only job he could get was at a fast food joint. Begrudgingly, he became a manager of a local pizza parlor, and he hated it. Paul was having a difficult time with women, with finding jobs, with life in general.

He got himself a small apartment and moved in with his girlfriend, Mindy, but that didn't seem to be working out either. One night, just out of boredom and rage, Paul put on a mask, armed himself with a handgun, and robbed the pizza restaurant after hours.

Tammy didn't realize it, but soon after that first robbery, Paul set his sights on the Alpha Beta Supermarket where she worked as a checkout girl. Apparently he noticed the Brinks trucks making pickups there, and he developed a hatred for the armored-truck guards, who were arrogant,

Paul thought, just because they carried weapons. The guards walked around the Alpha Beta acting like big shots, and Paul despised them for it.

"They'd come into the store with their revolvers pointing to the ground," Schneider confided to *Rolling Stone*. "They'd bump into people without even apologizing, and I wanted to show them that they weren't so tough."

After getting away with over $100,000 in cash, Paul showed up at their stepfather's house with a new souped-up motorcycle. According to Tammy, it was their stepdad who tipped off the cops about Paul's robbing the supermarket in 1985. Paul was twenty-three when his stepfather helped law enforcement send him to New Folsom State Prison.

Tammy never could forgive her stepfather for that. Even though Paul was dead wrong, she hated the man for taking pleasure in ruining her brother's life. It was repayment, she thought, for Paul not wanting their mom to remarry in the first place. At the tender age of fourteen, Paul had been traumatized by his parents' impending divorce, pleading with his mom to stay married to their dad. When his mom decided to work as a secretary and live on her own, it made Paul very upset. And when she soon thereafter married a maintenance man, this angry ex-military person, she broke Paul's heart.

Paul hated life from that point forward, and Tammy was well aware of that. She wished she could have done more to help her brother in those days, she wished they both could have found a way around the household abuse, but being a child herself, she was too young and vulnerable, too scared to say anything to their mom.

Now, as an adult, Tammy's relationship with her brother had grown increasingly strained. Paul had become a product of the system; prison life had turned him stone cold. He was different. He was nothing like he had been when he was first sent away. Back in the early years at New Folsom, Paul seemed happy with anything Tammy did to try to help. He was appreciative of Tammy's efforts to visit and send cash, to try to make life more comfortable for him. But once he arrived at Pelican Bay, Paul began writing with crazy demands. And he became paranoid, believing everyone, including Tammy, was his enemy.

As his years at Pelican Bay went by, Paul seemed to have lost all sense of conscience. He didn't seem to care about anybody, about how he treated people. He blamed all his problems on other people. It was always everyone else's fault, and he didn't care who he hurt or violated.

Tammy had promised she'd always be there for her brother, no matter what. So even though he would attempt to scare her, sometimes with powerful threats, she couldn't completely give up on him.

Tammy was, in a way, all Paul really had. But she was put off when, out of nowhere, she was threatened by one of Paul's cellmates:

Hello Tammy,
This is Mark, one of the guys you bought the TV for. Now, I figure you weren't expecting to hear from me, but I think it's high time somebody let you know what's going on. First of all, some of your most recent actions have placed a few people in bad situations around here. Your brother gave you a large sum of money, and this was done because he was counting on you to handle business.

Even though he thinks you are a slightly naïve girl, he assured us that you would never change up in mid stream. He promised that you were loyal. That you would never betray him. But unfortunately, you've given many of us reason to doubt that. It looks like you don't care about your own flesh and blood, looks like you care about your old man more than your loyalty to your brother. Now, you gave your word on certain things. And you haven't followed through.

Not good, Tammy. Not good at all.

You know, if a guy in prison gives his word and fails to follow through, he gets wacked. No ifs ands or buts. . . . That's the way your brother and I feel about people breaking their word to us. And to us, in here, out there, it's all the same.

Can you believe, that a lot of people really think we live in a completely different world than they do? It's a fact, Tammy, that some people are so dumb, they think we have to take a spaceship to get to their world. Isn't that funny?

But I can assure you, our world is the same as yours, and sometimes, we just have to reach out and touch somebody.

Because all it takes is a quick car ride. It's amazing to me, how stupid some people can be. They think none of us have any friends or family out there.

But you would never think that, would you? You know we don't need a spaceship to get to you, don't you. . . . You wouldn't give us your word, then go back on it, cause we have been asking ourselves that question.

Now, just so I'm confident that you fully understand me, let me go on and tell you about *my* sister. See, she did a really bad thing, and someone didn't like it. She was given something to hold and take care of, and she got warned by certain people about spending money that didn't belong to her, and let's just say, she stopped caring about her brother.

But then one night some people showed up, and let's just say she doesn't have to worry about anything anymore. There's not much else I can say about it. Yeah, it hurt me. But she did break her word.

But I don't want to think about things like that.

Let me tell you some good news, Tammy. I'm paroling in a month, and I'm going to be staying right in your neighborhood. Isn't that great! Your old man and me can go duck hunting with that *new* shotgun you just got him. Don't you think he would like that?

I know we'll have so much fun.

Now, maybe you're going to start seeing this my way, and do the right thing. Your too-trusting of a brother says I should have faith in you. Oh, and your brother asked me to give you a message. He'd really, really like to hear from you, and hopes you'll start sending him the $100 every week, like you said you would. He wants to think you'll come to your senses, Tammy.

Either way, I don't care. A job's a job. You know what I mean? And you can bet I'll be stopping by to visit as soon as I get out.

Me and your brother and a lot of people around here are tired of hearing all kinds of bad things about you. All kinds of bullshit. You know? A person can only take so much, before he shuts the bullshit up.

So think about it, Tammy, cause Paul hopes to hear from you, and I plan to come over for one of your good home-cooked meals.

Most sincerely,
Mark

If Tammy felt disheartened by her brother's evil ways, even if she felt she was being punished for doing him favors, whenever Paul would write to her with a new request, Tammy couldn't help herself. She would still try to respond.

But her husband felt differently. Greg had been burned by Paul more than once, and there came a point where he had had enough. In 1997, when Tammy got a letter from Paul asking her to raise dogs for him, Greg insisted Tammy write her brother and tell him they were not going to get involved.

No way in hell were they going to fall into another one of Schneider's wacky schemes, Greg said. Paul had caused them too much trouble already, and prisoners raising *dogs*? It didn't even make sense.

Immediately after the Whipple mauling, Greg and Tammy made statements to the press. They felt sorry for what happened to Diane Whipple. They needed the public to know they had nothing to do with Paul's dog-breeding business, reporting they were afraid of Schneider and his inmate friends. And with good reason.

"At one time, Paul got us into some deal where he sent us money from one of his legal settlements to buy TV sets for his buddies in prison," Greg told the media. "Next thing we know, FBI agents come to our door and said we were on someone's hit list . . ."

"I love my brother," Tammy confided, "but the guy's in prison for a reason." Of course with or without Tammy, Schneider would manage to continue to do "business." He and his Aryan Brothers had an interesting system going. They would use AB parolees to work with other "associates," setting up everything from drug deals to stock portfolios, and AB leaders would receive a percentage of the "take."

The Aryan Brotherhood had been around since the 1960s, and over the years, it became understood that AB parolees would do bidding for the "big boys" inside. This was considered an AB insurance policy, because if a parolee didn't comply, and then the guy just "happened" to wind up back in prison, the punishment would be death. It was that simple.

The AB payola system worked beautifully. It was a way to keep the gang organized; it was a way to have members facilitate AB business on the outside; it was a way to allow the Brotherhood to amass thousands and thousands of dollars. Whether gained by legal or illegal means, a percentage of all monies collected by Aryan Brotherhood members would go to the AB leadership, and the money added up.

Everyone understood that a membership in the Aryan Brotherhood gang was irrevocable, and AB leaders would enforce "hits" on anyone who broke the rules. Paul Schneider, one of the AB "shot-callers," was considered responsible for a half-dozen cell strangulations. That was back in the mid-1990s, when Devan Hawkes was working in a special Gang Unit Office at Pelican Bay under a gang expert named Jeff Briddle. They started finding evidence of Paul Schneider's leadership role.

Back then, the two gang investigators spent months studying Schneider's outgoing mail, looking at Schneider's elaborate codes to decipher what he was plotting. Even though Schneider used ancient runic symbols to confound them, eventually, between decoding his letters and using wiretaps on his phone conversations, Briddle and Hawkes figured out that Schneider was sending coded directives to have his "enemies" killed, both inside prison and out. But Schneider was so clever at making his demands, so sly in the way he intimidated people, that at that time there was no way to pin any crime on him.

Not that it would matter, because by the mid-1990s, Schneider was a "lifer" who would never get parole. Still, Hawkes and Briddle were frustrated by Schneider's ability to pull off killings right under their noses. Both dedicated corrections officers, they wanted to nail Schneider, not only to protect inmates, but for the safety of their fellow corrections officers as well.

But because they were unable to get any AB member to break the "code of silence," because they needed a witness to testify against Schneider in order to bring criminal charges against him, the guy was literally getting away with murder.

61

"Art Ruffo," a longtime Aryan Brotherhood member, was real tight with Schneider," Briddle recalled. "There was a significant relationship between them. Ruffo and Schneider had been celled together for a period of time. . . . And then Ruffo ends up dead."

One of Schneider's letters to his then girlfriend, Brenda Moore, included an order for a "check account withdrawal" from Schneider's stash. Also in that letter, written just before Ruffo's death, was Schneider's cryptic message about the season of vengeance.

"I have but one wish, and that is, I live long enough to repay in time tenfold all those who have come and gone," Paul wrote. "Gratifying to be there when arrogance collapses. How much more so to be the instrument."

"You just kind of surmise, with no hard evidence," Briddle confided. "Hey, you know what? Ruffo's dead. He's killed in his cell. It doesn't take a rocket scientist to figure out that it was probably a gang hit. But can you prove it? That's highly doubtful."

Nonetheless, the two gang investigators continued to monitor Schneider, certain he would slip up sooner or later. That was back in the time when Schneider had Brenda Moore wrapped completely around his finger. Brenda was seeing Paul quite often, showing off to other visitors. She had an attitude about her when she appeared at Pelican Bay on visiting days, and other female visitors disliked her. Brenda carried herself like she was the queen of the day. She felt a certain power, being the girlfriend of Paul Schneider. Of course, she had no idea how closely she was being watched, both in the prison and at her home.

From their letters and in-prison phone conversations, it was clear that Schneider and Moore were coming up with a different plot, one that didn't seem to have anything to do with murder. Schneider was hatching some kind of brilliant scheme, some kind of business plan, but the gang investigators couldn't decide what it was.

Between the runic symbols and the cryptic language Schneider used, often referring to his "saga," they had no idea what the criminal mastermind was up to.

"When we first started catching on to the letters, it was like, what's this? A saga? A book? Schneider's writing a book?" Briddle reflected. "We didn't have any informants giving us information about what might be going on, but we knew something was up. It took a long time, with the surveillance that we did, but then it all started coming together."

"You have to have icebreakers," Briddle said. "At the gang office we had at Pelican Bay, I had this crystal ball with a wizard on it. It was a battery-operated game piece, and if you passed your hand over it, it would say, 'Please consult me later,' or 'It's not in the cards.'"

Even though the Wizard was a game, it became a significant icebreaking tool with the inmates. At one point, Briddle was commanded to produce it as evidence in federal court during one of the lawsuits filed against him by a prisoner at Pelican Bay. Inmates loved to play games, and they enjoyed walking the edge with "cops," as they called corrections officers.

"You have to be able to be a gabber to talk to these guys. And that's where, as a gang investigator, you have to gauge their sincerity," Briddle explained. "We knew these guys could not be trusted. But there's always truth somewhere, and sometimes, you don't have the luxury of picking who you're in bed with."

Inmates found interesting reasons to sue the deep pockets of the California Department of Corrections. Whenever they confided in the investigators, if they believed Briddle or Hawkes said one wrong word, they would file a lawsuit, which meant, win or lose, the plaintiff would have something to look forward to.

For anyone serving life without parole, going to court was a chance to get off prison grounds—to go "sightseeing," so to speak. There was also gratification in being able to keep the court system tied up, and then of course, the possibility that money might be awarded. It was a very serious business, and everyone knew that. Lawsuits had become the chief method for inmates to make financial gains in California.

So there was a whole strange mentality, a dance that had to occur, in order for Briddle and Hawkes to wear an inmate down, to get an inmate to become an informant. Working in the Gang Unit Office, "debriefing" AB members and members from other prison gangs—the Mexican Mafia, the Black Guerrilla Family, the Noestra Familia, the Nazi Low-Riders—was a highly difficult task.

The officers had to get inmates to trust them, and then there would be these fine lines with confidence issues. If something went wrong in that Gang Unit Office, it could result in a lawsuit or the death of an inmate, and a gang war could break out. Briddle and Hawkes had been through a fair share of prison riots.

When it came to assisting Briddle, Hawkes was great at gaining intelligence about gang activities: murders, witness tampering, drug trafficking, racketeering. Every morning, he would sift through a box of mail—he was experienced at decoding information—and Hawkes and Briddle would make regular reports to the Department of Corrections, passing along intelligence to the FBI and the Drug Enforcement Administration as well. A brilliant guy with a photographic memory, Hawkes would look through his two computers, his microfiche, his reams and reams of stacked papers. He would stick his hand into a pile and pull out the exact letter someone was referring to, or find the particular file in question, even if it was from ten years prior.

People called Hawkes the "Rain Man," likening him to the Dustin Hoffman character, but Hawkes was much smoother than that. He was a tough guy with a heart of gold, a religious family man who at the same time gave the distinct impression that he had no problem using brute force.

When an inmate "debriefed" with Hawkes, spilling the goods on gang activities, naming names, naming locations, Hawkes would keep his end of the bargain and protect the guy. The prisoner would usually be moved, sometimes out of state; otherwise the inmate would be targeted by individuals from his own gang.

Working at Pelican Bay, Hawkes made things much easier for Briddle, and together they maintained things, security-wise, getting crucial information that would allow law enforcement to arrest violent predators. Yet they always kept their informants cool, calm, and collected—even when the inmates knew their lives were on the line.

Not that everything always ran smoothly. Pelican Bay had seen its share of gang-on-gang combat, and there were many correctional officers attacked. It was a violent atmosphere, and officers had to resort to everything from shooting rubber pellets to spraying tear gas . . . to severe beatings.

But Hawkes was one of the few correctional officers at Pelican Bay who never had been harmed by an inmate. People feared him. They revered him. As a gang investigator, Hawkes had become a powerful man. Because Hawkes was key in putting one of the leaders of the Mexican Mafia out of business, that successful operation would land him a promotion to Sacramento, where he worked as Special Agent for the Department of Corrections's Special Service Unit.

"The Mexican Mafia guy was sending hundreds of letters out. He had people on the outside," Hawkes said. "They were trafficking drugs, making assaults, causing riots. He had this entire network out there. He had a lot of Mexican Mafia members operating for him on the mainlines. And we shut down part of his operation."

Once Hawkes moved over to become a Special Agent, he and his hand-selected colleagues would keep tabs on parolees, escapees, and Level 4 inmates, the worst of the worst. Hawkes used SWAT teams and local police forces to help him bust crack houses, drug rings, all kinds of organized street gang activities that were being directed from the "inside" by gangs he tracked in California prisons.

Hawkes was incredible at getting people to spill. He knew how to work the likes of Brenda Moore and Paul Schneider. It wasn't just that he knew so much about the Aryan Brotherhood business dealings. He knew how to decode the leads they provided, and he got to know their affiliates.

With Hawkes on Schneider's heels, it would only be a matter of time before the predator's latest scheme—"the saga"—would be deciphered.

CHAPTER SEVEN

Hawkes and Briddle consulted with their colleagues at the American Bureau of Prisons, an agency that tracked gang activity across the United States. Back in the mid-1990s, they were looking to build a federal case against Schneider, if possible, to file a RICO case that could put the clamps down on Aryan Brotherhood criminal activities. Nailing Schneider would have a huge impact on the violence and crime inside Pelican Bay.

"The Aryan Brotherhood, they are the predominant white gang, with a blood-in, blood-out policy," a source from the Bureau of Prisons said. "Other gang members, of all races and ethnicities, know that when they deal with the AB, they are dealing with the ultimate group of control within the prison system."

Paul Schneider, an elder of the Aryan Brotherhood, was controlling members of other white prison gangs as well. With names like Dirty White Boys, Nazi Low-Riders, and Public Enemy Number One, these white prison gangs sounded tough, but they kowtowed to the Aryan Brotherhood, whom they looked to for leadership. Because the Brotherhood was in control of all insider drug dealing as well as mass quantities of cash, and its leaders were the "heavies" who negotiated with other prison gangs, the AB held all the cards.

"The major objective of a gang is primarily money and drugs," an anonymous source explained. "Ninety percent of Aryan Brotherhood gang members are hooked on drugs, methamphetamine, cocaine, whatever. And the only way to get the money to buy the drugs is through fear and intimidation and the power they gain over people."

Schneider was a gangster with a huge reputation. Not only could he have murders carried out, he could extort just about anyone he wanted. In particular, white inmates, white parolees, and white gangbangers were his targets. Schneider would use his powers to handpick certain white individuals, being careful that his "chosen people" understood their priority—always to take care of the Aryan Brotherhood's needs.

"That's what they do best, they profile people who can get the most done for them," a source confided. "Schneider, based on his characteristics and profile, is very effective at utilizing people. He could make people believe that they were being brought into the fold, make them believe that he would make them part of the inner circle, when in fact they weren't."

Back when Scott Erickson, a parolee friend of Schneider's, moved down to Sacramento, he was still paying "dues" to the AB and still active in illegal activities with the gang. Erickson made the acquaintance of Brenda Moore, a dark-haired voluptuous woman who worked out at Gold's Gym. Scott and Brenda became workout buddies, swapping stories. Eventually, Moore confided she herself was on "parole" of sorts, having been convicted of supplying weapons to a felon. Moore explained she escaped jail time by taking part in a parole-type "diversion program."

When Erickson sent a letter to Pelican Bay telling Paul about Brenda, including her photograph, Schneider was pleased. He liked the picture, her recent history, and her ballsy attitude. Certain that Brenda Moore could suit his needs, he sent a message to Sacramento that he wanted to meet her. And he wrote Brenda a postcard.

In his first note to her, Paul was very flattering, telling Brenda he was inspired by her beauty. Soon, Schneider would gain Moore's sympathy by telling her about the *hard time* he had to serve. In his own special way, as his notes progressed to letters, Paul told Brenda how much he wanted to get to know her. Paul thought they might wind up liking each other. He felt he could confide in her, and he began telling Brenda some of his inner desires. Brenda could relate to him. Paul and Brenda seemed to be made of the same cloth.

Paul was slowly luring her in, insisting that he wanted Brenda as a new "friend," nothing more. Of course, Brenda became determined to seduce Schneider, but Paul didn't respond to that. He insisted that they be "friends." Schneider offered to do her favors; he offered to pull strings for her. Paul promised Brenda the moon, all in return for her friendship. He would ask if she needed help in any way, wondering if she ever had any problems with money.

"At the beginning, people like Schneider start with things seeming equal," a source confided. "Schneider would make someone like Brenda Moore feel that they could help each other. He would hook the fish, then let it go back out and play. It's no different than an expert fisherman. You don't automatically reel any fish in the boat. You've got to give it play."

After numerous letters back and forth, Paul confided to Brenda that, against his wishes, he thought he was falling in love. He asked her if she wanted to see him in person, and he had Scott Erickson bring her up to Crescent City for a visit. Physically, Paul and Brenda were well suited for each other. It was obvious to the corrections officers monitoring the visits that their meetings were sexually charged, even from behind the glass wall.

In no time, Schneider became Moore's puppeteer. She fell head over heels with the strapping young man, about six years her junior. For Brenda, Paul seemed to be the answer to her prayers. He was brilliant, sexy, tall, and handsome. He sure didn't seem like a criminal. Quite the opposite, he was sophisticated and educated.

Brenda didn't care that Paul was behind bars. She didn't give it any thought at all. Brenda believed, in her heart, that Paul would get out somehow and the two of them would be able to run off together.

Because Moore was using fake "Department of Justice" stationery to communicate with Schneider, she was able to help plot all the details with Paul (she could even smuggle him drugs) and the Department of Corrections was completely in the dark about it.

But once Hawkes and Briddle had confirmed that the "official" Department of Justice stationery was bogus, that Brenda Moore and her cohorts had manufactured the phony "official" envelopes on a printing press, the Gang Unit investigators did some serious reading and they got the goods on Moore and Schneider. Looking through the next batch of false "Department of Justice" envelopes, they were finding things like plastic bags of marijuana and plastic bags containing white powdery substances.

With the new evidence they had, things were starting to heat up, and Schneider was becoming the centerpiece of an array of criminal activities. Briddle and Hawkes wound up making some phone calls and discovered that Brenda Moore was working with parolee Scott Erickson. It was alleged that Moore and Erickson had already robbed a store in Crescent City, and authorities believed that the pair had stockpiled stolen firearms, sawed-off shotguns, and were ready to pull off a string of crimes in Northern California.

Prison officials wasted no time in monitoring Schneider's associates. Hidden in a stairwell inside Pelican Bay, the Gang Unit discovered a piece of steel, one of the ceiling vents in the prison law library, had been stolen and replaced by a perfect cardboard replica, that had been used by Schneider to manufacture lethal weapons.

Hawkes and Briddle were able to get through red tape to quickly put new wiretapping into place in order to monitor Schneider's elaborate escape plot. They had their hands on Schneider's weapons, on his contraband, and everything was falling into place.

Simultaneously, Hawkes found a note floating around the prison which indicated that Schneider was involved in a conspiracy to kill another inmate. Briddle sent the note to the Department of Justice handwriting analysis unit, which confirmed that Schneider was the author. The details were very specific: Schneider instructed somebody to kill an inmate, stab him with a knife, then claim it was done in "self defense." Also in the note were instructions to contact Brenda Moore.

At that point, Briddle reflected, the investigators were "cuing into Schneider. We always knew he was really active but now we're discovering significant pieces. Then we have this note wherein he tells people, 'Hey, we're going to kill this guy.' So we found the weapon, we have that going on, and at the same time, we have this escape plot in existence."

———

At Briddle's beckoning, the Del Norte County Inter-Agency Narcotic Task Force issued a search warrant at Brenda Moore's place in June 1994. She lived in a back-lot trailer, cluttered with trash. And when the task force busted down the door, Brenda had locked herself in the bathroom, thinking no one would come bother her, naked in the tub. But, familiar with that ploy, law enforcement called female officers to the scene, who busted down the bathroom door and watched Brenda as she dressed. Other members of the task force searched Moore's bedroom drawers and closet. They located a double-edged knife, a Smith & Wesson nine-millimeter handgun that was reported stolen out of Eureka, and a black leather fanny pack filled with empty Ziploc baggies, some containing a few grams of methamphetamines, and a few grams of marijuana.

"You could tell that she was packaging drugs. It's in small amounts," Briddle explained, "so whether it was in the community or in the institution, she was distributing drugs."

Moore was arrested and thrown into the Del Norte County jail. But apparently, there wasn't enough evidence to get Moore on a felony charge for drug dealing, and they couldn't pin a felony charge on her for having a stolen gun. It was odd. The only felony charge that came out of the search warrant was based on Brenda Moore's possession of an eagle feather sitting on her nightstand.

"She appeared to be in some kind of mystic frame of mind," Briddle confided. "I don't know the proper word for it. She had rune stones, and things with wizards, and she had this eagle feather, which is illegal. It's a federal crime."

Brenda Moore wound up spending just seven days in jail. Apparently the Del Norte prosecutor, Jim Fallman, thought it was a stretch to bring her up on a felony charge for having a bald eagle feather, even if it was a national symbol. So, after what amounted to a slap on the wrist, Brenda Moore walked.

Fallman had offered her a plea deal.

Brenda Moore plead guilty to an amended misdemeanor count of possession of illegal narcoties. When she was convicted in the summer of 1994, her punishment was "community service" along with a $250 fine.

Briddle and Hawkes were disappointed by the Del Norte prosecutor's decision, but were still determined to go after Moore. Once she'd been arrested, they officially classified Brenda Moore as a "runner" for the Aryan Brotherhood, especially in light of one of the items they seized: a circular leather handmade piece of art, inscribed with Schneider's birthdate in runic symbols and the English words:

CORNFED
PAUL JOHN SCHNEIDER
RELEASE FROM PRISON
1994

After the raid on her home, Brenda Moore flooded the Gang Unit Office with complaints; she did everything she could to thwart them, filing citizen's complaints with the Department of Corrections in Sacramento, claiming that Pelican Bay officials were violating due process rights. Schneider and his AB associates also filed similar complaints claiming their due process, as inmates, was being interfered with. It was yet another brilliant ploy by Schneider, and it was effective.

"Because we had to respond to all the complaints," Hawkes recalled, "they were taking away from what our function was with intelligence gathering and interdiction. They inundated us, not with one complaint, but with fifty complaints. They were writing to the warden, to department headquarters, to their congressmen, to their senators."

But Briddle and Hawkes would not back down. They had enough evidence to believe that an escape plot was real, and though it was difficult to go to the warden and explain that a bunch of letters describing a "saga" translated into an impending escape, that's exactly what they did. Even though on the surface, the letters looked like they were planning to write a book, the gang investigators used charts and diagrams to prove that Schneider and Moore were using codes, that this wasn't any "saga" they were writing.

"The escape plot called for Schneider to get out of his cell," Briddle recalled. "At Pelican Bay we had this access system where the officer would electronically open the door and inmates would come out to go to the shower. There were indications that Schneider would use that opportunity to go to the roof. There was also an indication that Brenda was going to bring a jeweler's saw, a piece of wire embedded with a diamond. She was going to attempt to get that in to him."

According to the initial plan, Brenda was going to slip the jeweler's saw to a mainline inmate whom she could have a "contact" visit with. Once Schneider received the tool, he was going to cut through the roof of the Security Housing Unit, and then get out to the perimeter of the SHU, where Brenda would be waiting with two minibikes.

Investigators believed the escape was to be pulled off sometime around July Fourth. Schneider chose that date because there was a clock ticking: Pelican Bay was about to install a lethal electric fence later that summer.

But Briddle and Hawkes were one step ahead of him. They were decoding his messages, one by one. And they had gotten good at deciphering the runic symbols and the twisted language that read like a "fantasy" plot.

What struck them was the criminal mentality Schneider was able to instill in someone like Brenda Moore. The woman had no idea what danger she was in. She had zero knowledge of the workings of a super-max prison. She clearly didn't comprehend the extent of the security at Pelican Bay, one of the most highly guarded facilities in the nation. She was in way over her head, and she didn't know she was putting her life on the line.

"As far as the escape plot, Brenda Moore had others involved," Briddle said. "She had someone accompanying her, actually surveilling the prison from inside the institution during visits. And you can see the masterfulness of Schneider if you look at all this stuff he had going. He's got mainline people working for him, he's got Brenda, he's got a scheme set up to rob a Marshalls store, and that was all about money for the escape."

Schneider believed he had everything figured out. Having used a girlfriend years before in Oregon to help him escape from a maximum-security prison on minibikes, Schneider was confident his plan would work again. Behind prison walls, Schneider was collecting as much cash as possible, ready for a new incarnation down in Mexico. As a safeguard, he kept pressuring Brenda to carry out an armored-car robbery at the Marshalls store as well. Paul wanted to make sure he and Brenda would have enough "collective" moneys before they made their way south of the border.

Authorities learned that Brenda Moore also went by the name The Lady of Avalon. She had a pink business card printed up, which she handed around, claiming that she was some kind of mystic. It was all in keeping with the gothic sensibility of Paul Schneider, who was obsessed with that genre.

Paul identified with a significant gothic premise: the renunciation of society's rules. He saw himself like a gothic protagonist, as someone who could stretch beyond human realms. In his elaborate self-portraits, Schneider fancied himself not as an egomaniacal villain with the power to terrify, but as a depraved nobleman from another era, reduced to a life in chains.

The Lady of Avalon loved to play into Paul's fantasy. To her, Schneider was a gothic hero, with an impenetrable aura of mystery. Filled with Paul's sense of confidence, Brenda was convinced that her "nobleman" was omnipotent. She believed they had lived together in a previous life, and that in another incarnation Paul was an aristocrat and she was his wench.

Just as in any gothic story, Schneider's tale was one of horrific perversity. Like a gothic character, Paul claimed he had been wronged by the system. His imprisonment at Pelican Bay evoked, in Brenda's eyes, the gothic image of a giant castle, with its maze of dark hallways, and whatever forms of fear and punishment Pelican Bay might represent.

Because Brenda completely identified with Paul's gothic ideology, which promoted the perverse, the mystical, and the deviant, she felt she understood his plight. Schneider felt depraved and debased, and Brenda was fixated on the idea of saving him. She wanted a life with Paul, but in the interim she satisfied herself with the belief that she was his gothic lady. Perhaps Brenda was titillated by the idea that Paul was an enslaved and entrapped Dark Prince. Perhaps she thought she could save him by sharing in his darkness.

Ironically, in real life, Paul tormented Brenda, so on a twisted level, she did share in his darkness. Brenda had gone over to the dark side. Paul had her begging to stay in his life. After their initial courtship, after the letters of love subsided, Paul began writing abusive letters. Schneider insisted that she stop visiting him, claiming he didn't want her around because he didn't want to hurt her emotionally.

But really, it was all about him—and his "saga," which Brenda wasn't making a priority. Brenda wasn't getting things done fast enough for Paul, and since she wasn't operating on his schedule, he was threatening to find someone else to fill her shoes. He wasn't going to sit around in prison and rot.

"You're out, love," Paul wrote in one nasty letter. He was sorry to tell Brenda that it had all been "for naught." He hoped that love could prevail. But he couldn't justify her unreliability. He warned her *not to talk*, saying, "remember, no witnesses."

"Schneider played with her like she was a damn puppet on a string," Briddle later said. "You read the letters, and you can see it. He tells her how much he loves her in one letter, and then beats her up in the next. He would keep Brenda on pins and needles."

During their visits, Paul would promise to love Brenda until his last breath. He would call her his best friend and tell her how much he missed her. But then in other letters, Paul would change his tone completely. He'd become cold and uncaring, disconnected from Brenda and her problems.

If Brenda complained that she was being watched, that she wasn't writing the "book" because she was frightened or paranoid, Paul would fly into a rage. If she wrote and whined to him about being unable to get certain moneys or objects, if she had difficulties with people "coming through" for her, Schneider didn't want to hear it. He would cut her off. Refuse to accept her visits. Paul was great at head games.

From jail, after she'd been arrested for the eagle feather, Brenda wrote, telling Paul that things had gone from bad to worse—the DA's office had really surprised her. She called herself the "wench" who got out of the bathtub "buck naked."

Brenda told Paul about the way police busted down her bathroom door and how she had to stand there, nude and frightened. She said police put her son in handcuffs, and she was crying about how upsetting it was to see her child treated that way. Brenda said police asked her about gang affiliation. She said police made her nervous. She also claimed that the police made her strip so they could see her "pet cat," which didn't seem to fit her story, since she mentioned she was already naked when they arrived on the scene.

"I'm scared, Paul," Brenda wrote. Apparently one of her cellmates was paranoid, claiming that the DA would add more charges, that the DA would really screw her by the time she went to court.

Brenda was outraged that authorities were pressing for felony charges based on a feather, writing that it was such "bullshit." Still, she confided that she was creeped out about the whole thing, and she listed the charges against her, very upset that she didn't have bail money, very paranoid about the "the rat in the cellar."

"The eagle feather was the most substantial charge, because it's a federal violation to possess an eagle feather, period," Briddle explained. "And we wanted her on a felony, because if she pled guilty or was convicted of a felony, then we could preclude her from visiting Schneider. We would have taken out a major player in terms of prison drug trafficking, the robberies on the streets, and the escape."

"I don't know if I'll ever get to see you again," Brenda wrote, signing off. She didn't think it was funny, not at all. She was in jail, and no one would help. In her letter, Moore indicated something about "snitches." She was talking about two people specifically who she thought had "sold them down the river." She used code letters to indicate the names.

At first, Paul promised he'd take care of it, but then suddenly he changed his mind, and let Brenda know that he blamed her; he was sure it was her big mouth that got them caught. He was angry that Brenda could be stupid enough to blow three years of his planning. He was just furious. As Paul became more abusive, Brenda tried to placate him, but the more she did that, the more he would push her. Hot one minute, cold the next, Paul could turn emotions off and on, and keep Brenda dangling by a thread.

Briddle and Hawkes couldn't understand Moore whatsoever. To the investigators, Moore's fantasy life with Schneider was ludicrous. They thought it was absolutely insane that this attractive forty-something woman, who had started off as an average citizen, with a decent job, an IRA account, and all the other trimmings of middle-class life, could connect with a man like Paul "Cornfed" Schneider and, in a short period of time, become a violent threat to society.

Somehow, Schneider had transformed Brenda Moore into a key player in a major criminal scheme. By late summer 1994, Moore had moved from Crescent City out to an isolated region of Del Norte County. She was making her next step, as she continued her plans to help Schneider escape. Brenda thought she found the perfect hideaway. She was sure she had everyone off her trail. But not only was she being watched by Department of Corrections units and county law enforcement, she also had the FBI and DEA interested in her whereabouts.

"There was one map, a map of Brenda's house," Briddle confirmed. "She sent it to Schneider, purportedly to show him how she was living in this isolated area, to show him what her layout looked like." This hand-drawn map of Del Norte County, sent to Schneider in a "Department of Justice" envelope, provided specific directions about how to get to Brenda Moore's property via motorcycle.

"If Schneider's going to be escaping, and Brenda's not going to be there to pick him up, he's going to need to know a layout of her area," Briddle explained. "She was writing these letters to let him know that she had a safe haven for him. If the escape was going to be accomplished, she had someplace isolated and out of the way."

Brenda's map described the logging road that led to an old gold mine. The drawing she sent to Schneider was almost like a treasure map, detailing her landlord's property, the main house, her trailer, the pond, and the meadow. Brenda told Paul how happy she was to be there, hidden in the Smith River National Recreation Area, a place with the world's tallest trees. Her backyard had trees as big as skyscrapers, she wrote him—it was just amazing.

Though it was only twenty miles outside Crescent City, Brenda had indeed moved to a far-away land. She lived at the junction of the North Fork Smith River, just off Highway 199, near the ranger station, in a small town called Gasquet, where there was nothing more than a general store and a gas station. Brenda had no neighbors around for miles. Her landlord was so far off in the distance that she had complete privacy. She wanted Paul to know she was safe there, in complete peace and quiet.

From the main house to her trailer, the road sloped down for a half mile, taking her to the backside of the mountain, and she wanted Paul to imagine her there, just nestled in such a wonderland. There was so much beauty around her, and strange animals that people never saw, like spotted owls and flying squirrels. Brenda thought she was on top of the world. She could hardly believe she was four miles up a mountain, where she had crystal-clear waters flowing down from snowy peaks.

Trying to impress Paul with just how enchanted the place was, Brenda wrote that she was busy putting in flower beds and a new lawn to help keep the dust down. She was making things very comfy, starting a new life for herself. She hoped to build on an additional room and planned to add a woodstove before winter.

Paul wrote a letter back, asking nothing about the new place. It was "business" he wanted to talk about. Schneider wanted Moore to come visit again, so he was apologizing for being angry. If she would come see him, Schneider wrote, everything was going to be okay. Schneider couldn't get more detailed than that. He didn't trust the prison mail-delivery system.

"Brenda was stupid enough to believe that we wouldn't have the authority to stake out her house," a Department of Corrections source said. "In her mind, because there was only one dirt road going to her house, she thought the place was inaccessible. She didn't even fathom that we would end up at her house looking for him."

Gang Unit investigators knew Schneider was spending every waking minute coming up with new escape designs. In another note to Moore, he said something about a certain paint color he was interested in. He made it sound like he needed the paint for his artwork, but the unusual color matched with the metal door frames in the SHU.

The messages Schneider began sending Moore became more double-edged and deliberately confusing. Regarding the paint, Paul started out just being curious about whether Brenda could go search for it, but by the end of the note, he seemed to change his mind, and said he wasn't sure he needed it for the portrait he was working on.

Paul was pushing the envelope. Knowing investigators were reading his mail, he wanted to throw them off track. At the same time, he wanted to keep Moore guessing. It was his way to prevent her from blabbing. Schneider wasn't about to risk giving her new information. Paul told Brenda just enough to keep her holding her breath.

Brenda wrote that she "cringed" and actually felt like she died inside every time Paul expressed doubts about her. She told Paul how much she loved him, and wanted to know if Paul missed his "wench." She wondered what was wrong with Paul, why he'd stopped writing as much.

She wanted him to know, in his heart, how much he really meant to her, gushing about her unconditional love. She said she loved him "so darn much" she was at a loss about where to begin.

But Brenda was worried. She wasn't sure if their wedding plans were still on. She wondered about their getting married. She hoped that was still going to happen. She hated being in limbo about things, and she really wanted to discuss it.

When Brenda didn't get a response, she wrote Paul again to let him know that she'd gotten herself a guard dog, a Rottweiler, to keep unwanted guests away. This suggested to Briddle and Hawkes that if Schneider did escape, he might consider Gasquet as a quick turn-around location.

"I don't believe we had enough evidence to show Brenda Moore was involved in a conspiracy," a Department of Corrections source explained. "There was not enough evidence to withstand the scrutiny of the court, or we would have arrested her for that. We had a lot of supposition. We had a leather patch with writing, and that was the only physical piece of evidence we had. We didn't have proof of her bringing a jeweler's saw. We didn't have any motorcycles or minibikes out there."

Briddle knew that if Schneider did manage to escape, it would be very easy for him to lose law enforcement up in those mountains. They knew it was possible for Schneider to steal a guard uniform and just walk out of the facility. If Schneider managed to leave on foot, if he had a parolee waiting somewhere with a car, Moore's house was just a quick thirty-five-minute drive away.

"You look at the guys who escaped from a super-max in Texas," a source explained. "They just took off in a vehicle. Well, Schneider could do that too."

If he made it to Brenda's, Schneider would have about two hundred miles of wilderness all around him. There were plenty of places for him to hide.

"He had military status and training, and that means he would have taken a course on survival up in Washington, where he was stationed," Briddle surmised. "So knowing the guy's physical fitness and his education and experience, I always figured he would head for the Coastal Range at the very top of the Sierra Nevada, where it's very rugged."

"The guy always talked about Mexico," a source confided, "but he would first have to go into seclusion for a period of time. He'd have to hide out and then make his move quietly to Mexico, where he could kind of vanish."

CHAPTER EIGHT

With every new conversation and letter, authorities were getting closer to bringing conspiracy charges against Brenda Moore. All they needed was one piece of concrete evidence, and they were sitting tight. But Schneider was brilliant when it came to appearances. For instance, he had arranged things in such a way that there was not enough evidence to withstand the scrutiny of the court, and yet it appeared that he did have Moore sneak a jeweler's saw to a mainline inmate.

"Most of these people only know prison," a corrections official explained. "They don't know anything else. So even though they might be getting out, they know they're going to be back in a minute. And they figure they might as well be 'in good' with the inmates running the system."

Schneider would be careful not to let certain details pass his lips, but people around him knew that Schneider had big plans. No one dared to question or contradict him. Schneider had others carry out his commands, and if an inmate didn't comply, the guy would be considered effeminate and cowardly. And that would have horrible repercussions.

"Schneider could raise his hand for somebody. He could suggest that someone be made a member of the Aryan Brotherhood," a source confided. "So when he'd send people out on the street, these guys would bust their butts. They'd rob, rape, do whatever. They'd follow his orders at all costs."

What was interesting was that Schneider, for all his promises, never "raised his hand" for anyone. Most white inmates thought Schneider was helping them, that he was their best buddy, their true protector, but in reality, they never stood a chance of being "blessed" with AB status. That was something to be bestowed only upon the elite few.

Schneider and his AB council would operate in stealth, keeping everyone in the dark regarding their "status" with the gang. Some inmates were considered "associates," others were just "wannabes," but the brothers running the show would never outwardly inform anyone about who was officially in or out with the gang.

To prison officials, Schneider was an enigma. He would use his "authority" to offer memberships to the AB, and though officials realized Schneider's offers were bogus, none of the inmates ever seemed to catch on. Schneider would get parolees to accomplish all kinds of dirty deeds, then he'd stick a knife in their back, without the parolees ever suspecting that it was *Schneider* who was the ultimate backstabber. Schneider would act like he was defending parolees against the threat of the AB council, when in reality, behind the scenes, it was Schneider pulling all the strings.

It was a system that worked beautifully for Schneider. Because none of his patsies ever suspected him, he would wear the white hat, he was Mr. Congeniality among the inmate population. Then all of a sudden, a parolee would find himself on a hit list, either because the person "disrespected" an AB member or because the guy didn't carry out his assignment to the AB's specifications. But, of course, Schneider would know nothing about it.

Of the fifteen hundred inmates at Pelican Bay, Schneider's name would come up often. He was secretly feared throughout the prison, but in person, inmates liked him. They thought he had a great demeanor. Paul Schneider was filled with personality; he rarely expressed anger and always seemed to act in a cooperative spirit. Inmates thought they knew what to expect out of Schneider, but they had no idea who the real Schneider was.

"Instead of bringing in new members, if Schneider thought someone was played out, he'd just get rid of them," a prison source explained. "Every once in a while, he would bring someone into the AB, just to keep all this business going. But he wouldn't take just anybody. He would bring you in only if you fit the AB's elite profile."

To get into the gang, an inmate or a parolee had to "make his bones," which meant he had to kill somebody. That was the requirement—blood in, blood out—and that was how Schneider and his AB council members kept the terror and devastation going. Whenever a white guy would get paroled, Schneider would ask for favors, promising that in return, he'd make the guy an AB member.

And it was under that pretense that Schneider sent several parolees over to Brenda Moore, ordering former SHU inmates to help her with the Marshalls store armored-car robbery. Schneider needed that cash. He was ready to bolt from Pelican Bay, the clock was running. The July 4 date had passed, and by the end of that summer, in 1994, the lethal fence was already halfway up.

It was around that time that Robert Scully, a former heroin dealer and friend of Schneider's, was paroled from Pelican Bay. A bad ass, Scully was known for inciting riots among inmates and for attacking people with homemade knives, hacksaw blades, and whatever weapons he could, to create pandemonium in the prison. Because of Scully's gladiator-type combat, he'd been shot twice by prison guards, and locked away in the SHU.

Out on the streets, Scully would be a ticking time bomb, and Schneider knew that, but nonetheless Scully had been given orders to escort Brenda Moore to Sacramento to stake out the Marshalls store. Scully told Schneider he was only too happy to oblige, but somehow he got caught up in another criminal enterprise, and Scully never hooked up with Moore.

Just one month after his release from Pelican Bay, Scully was arrested for violating parole. Caught consorting with an armed acquaintance, he was sent straight back to the SHU. But when he emerged from Pelican Bay again, in March 1995, Schneider arranged for Scully to be picked up by Brenda, and the three of them had a string of robberies planned. Moore and Scully were going to hit a bunch of little stores on the way down Highway 101, and Brenda would send a portion of the take back to Paul.

Brenda didn't see Scully as a brutal creature, as a product of the sensory deprivation and social isolation of the SHU. In Brenda's eyes, Scully was a guy who, after growing up in Ocean Beach, an affluent part of San Diego, had been thrown into prison for being a drug addict. He was another victim of the Department of Corrections, just like Paul. Brenda felt safe with Scully. He promised he would be her protector, and Brenda believed him. They were headed toward Scully's hometown, where Scully was to check in with his parole officer.

But the duo never made it down to San Diego. Having bonded during their drive along the California coast, the two of them started to fall in love. With Scully assuring Brenda that Schneider didn't care about her anymore, Brenda became enticed. She wanted to get to know Scully better. She decided that her interest in Schneider was over.

As the two of them made their way down Highway 101, staying at cheap motels, fucking each other's brains out, Scully and Brenda enjoyed the high of new love. And they both reveled at the idea of pulling off robberies together.

However, they got sidetracked along the way, and just five days into their little road trip, they landed in Sebastopol, a small town in California wine country, surrounded by vineyards, a place with quaint shops and restaurants.

Scully and Moore loitered around the Sebastopol Bar & Grill until almost closing time, making the owner quite nervous. Fearing a robbery, the proprietor called the police. But Scully noticed the strange call, and he decided to take off and lie low in a nearby parking lot. Minutes later, as he and Brenda sat in their truck in front of a saddlery shop next to the restaurant, Deputy Sheriff Frank Trejo, a middle-aged grandfather looking forward to his retirement, pulled into the lot.

Trejo asked to see Moore's license and, according to Sonoma County investigators, as Moore fumbled through her purse, Scully pulled a sawed-off shotgun on Trejo, placing it directly on the deputy's face. Trejo was made to back up between the two vehicles, and get on his knees. As the man begged for his life, Scully shot the deputy in the forehead, smack between the eyes. Scully and Moore then ran across wine-country fields, broke into a house, and took a Santa Rosa family hostage. The next afternoon, with police surrounding the Santa Rosa house, Scully negotiated his surrender, and the hostages were released unharmed.

Scully and Moore were both brought up on murder charges. At his trial, accused cop-killer Scully would use everything in his power to deflect his culpability, blaming Moore for inciting the incident. Since he was accusing Moore of being his accomplice in the slaying, Moore's counsel called Paul Schneider in the courtroom to testify. It was Moore's understanding that Schneider would provide testimony on her behalf.

Brenda Moore claimed that she did not willingly participate in the murder of the deputy, insisting that she was an innocent bystander. Schneider had agreed to take the stand to explain Scully's violent nature, to say that he regretted not having warned his thirty-nine-year-old "fiancée" about Scully, that he should never have asked her to drive Scully from Pelican Bay to San Diego. But as things played out in the courtroom, Scully used hand signals to block Schneider's testimony. During almost an hour on the witness stand, Schneider went from openly discussing his relationship with Moore to balking at questions.

It was obvious to everyone in the court that Schneider was responding to Scully's signals, who was shaking his head, mouthing words to Schneider, and putting an index finger to his lips, indicating that Schneider had better be quiet. Though Brenda Moore's attorney ordered Schneider to ignore Robert Scully, Schneider made the decision to protect his gang brother.

For the murder of Deputy Frank Trejo, Robert Scully would eventually be sentenced to death, banished to the horror of death row in San Quentin. However, Brenda Moore would elude that kind of severe penalty.

For her part in the murder of a deputy, Moore was sentenced to serve a minimum of fifteen years. Moore would serve her time in a harsh California women's prison, and seven years later, Schneider's next "girlfriend," Marjorie Knoller, would wind up joining Brenda there . . .

Note: here's a portion of a letter written to "girlfriend" Janet Coumbs from Paul Schneider just after her first visit to Pelican Bay:

Dear Janet,   1-8-98

Hey there woman, whom I've seen now, luckily, and who
pressured a New Year's resolution out of me. Boy, that was *real*
good to see you and speak to you, Janet. I'm very much in love
with your voice and enamored by those eyes, Lady. Made my
month, nay, my year, seeing you . . .

Paul John

For months, before, during, and after the Moore and Scully trial,
Schneider had Janet Coumbs sending him calendars filled with pictures
of animals—horses, large wild cats, and dogs. He used the calendars to
draw pictures for Janet and Daisy, sending them little gifts of artwork,
encouraging Janet to try her own hand at sketching, telling her he was
having "tiger withdrawals" whenever he didn't receive new magazine
photos.

He loved to stay in touch with Janet, and he wanted her opinions of
his art. Paul said he trusted her point of view, being that she wasn't all
tied up in "prison crud." Janet could offer him a fresh perspective, and he
hoped she didn't think his drawings of animals looked too fierce or too
mean. He just wanted the animals to look "protective."

"I get tired of making all those sad, begging, don't-you-love-me-
cause-I'm-so-cute eyes of the animals," he wrote, "though I prefer those
type animal drawings."

Secretly, Paul was keeping his fingers crossed that Janet and Daisy
would make another trip to Crescent City. They had been there once,
and he felt sure he'd find a way to talk them into becoming dog owners,
if they would keep visiting more regularly.

From their first "in-person" visit, Paul was starting to act like family.
He told them how much he wished he could live near them. He looked at
the pictures that "Calamity" brought of her farm—a place with sheep,
goats, and chickens, a place up in the middle of nowhere. Teasing around,
Paul told Daisy he could easily live up on top of that mountain and
become "Grizzly Adams."

It would take a few more prison visits before Schneider would start to
drop hints about owning dogs. Paul thought it was smart for Janet

Coombs to have a dog around for protection. He was thrilled to hear Janet might consider buying Daisy a puppy. And Daisy loved the idea.

If they wanted a good strong dog, Paul suggested, he might even buy one for them, as sort of a "gift." That way, it could be their dog, together, and Janet could send him pictures every week so he could make new drawings and see the pup grow.

This friendship with Janet had blossomed after Brenda Moore's conviction, when Paul Schneider had to find another route to getting himself drugs and money. During Janet's initial in-person visit, he wasted no time in praising her to the max. He told Janet what a great person she was, he reminded her that other missionaries had the "lock 'em up and throw away the key" attitude, insisting that Janet was special, *more Godly*, that she was a gift sent to this world.

Having given up on his original plan to escape, the lethal fence having foiled him completely, Schneider worked hard as a jailhouse lawyer, filing endless lawsuits against the California Department of Corrections. That was his best chance at ever escaping, because during transport to any courtroom, there was always the possibility of stabbing the guards, grabbing the keys, and making a run for it.

Paul found litigation served another purpose as well. Not only did it help occupy all the endless hours he spent in the SHU, it allowed him the luxury of spending an hour a day in the prison law library, which was a significant outing for him. Otherwise, he'd go insane, and he definitely didn't want to lose his marbles just because he was locked up in a solid concrete box all day, looking at the world through a steel mesh door.

It was lucky for Paul that he was so smart, because Schneider had so many cases going that it would have been hard for most people to keep track of them. Schneider had filed and won a couple of his cases, so, in his mind, he rationalized being in the SHU as a good thing. Not only did the isolation keep him away from the rapists and child molesters on the mainline—the people he hated—but his life in the SHU was so nice and quiet, affording him the time to continue with his legal filings and his precious artwork, which was becoming an important pastime.

Since he was forbidden art supplies by prison officials, Schneider was a genius at making his own colors by collecting scraps of magazine paper, soaking it in toilet water until the ink ran, then making pigments by mixing the colors off the print ads. Over the years, Schneider would pester Tammy to send him all kinds of magazines, especially nature publications like *Field & Stream*. And Tammy would oblige, always looking for good photos of animals, knowing that Paul enjoyed seeing large animals in the wild.

However, when *Field & Stream* was banned by the prison because of the photos of guns it contained, Paul was forced to look for other outlets. Famous animals could be found in everyday magazines, Schneider realized, and he became partial to Siegfried and Roy's white tigers, whose photos were available in magazines such as *People* and *Us*.

By tracing over magazine art, Schneider fancied himself a great artist. He and Bretches worked together, looking over each other's shoulders to produce intricate drawings that looked like airbrushed erotica. Some of the art they depicted were simple tracings of animals—tigers, cougars, and dogs—which were good enough to be sent to people as gifts, and occasionally to be sold through the Internet.

Then there were Paul's personal artworks, where he depicted his fantasies of gothic scenes. There were drawings where he fashioned visions of women who might have had erotic encounters with animals—it was all just suggestive. Then there were other drawings where he presented himself as a Norse god, protected by guard dogs on each side. His godlike image would be accompanied by cryptic symbols, runic letters, and elements of Odinism, a pagan religion Schneider played with.

Associated with warfare and magical knowledge, Schneider called himself an Odinist, believing that he had mythological powers like the pagan god Odin. Schneider was occasionally referred to as "Loki, the son of Odin," and drew pictures of himself to indicate he was the "god of mischief." Schneider used gothic rune symbols from an extinct Germanic language, to signify codes about *supreme white power* and a *new world order*. It was the ancient runic alphabet that allowed him to communicate to other inmates and associates.

But oddly, it wasn't his mythological enchantment with Odinism, nor was it his obsessive belief in white supremacy, that got Schneider into any trouble. It was when he came across an innocuous magazine called *Dog Fancy* that his life would take a dark turn.

"Looking at dogs made me forget I was in prison," he would later grumble.

In early January 1998 when Paul Schneider wrote Janet Coumbs asking her how things were going at "Green Acres," he was jovial in his tone, telling her that her farm reminded him of that old television show, and he wanted to know what Janet thought of his "banana suited self." Paul hoped Janet would send him more animal photos. He needed them to be able to draw, and he was trying to figure out what to draw for Janet's birthday. Paul said he already had a "killer cougar" laid out.

He hoped Janet and Daisy missed him, he wished them well, and wondered if they might come back to visit again on the fourteenth of that same month. When the fourteenth came and went, Schneider wrote Janet another letter, this time a bit annoyed by not having heard a response from her. He hoped that everything was okay at the Hayfork farm and that Janet had gotten her IRS refund check in the mail. He still planned on making a drawing as a gift for Janet's birthday, and was thinking of drawing a cougar with a cub.

Paul wanted Janet to know how much he liked her New Year's resolutions, especially the one where she promised to visit him once a month. He thought that was really cool. He was "tripping" on the possibility of Janet making a weekend visit. He could hardly imagine the two of them having three straight days of talking to each other in person. He wondered if Janet had figured out a place to sleep overnight. He wondered if Daisy would be coming along.

In another letter, Paul said he was a dog fanatic, and he hoped Janet would get a dog. Paul didn't like small, yappy dogs, only big dogs, he wrote. Paul thought little dogs existed only to feed big dogs (only kidding).

Paul was disappointed that he hadn't heard much from Janet. He was pacing around in his pod, waiting for the mail to arrive, waiting for "the cops" to come open up each of the pods, listening for the sound of the electronic chain-driven steel doors.

When the mail finally arrived, Paul received a surprise from a friend. It was a Rottweiler calendar from his friend's girlfriend. He wrote Janet to tell her how happy the calendar made him, he wanted her to know that it was sent just out of the blue, that it was a kind act on the part of a woman that made him "see the world anew." He wished he could show it to Janet.

Paul was running out of things to say, not wanting to get too personal too soon, but he did tell Janet how busy he'd been, filing new court cases against the Department of Corrections, bragging that he'd won three out of four personal lawsuits, and helped three other inmates win cases. He told her his victories in court were like a "one in a million" chance.

Before he signed off, before urging Janet to come visit again, Paul mentioned that he might just have to buy her and Daisy a purebred dog. That way, they'd be sure to have a good dog to protect them.

Janet Coumbs didn't go to see Paul as often as he would have liked. She had problems with her car, she owed money to her mechanic and a half-dozen other people in Hayfork. Between her meager farm income and her Social Security benefits, it seemed she just couldn't make ends meet.

Janet was never good about money. Thoroughly naïve, she had no real experience in the workplace. She'd been to business college in her younger days, she learned to type and take shorthand, but that was back in the late 1960s, when certain women went to college as a formality, not necessarily expecting to get a job.

Like many women of her generation, Janet left business matters to men. She went to college "just in case," and that was a reasonable plan back then. She was biding time in business college, just long enough to find a boyfriend, get married, and have kids. Janet just couldn't make it in city life. She had animals in her blood, and she wanted to live back home on a farm and raise a family.

It seems she lost her secretarial skills almost as soon as she learned them, returning back to Hayfork to get married and train her horses. A country girl who grew up with cougars and coyotes surrounding her property, even as a kid, Janet was fascinated by the wild. At age five, she followed a cougar up a trail on her horse. She would recall the horse's being restless as she got up close enough to make the cougar roar, but even then, she felt perfectly at ease, as though she was spiritually connected to the wild animal.

When Janet landed back in Hayfork, she and her first husband bought a two-acre lot with a creek running through it, right next to the lumber mill in town. Janet was the one who had the money for the property, and they lived the American dream, decorating a two-bedroom house with quaint Americana furnishings. Her husband was a day laborer, and Janet raised livestock. She tilled the land, tended to the vegetable garden, and got herself pregnant, and things went along fine for about a year. But when Janet gained a ton of weight, the fighting started, and her husband became violent. The guy threatened to kill her. He took off before Daisy turned two, just after Janet had given birth to their son. By then, Janet Coumbs had gotten even larger, and her self-esteem was shot.

Left to raise her kids on her own, Janet did everything from baby-sitting to firefighting to bring in cash, but she was having a rough go of it. Her horses were dying—she suspected it was caused by the run-off pollution from the local mill, but she couldn't prove it. She lost eight horses and thirty rabbits because of the chemicals the mill was using, and eventually Janet and Daisy were both feeling sick. Unfortunately, their hometown doctor was paid by the lumber mill, so the physician wouldn't confirm that the mill was causing the problem.

Janet was smart enough to go to the mill and complain, showing them how runoff from their chemicals would fill her pond. Eventually, the lumber mill traded properties with Janet and she wound up with her four-acre place. Her old house was literally picked up and moved by the mill. It was an odd settlement, Janet thought, especially when she watched the lumber mill cover up her old property with a twelve-foot layer of rock.

Nonetheless, Janet had her new farm, she met and married her second husband, and after a few years, she had another baby girl. Her older kids helped her with the farming and Janet was happy enough to raise chickens and vegetables. She rescued horses on the side; she had a half-dozen on her land, and Janet had a good life for a while. That was until her weight started creeping up even more, and eventually her second marriage was destroyed.

Depressed and lonely after her divorce, Janet's continued eating caused her knees to give out. Her knees made it difficult to work on the farm, her life became unbearable, and before she knew it, she couldn't afford her horses or tend to her chickens.

With three kids and no decent income, Janet was desperate. She received welfare moneys and she scratched by somehow, but life was pretty miserable. But then a neighbor friend, a guy she'd known for three years—a widower with a lot of problems—came along, and asked Janet to marry him. It would be the third marriage for both.

Of course, Janet never did choose the right men, so the marriage didn't last long. The guy was violent, and when Janet caught him abusing his own children, she went to the authorities. Janet's third husband skipped town, taking his kids with him, and was never to be seen again.

All Janet had left of the man was his herd of sheep. Janet didn't want the animals; she thought sheep were stupid creatures. But she was stuck raising them, and it became profitable for her, selling the lamb and mutton to the markets, shearing their coats for wool. It was funny, the animals were her livelihood, but at the same time, she would also consider them her pets. Janet was like that. She could raise sheep and pigs and rabbits, and she would love them and consider them a part of her family. But when the time came for them to be slaughtered, that was that.

Such was the way of life on Janet's farm in Hayfork.

By the late 1990s, when Paul Schneider offered to buy Janet and Daisy a set of dogs, Janet was considering it. Her other two kids were no longer in the equation, both of them having moved in with relatives, and Janet felt the dogs could breathe new life into the farm.

"So Paul starts telling me about these dogs, big bull-nosed dogs, and I don't want them on my ranch because of the sheep," Janet reflected. "Then he told me about these companion guard dogs called Presa Canario. The up and coming dog of the world."

"Well, the pictures of the puppies look really cute," Janet admitted.

"They're terrific dogs and they're very well mannered," Paul promised, his voice sounding upbeat and sincere.

"But I'm worried about my sheep," Janet told him, "they're fragile."

"What you don't realize is, these are protection dogs. They won't let anyone on your property, they won't let anyone come after your animals."

"Well, how big do they get?" she wanted to know.

"About a hundred forty pounds. Didn't you ever look at the Web site?"

"No. I still don't have a way to get to a computer."

"Okay, well, let me get right to the point, Janet. You would be one of the first people in the United States who would have these dogs. I think you'd be one of four breeders in the country."

"Really?"

"Yeah. And I'm telling you, these dogs are going to catch on. Everyone's going to want one, because they're better than Rottweilers."

"Well, I think it might be too much of a job for me, I mean, I've got my knee problems and all."

Paul and Janet went back and forth in their discussions for weeks. By that point, Paul was sending her money so he could call her collect on the phone, and still, Janet wasn't convinced that she should get involved in dog breeding. She knew nothing about the business, she kept telling him, and she didn't like the idea of raising big huge dogs.

But Paul was pushy and told her she'd make good money out of it. He promised he would pay for the food and everything. All she had to do was sell the pups, sit back, and enjoy the profits. Paul told Janet she could choose whatever type of dog she wanted, but he seemed to be forcing the Presa Canario on her. When she balked at the breed, Paul gave her instructions to look at *Dog Fancy* and check out other massive breeds. Because Janet couldn't find the magazine, Paul sent her a few photos with other suggestions: the Dogue de Bordeaux, the Fila Brasileiro, the Japanese Tosa.

Of course, Janet didn't have a clue about any of these breeds, but from the pictures alone, she wanted no part of them.

"Paul sent me pictures of these really big ugly dogs. I mean, they were horrible looking," she recalled. "The one with the French name had all these wrinkles and drool, and then the Tosa was like a sumo-wrestler dog. The picture showed this Tosa with two big ropes holding it. It was just huge. The only one that looked cool was the Fila, but that was giant too, and I saw they were used to herd cattle. I told Paul I didn't think they were supposed to be raised around sheep."

Paul wanted to make Janet feel comfortable. He was trying to give her a quick, easy guide to dog breeding, explaining that she was wrong about the large dogs mixing with livestock. He began to write more often, explaining the differences between cattle dogs, sheep dogs, herding dogs, and hunting dogs.

Paul wanted Janet to know how important it was for them to breed a rare type of dog. He said he and Dale planned to make a lot of money with her. They intended to buy her champion-sired puppies, and they needed Janet to comprehend the significance of certain bloodlines, the working abilities of each breed, their temperaments, and their soundness. It was no game for him and Bretches.

But Janet felt the dogs Paul was asking her to raise looked scary. She was really on the fence about what to do when something happened that made her finally give in. The Rottweiler she'd bought Daisy was killed on the road, and just days later, a mountain lion got on her property and killed some of her livestock.

"So I'm writing Paul and telling him about losing my sheep," Janet confided, "and he's telling me how terrible that was, and how if I had guard dogs, they would protect my animals. And he tells me the Presa Canario is going to be just like a Rottweiler, that they were championship dogs, that they would help me, they could keep me company and ride around in my car."

Traditionally used for dog fighting, the Presa Canario breed was almost extinct by the 1960s, having been banned in the Canary Islands for humane reasons. But when the breed was introduced in the United States in 1990, it quickly became known for its strong temperament and ability to seize other animals, and soon it became popular again back in the Spanish province.

Always strong and decisive, the Presa's real disposition could be seen when the animal would defend or protect its territory. Notorious for its territorial and determined nature, the Presa Canario was fearless. The breed seemed to be an enigma, unlike any other. They were impetuous, yet reliable. What impressed American breeders was the fact that the

Presa would remain docile but could move suddenly with great speed and action. The Presa Canario breed was a result of the crossbreeding of the pre-Hispanic Molosoid dog with a dog native to the Canary Islands that had been bred for fighting purposes. The cross mix created a Presa Canario (or Canary dog) that was a powerful, muscular, well-proportioned, and robust animal.

When Janet received photos of Presa Canario pups, they were accompanied by Web site print-outs from U.S. Presa dog breeders. The Presa Canario Club of America talked about the Presa as a valued guard dog that could be counted on to protect the home and family. Janet was sent photos of young children riding on Presa Canarios' backs, along with tales about how friendly the dogs could be. She was never told that these dogs were considered dangerous or that, among other things, owners were required to have insurance for them.

From the photos of the pups, it was impossible for Janet to see how powerful the dogs were, how severe and frightening their gaze could be. She read Internet excerpts that described the Presa as "affectionate, docile, and well-behaved with its owner and family." She understood the Presa Canario to be a most loyal dog, a rare breed that could be trusted to stay by her side at all times.

That the Presa would not hesitate to attack anyone whom it perceived to be a threat—that the Presa's attack could be deadly—would remain completely unknown to her. And Janet would give Paul the go-ahead.

Schneider called with a list of three Presa breeders for Janet to contact: Red Star, Dark Force, and Hard Times Kennels.

CHAPTER NINE

Prey Drive is a catchphrase in training seminars for canines. Animal behavioral experts can determine, on a scientific level, what various canine drives are, and how they fit into protection training. Experts specify that while Prey Drive can be enhanced, it is *inborn*. One might say it is a trainable instinct. Prey Drive is part of a dog's food-gathering behavior, which means it rules a dog's hunting and killing techniques.

In order to understand the Prey Drive instinct in a dog, experts say, one might consider what a real prey does when it's hunted. Always on the move, in an evasive way, the prey is panic-stricken. This type of behavior sets off the response of pursuit in a canine, which, in turn, triggers pouncing, biting, pulling, gnawing, and *shaking-to-death* action.

CHAPTER TEN

Bane was thirty pounds when Janet first got him. She would remember seeing his huge paws, and thinking how big he would grow, but she could never imagine that his head could get as big as a steering wheel. Luckily, Janet knew enough about dogs to contain him. Bane understood "no." He understood "sit."

Bane was clumsy, however. As much as he tried to heed Janet's commands, he was not quite as graceful as the female, Isis. Bane tried to be obedient, but he would knock things over; he was a bull in a china shop. Isis, on the other hand, moved almost like a cat, able to stop and turn on a dime.

Bane was the opposite of Isis in every way. Bane was almost sheer black; Isis was light tan. Bane was a clown; Isis was a princess. Both of them were beautiful canines, both were good at responding to verbal praise, but Bane wasn't as adept as Isis, nor was he as adaptable to his new surroundings. Bane had a more difficult transition and was leery of being around other animals.

"When we first got him," Janet said, "Bane was not even here a week when he bumped his head. We didn't know what happened to him. He was fine when he went to bed that night, out in his little yard that we built for him, but when I got up in the morning, he's got this big lump on his head."

Janet had to drive Bane twenty-two miles to the veterinarian. When the vet shaved Bane's head a bit, he discovered a huge knot and was concerned that Bane might have some brain damage. But once back in Hayfork, Bane seemed to do fine, and after a while, Bane became part of the fold, just like Isis.

The two pups played well together, even though they were very much different creatures, and Janet was fascinated watching them in action, trying to learn about their unusual personalities. Always goofing around, Bane would run without looking—he would trip and fall, he would wind up soaked in the pond, covered in mud, he was just a mess. Isis, on the other hand, was elegant and reserved, even regal, in the way she carried herself. From the age of three months, Isis preferred to keep her distance from all the muck at the farm.

Whatever their differences, whatever their flaws and attributes, Bane and Isis were Janet's babies. She and Daisy had driven eight hours through the mountains to get them, and she fell in love with the pups at first sight.

At first, having these two pedigreed dogs seemed like the best thing that ever happened to Janet. They were so much fun to cuddle, so soft to touch, so loving and friendly. They were both regal beings. But as it turned out, they had strong personalities, so it didn't take too long for Bane and Isis to "take over" the farm. They were the keepers of all the animals in the land; they protected everyone—even the cats Janet had running around. Daisy would squeal with delight when she saw Bane walking around with one of her kittens in his mouth. She thought it was hilarious, the way Bane would carry the little fluff ball, like the kitty was his personal "pet."

All along, Paul was keeping track of his Presas in Hayfork. The initial pictures Janet sent him of the dogs were exquisite, and he wrote Janet often, with questions and instructions about their growth, their weight, the way they were being handled. Paul wanted Janet to remember that he shelled out a lot of money for the animals, they cost a couple thousand apiece, and he planned to keep strict tabs on her.

Paul couldn't trust Janet to raise such blue-blood champions on her own. He wanted to be sure the dogs were being treated with kid gloves at all times, and insisted Janet feed them special "growth" food and dietary supplements. Schneider had all kinds of demands, for special this and special that.

Janet wasn't too happy about Paul's bossy ways. He seemed to want an awful lot from her, yet he wasn't keeping her well stocked with cash. The dogs were costly, between vet bills, collars, dog beds, and the inordinate amount of food they consumed. But Paul didn't seem to care. That the money was always running out became Janet's problem. Janet did realize she was becoming overwhelmed, and she was getting behind on things. Bane and Isis just ate so much and were growing so fast that they were hard to keep up with.

Even from the initial contact, Janet had problems with the two dogs. A few days before Bane and Isis were to arrive, Janet's car wouldn't start. She was in a panic when Paul phoned her. On short notice, Paul got his friend Brenda Storey, the mother of one of Paul's fellow inmates, to "rescue" the two pups from the Sacramento airport, signing officially for them.

It was a few days before Janet could make it down to the Storey residence in Fairfield.

When Janet finally borrowed a truck and got to Brenda and Russ Storey's place, she and Brenda didn't take to each other very well. Brenda blamed Janet for being unreliable. She blamed Janet for having been put upon by Paul, who was barking orders from Pelican Bay. Brenda didn't want to have anything to do with the dogs, but she felt compelled to comply. Her son was in prison with Paul, and Brenda Storey knew Schneider was a threat. She didn't like the whole idea of Schneider and Bretches being in the dog business, but she kept her mouth shut. Storey sure hadn't bargained for all the problems the large dogs brought, and she just wanted them out of her house.

Schneider sent a money order to help Mrs. Storey pay for her time and trouble, but the money didn't arrive for weeks, and in the interim, Russ and Brenda were stuck paying for the special food, the special supplements, the big dog collars, and the big leashes. It was too much. The Storeys were spending all this cash, their house was being turned upside down by these tremendous unruly dogs. The Storeys were outraged. It took Janet almost a week to get Bane and Isis out of their hair, and by that time the Storeys were at their wit's end. Practically shoving the dog crates into Janet's truck, the Storeys were glad to see the motley brood go.

Of course, when Paul received Brenda Storey's report, he wasn't too happy with the way the dog pickup went. He felt Janet had been irresponsible, and couldn't be trusted anymore. He was insistent that the Storeys keep an eye on Coumbs. The couple, worried about the safety of her inmate son, knew they had to comply. They promised to help Schneider in any way they could.

In the first weeks that Janet had the dogs, when Paul heard reports of Bane walking around with a kitten in his mouth, he was mortified. He didn't want Janet raising "sissy" dogs, he told her. Bane was not to be "friends" with kittens or anyone else. He reminded Janet about Bane's pedigree. His father was Stygian's "Thor." His mother was Red Star's "Karma." Bane's bloodlines had been traced by the Federation of International Canines all the way back to the great Presa Canario "Urco," the Spanish champion of champions.

When further reports came that Bane was being used to carry firewood around the ranch, that he was pulling a little red wagon by a rope, Schneider started getting antsy. He didn't want to do anything to scare Janet, but at the same time, he needed his dogs to be aggressive, and if Janet couldn't handle it, he'd figure out another way.

It didn't help matters that Janet was lagging on her promise to keep Paul up to the minute on the dogs. Schneider didn't like the new sets of photos she was sending, and he didn't think she was taking the enterprise seriously enough. He was getting ready to threaten her, to have the Storeys pull the dogs out of Janet's hands, but he decided to give her one last chance.

"You were *standing* when you took the last picture of Bane," Paul harped, yelling over the phone. "You're making the dog look smaller than he is."

"Well, trust me, he's not small," Janet promised. "He's one of the biggest puppies I've ever seen."

"You're not getting the right angles," he argued. "You need to get down on their level so I can see the dogs. We don't have any good close-ups here."

"If I get down on their level, they want to see what I have in my hand. They get right in my face, so I can't get the picture anyway."

"If these pups are growing as much as you say, Dale and I can't tell. From these crappy shots you've sent us here, we can't see shit. Half the pictures are fuzzy and washed out."

Schneider was angry that he had to deal with such ineptitude. He couldn't stand it when people promised things, and then didn't get them done. It made him furious to think that his champion purebreds were not being tended to properly.

But the days passed quickly, weeks turned into months, and before Paul knew it, it was time for Bane and Isis to breed. Paul and Dale just had to hope that Janet wouldn't screw things up.

But as Paul continued to hear new details about Isis, he grew angrier and angrier at Janet. From the cell in Pelican Bay, Dale was trying to calm Paul down, but Paul couldn't be consoled. These were their "Dog O' War" champions. They were tenacious dogs with ancient bloodlines from the Spanish "dominion islands" and this Dog O' War Kennel suddenly meant the world to Schneider. If the ferocious dogs were bred well, they would be his ticket to the rainbow.

Dale suggested Paul write Janet a list of explicit instructions regarding how the dogs should be fed. Paul did that. He sent Janet a note, explaining to her how important it was that the dogs grow "mighty." If Janet did things correctly, he reminded her, Bane and Isis could stop any predator dead in its tracks. Janet would have no more troubles with wild animals invading her farm. No mountain lion or coyote would be a match for his Presas.

"It's very critical, Calamity, that you feed each of the dogs a half pound of ground chicken or ground beef daily," Paul wrote. "Plus you need to give them Peak Performance, the powdered supplement. That's very important."

Janet was becoming ever more frustrated. She was trying so hard to please Paul. But nothing she did ever seemed good enough.

Paul feared Isis was too small to have puppies. Paul would cite his books and the training manuals he had. According to his charts, Bane and Isis were of the right age, and he was paranoid about Janet's motives and interests about the breeding scheme.

"Well, honestly, I don't know if me and Daisy are ready for puppies yet," Janet told him. "And, I mean, *what if Isis doesn't want to breed with Bane?*"

Paul was counting his chickens before they hatched, Janet said, half kidding, but Schneider had this whole kennel-breeding plan laid out. He knew just about how many pups would be born, and how often. And he was counting on all the money they would sell for. If Janet Coumbs couldn't breed them, Paul had no intention of letting her get in his way.

Janet tried to explain that it wasn't as easy as Paul thought, that Bane and Isis had minds of their own. Janet reminded Paul that animals didn't necessarily operate according to a specified time clock and that, as it happened, Isis was very late going into heat. Her system didn't tick according to Paul and Dale's charts whatsoever, but Paul was just freaked out over it, yelling at Janet like it was her fault, certain that Janet was lying or just plain stupid.

"What am I supposed to do? *Go out and stalk her?* You can't do that, Paul. You have to wait."

But Paul didn't want to hear that.

Paul decided they needed to increase their chances by adding two more female Presas to the equation. Janet balked at first—these dogs were getting huge, over one hundred pounds each, and she couldn't imagine having four of them running around, not to mention all the large pups. However, Paul was persistent. He became adamant with Janet, informing her that he was already in contact with two breeders.

Paul said he was close to setting up the purchase of two Presa champions from a breeder in Ohio, informing Janet that he was ready to put a $900 deposit down on the dogs. If Janet didn't like the idea, he'd have someone else raise the dogs for him. Paul was basically forcing her into helping him purchase the next pair of Presas. Whether she liked it or not, Janet Coumbs was in too deep. She couldn't back down at that point.

"He wouldn't listen to me when I told him," Janet recalled. "I said her time would come to be in heat, and Isis would be bred. But that wasn't good enough. He wanted it on his time schedule."

Paul and Dale wrote threatening notes to Janet. They said they would fire her, they claimed she was violating their civil rights. They threw around all these big legal terms that Janet didn't understand. Janet didn't know why it was so important that Paul and Dale have crystal-clear pictures. She had no idea about how serious they were in their business plan. She was never told that they already had a "Dog O' War" Web site, that they had pictures of the pups *"El Supremo Bane"* and *"Ice Lady Isis"* being advertised as fighting dogs.

Even with the shoddy pictures from Janet, the Dog O' War Web site was impressive. There were reports on how the dogs were growing. There were charts about their ancient bloodlines, showing their famous ancestors: Presa Canarios who'd won numerous national and international dog shows. El Supremo Bane, aka the Tiger, was said to be 150 pounds and growing. The ad copy described the dog's character as arrogant and severe, and claimed he was a dual-champion offspring:

```
BANE: 1. One who causes death or destroys life.
2. Death: destruction, ruin. 3. One who ruins or
spoils.
EL SUPREMO BANE
For information Contact
www. DOGO' WAR. com
```

It was snowing like mad in the mountains, which made life even more difficult for people in Hayfork, the place was so remote, isolated like Appalachia. The roads were still rugged and dangerous to begin with, and bad weather kept everything at a standstill. With the onset of winter, the wind whipped through the town at high speeds. Outsiders tended to stay clear of that region of wilderness, unable to travel the slick mountain roads, where four-wheel drives weren't sufficient.

As the months turned colder, Janet was having more and more problems with Paul and the Presas. Isis was finally pregnant, but Janet couldn't contain her. The house was getting too small for all of them, the outdoor cages weren't warm enough, things were spiraling out of control. But Janet's concerns hadn't stopped Schneider from forcing her to accept two more female Presas. Schneider told Janet she just needed to build better-insulated doghouses. Schneider had a lot of people interested in buying the pups, he had promoted the dogs all throughout the prison system, and he planned to deliver.

No matter how much Janet insisted that Bane and Isis were becoming more difficult, no matter how much she claimed that the dogs were changing personalities, Paul wouldn't listen. He would find ways to lay blame on Janet, insisting that she was too hard on the animals, that she didn't understand them.

These were "regal" animals, he'd remind her, descended from fighting champions. She would have to expect them to be a bit ferocious. That was their nature. If she was having problems containing Bane and Isis, she'd have to beef up her fencing. Paul ordered her to contact Hard Times Kennels in Ohio, to arrange for the shipment of Fury and Hera.

Janet was finding holes in the fences she had built for Bane and Isis. The Presas were getting restless, and with puppies on the way, Bane and Isis seemed to be more protective. Janet was worried. Bane and Isis weren't doing just normal puppy things anymore. They weren't just eating her shoes and terrorizing the house. They were starting to become really aggressive.

When Janet told Paul a story about her neighbor's dog who charged at Daisy, reporting that Bane and Isis felt it was a violation of their turf, Schneider was fascinated to learn the details about the way his Presas attacked: Bane bit at the head, Isis bit at the hindquarters, and the neighbor's dog wound up with ten stitches.

The neighbor's vet bill was only eighty-four dollars, but Janet really couldn't afford it. She had little money left, and was wondering what happened to the new money order she'd been waiting on. Paul promised that cash was on its way; he told Janet to take the vet bill money "out of the pot." But he was leaving Janet with less and less cash, expecting her to "just hang in there." If the food and whatnot were costing more than Janet expected, Paul was sure she'd find a way to take care of it.

Janet didn't like the way things were going at Hayfork. She felt she had lost control over her life. She was frightened of Paul, and she found herself arguing with him on a constant basis. Coumbs and Schneider were always on the verge of a falling out. Meanwhile, Bane was becoming the "master" of the land.

Schneider was well aware that Isis was pregnant, but he still threatened to take the dogs away. By then, Janet had grown so attached to Bane and Isis that she couldn't stand the idea. In an effort to keep peace, she called Hard Times and left a message saying she was calling about two Presa Canarios they were holding for her "eccentric artist friend."

It was Paul who directed Janet's correspondence with the kennel, and it seemed to calm him down, knowing that Janet was providing him with a beard, knowing his breeding plan was being fortified. Paul wanted Janet to close the deal, promising her that the purchase of Fury and Hera would ensure her status as one of the "major Presa Canario breeders" in the country.

When Janet finally had a long talk with Hard Times's proprietor, James Kolber, explaining that she was familiar with the breed, that she was already a Presa owner, Kolber was happy to hear from her. Janet would be taking over the purchase of the two female Presas, she explained. They would be companions for Bane and Isis, but she just needed some time to work out the details.

"At first, I got to know Janet because I was trying to get the rest of the money," Kolber recalled. "I told her the dogs were growing. I'm sitting on money and these dogs are gaining several pounds a week, eating me out of house and home."

Janet promised Kolber she would send the balance of the money as soon as she sold her truck. She said she needed to make certain arrangements and was waiting for a release letter from the person who'd originally sent the $900 down payment. But as weeks passed, Janet had all kinds of excuses about why she couldn't send the money, or obtain the release letter. She ultimately told Kolber that she was buying the dogs for her business partner, that there was someone else in the mix—Paul John Schneider.

"Well, why don't you let me talk to your partner," Kolber insisted, "because someone needs to get me the rest of this money, and I need to know who I'm dealing with."

"Paul doesn't have a phone," Janet said.

"He doesn't talk on the phone?"

"He lives in the woods," she told him, which was partially true. "He's an eccentric. He stays holed up by himself."

"Well, give me his address, then," Kolber said, "I'll send him a Fed-Ex."

When Janet was forced to reveal that her business partner, P.J.

Schneider, was incarcerated, James Kolber had no problem with that. An eccentric himself, Kolber soon began receiving letters from Schneider, who claimed he just loved and admired the breed and wanted to own the Presas so he could be a long-distance "dad" of sorts. The pups would be his connection to the outside world; they would provide him with something to look forward to.

Kolber understood. Having dealt with inmate family members himself, the dog breeder felt inmates were often mistreated, misinterpreted, and misjudged. As Kolber and Schneider exchanged letters, the dog breeder came to like the guy, and Schneider seemed grateful for Kolber's friendship.

As it turned out, Paul sent letters to James Kolber for quite some time. The two corresponded during the purchase of Hera and Fury, and Paul would write to his new buddy, questioning Janet's breeding ability, reporting on the progress of the four Presa Canarios, constantly asking for new tips about the best ways to handle the champion canine breed.

Schneider thought it was great that Isis was about to have puppies, but had a lot of concerns regarding what kind of care the puppies would need, what type of shots, what kinds of special food. Paul needed free advice, so in return for Kolber's words of wisdom, he'd sometimes send the Ohio breeder small pieces of art, interesting images of Presa Canarios in unusual postures. Schneider was focused on drawing Presas in medieval settings, and Kolber found the artwork intriguing.

The dog breeder thought nothing of it when he received funny little cartoons from Paul. There seemed to be no harm in Schneider's intentions. The inmate was always kidding around, sending postcards and cartoons with cute captions, such as "FOUND . . . Very Large Dog with Human Foot in Its Mouth."

Janet and Daisy rented a trailer to haul Fury and Hera to the farm. They'd filled the back with hay so the puppies could play together, but when Janet arrived at the local airport, a bag handler told her she'd better be careful. She had "Cujo" back there, the man said. The one dog was "just going berserk."

At three months old, Fury was a big pup, but she scared the bejesus out of Janet. During their ride back up the mountain, Fury was lunging, she was barking, she was shaking the whole crate. Hera seemed more reasonable, she was just kind of sitting back, watching Fury most of the time. But, still, Hera was barking and growling as well. It was an ordeal to get the two females back to Hayfork. It took Janet eight hours to get Fury out of her crate, the animal was so resistant. Janet had to unscrew the bolts and take the cage apart, finally. That was the only way.

"Hey, what did you send me?" Janet asked in a panic, calling Kolber the minute she got a chance.

"Well, I didn't socialize the dogs," Kolber told her. "If I did, they would have bonded to me, instead of you."

"Well, they're going nuts up here. They won't even take any food."

"They're not people-ized," he said. "But it's okay. Just give them a little time and they'll chill out."

But they didn't chill. They were agitated, they were displaced, they didn't like the cold weather, and they especially didn't like the strange animals around. It didn't help that Bane and Isis were jealous of these new dogs. The Hayfork farm was Bane's territory, and he would bark and growl at the two female pups, bullying them both, picking on Hera in particular. The smaller of the two, Hera seemed really afraid of Bane. And Bane must have sensed that, because he'd go over to Hera's cage and lunge at her. He'd raise his leg and piss on her. Hera found ways to avoid him, but Bane was sneaky. Still, Hera was good at finding places to hide.

Janet was at a loss for what to do, the four dogs being at odds all the time. She had to resort to chaining Bane and Isis on one side of the house and chaining Hera and Fury on the other. But it didn't really solve the problem. The dogs would break free of their chains, they would eat right through their fences, they would eat through the wood.

It was a strange situation. Janet felt that her "teenager" dogs, Bane and Isis, were acting badly. They wouldn't stand being chained, they found ways to break out and roam around the farm. And soon, Hera and Fury were following suit. Janet was concerned about her sheep and chickens. No matter how much reinforcement she put on their "pens," no matter how much lead space she tried to give them, the four Presas would get loose. Isis was still pregnant, which scared Janet even more.

Soon, there would be newborns to contend with. Coumbs didn't think she could handle it. From Schneider's letters, one could gather that he relished the notion of Bane becoming "dog aggressive." Paul would write to his associates on the outside, bragging about how Bane was "Bad to the Bone," about how Bane was lording over the three females, about how he would beat on the pregnant Isis.

Paul thought that Bane's pulling Isis out of her doghouse and pissing all over the inside of it was hilarious. For a canine, Bane was exhibiting aberrant behavior, but Paul found it amusing. He loved hearing reports that Bane was lunging at anything on four legs.

Isis, on the other hand, wasn't anyone to brag about. In fact, Schneider was disgusted with Janet's reports on her. It was early spring when Isis gave birth, and according to Janet, for some odd reason, Isis chose to deliver the pups out in the cold rather than in her doghouse. Isis disliked her offspring, Janet insisted. Isis would let some of them die, leaving them out in the cold.

Isis had delivered ten puppies, but supposedly, she'd killed some of them. According to Daisy, there were bite marks on six of the ten pups. Daisy was horrified, screaming for her mother to help. When Janet got to Isis, she realized the six pups were unsalvageable. Janet found one pup that Isis had dug a hole for, burying the newborn alive, so Janet and Daisy worked fast. They "unburied" the newborn, kept him breathing, and put the pup in warm water. They managed to save Scruffles's life.

"Isis didn't want anything to do with her puppies," Janet confided. "She killed them. But they say that happens. I've seen rabbits do it, and it's not unusual."

Janet figured Isis just wasn't ready to be a mother. She tried to help by taking the remaining pups into her home, keeping them in her library, along with Scruffles, but she and Daisy just didn't understand why Isis was so antagonistic. Isis had bitten the jaw of one of her newborns, she'd shredded and ripped up four of her other pups. Nonetheless, there were four pups who survived, and Isis eventually came around, spending her time in Janet's library where she learned to mother and protect them.

Of course, Schneider didn't believe one word of Janet's dead-puppy tale. As far as he was concerned, Janet had taken the six missing pups, had put them up for sale at $1,000–$2,000 each, and was hiding the money.

Paul was not going to bother with threats anymore. He wanted his adult dogs returned, he wanted the remaining offspring, he wanted Fury and Hera, and he wanted the paperwork on all the dogs. Paul meant business, and he had the means to go after Janet Coumbs.

But Janet didn't want to give the dogs up. Even though she'd grown afraid of them, she still loved Bane, she was attached to Isis and her pups, and she wanted to keep her dog-breeding enterprise going. She called James Kolber, who assured her that Fury and Hera were registered in her name. Kolber reminded Coumbs that she possessed all the paperwork and had the pedigrees. The dogs were hers, Kolber promised, and she had every right to keep them.

"I'm afraid of Paul," Janet admitted, whispering to Kolber over the phone. "He wrote me a letter and said he knows people on the outside."

"Well, he's not going to do anything," Kolber said. "Paul knows this is all out in the open."

"He threatened that something could happen to me," she said, "that something could happen to one of my loved ones."

"Well, maybe you should consider giving the dogs up," the breeder told her. "From all the problems you're having, you were obviously unprepared for these dogs. You know, Presas aren't for everybody."

"No. I won't do that. I have them chained to a fence. I put big stakes in the yard, and I can deal with Hera and Fury," she insisted. "If they're mine, I'm going to keep them."

"Like I said before," Kolber warned, "if you're going to do that, you need to realize these are highly intelligent, independent dogs. They can't be chained up."

"Well, I'll try building them bigger pens. I'll give them more room so they won't feel chained."

"If you don't show them who's boss, they are going to walk all over you," he warned. "Chains won't hold them back."

Janet didn't like the dog breeder's advice. She stopped corresponding with Kolber after that brief conversation, and she never sent the Ohio dog breeder the balance of his money. Kolber stayed in touch with Paul, hoping Schneider would make good on his word, but the inmate was stalling. From what Kolber could gather, Schneider had enlisted an intermediary, Brenda Storey, who was in contact with Coumbs. Schneider promised that once he got his dogs back, Kolber would be paid.

Apparently Brenda Storey was relaying messages back and forth between Paul and Janet, and Schneider said there would be hell to pay if Janet didn't relinquish the animals. When Coumbs refused phone calls and failed to reply to Brenda Storey's letters, Storey threatened Coumbs with a lawsuit. Coumbs had received the paperwork in "certified" mail. She had signed for it, return receipt requested, and she was heartsick when she opened the document, learning that people could threaten to take everything away from her, including her farm.

All the time and energy Janet put into these prize dogs, all her love and care, now seemed to be blowing up in her face. Janet was becoming afraid for her home, for her daughter, and for her life.

Coumbs felt Bane and Isis were her babies. She had raised them, they had bonded to her, and she got on the phone with Storey, telling her she would not release the Presas. Coumbs informed Storey that she planned to keep the dog business going, calling it Happy Times Kennels.

But Brenda Storey had her own instructions. She was asserting her rightful ownership of the Presa Canarios, being the person who originally signed for Bane and Isis at the airport, being the person who signed the original money order that had been used to purchase Bane and Isis, she was claiming them as her property.

Janet pleaded with Brenda, telling her it would be a big mistake to remove Bane and Isis from their home setting. Janet thought the dogs would be traumatized for life if they were ripped from Hayfork. But Brenda Storey was hell-bent on following Schneider's commands. If Janet wouldn't hand the dogs over, they would be physically removed by law enforcement.

Storey was dead serious about her lawsuit. From that point forward, Coumbs would have to deal with Noel & Knoller, the San Francisco law firm that was representing her. Storey had nothing more to say.

The Noel & Knoller firm was prepared to go to court if necessary.

Of course, Storey hoped it wouldn't come to that.

"Hera was the one that killed Daisy's cat," Janet explained. "We had a Persian cat, Chippy, and he ended up in the pen with Hera. I heard a noise outside, but I couldn't get Chippy away from the dog fast enough."

Janet and Daisy were devastated. They had Chippy for two years, had watched him grow from the time he was a kitten, and now they saw Hera rip him apart. They never knew how Chippy got himself in Hera's chain-linked pen, they couldn't understand it. But how he ended up with Hera—whether he fell in there or slipped through a hole—really didn't matter. Chippy was gone.

"Mom, I don't think we should feed Hera anymore," Daisy said, in tears. "I think we should let her die."

"I don't know why the dog did a horrible thing like this," Janet consoled her, "and I know you're mad about it right now. I'm so sorry, honey, but I'm sure Hera didn't mean it. She's still a puppy."

"I don't want to look at her ever again, Mom," Daisy said. "She's mean."

"Well, we can't stop feeding her. I'll be the one to take care of her from now on, okay?"

But it wasn't okay. With each passing day, Hera and the other Presas were getting more stirred up. The taste of blood had done something to them. Things were getting eerie, and to make matters worse, about the same time that Chippy was killed, Marjorie Knoller started calling.

Knoller left nasty messages on the answering machine, threatening Janet and claiming her San Francisco law firm had proof that Brenda Storey was the rightful owner of Dog O' War Bane and Dog O' War Isis. Knoller insisted that if Coumbs didn't return her calls, if she wasn't willing to turn the dogs over, a lien would be placed against the Hayfork property.

Janet Coumbs was terrified. She had no idea what her rights really were. She didn't have the money to hire an attorney, and without anyone professional to turn to for advice, she asked people at church what they thought about it. Her church friends had mixed sentiments. Some told Janet she should stand her ground. Others, who had been to the farm and had seen the huge dogs, thought Janet should just get rid of the whole strange lot. For Daisy, the Presa Canarios had become frightful; they were causing more trouble then they were worth.

"I don't remember when they killed the first sheep, but Hera and Fury had both gotten out," Janet confided. "There was a dead sheep, and we didn't see who did it, but both Hera and Fury had blood on them."

After the first sheep was slaughtered, Janet realized she'd have to drastically change things at the farm. She *had* to take back the upper hand at Hayfork. The dogs had ripped up all the Cyclone fencing and had managed to get loose from their stakes. They were destroying her property, ripping up the ground, chomping holes into the side of her house. Janet needed to find a way to keep them locked in their pens, so she bought big strong fencing, heavy collars, and heavier chains, hoping that would do the trick.

"We were taking care of everything, we were hammering and stapling wood and fencing, to keep the dogs in place," Janet recalled. "We thought we had it under control, but then Hera and Fury started climbing over the fences.

"Fury got loose and ran my male sheep over the fence," Janet confessed. "Fury had jumped over the fence with her chain dragging, and I had just gotten back from town, and my male sheep was dead. Fury was locked to Bane. Their chains were locked together, and Bane was bouncing on the dead carcass of my ram. He wasn't chewing. I think he was trying to get life back. I don't know."

Janet wanted to believe that her dogs were just playing with the sheep. That her ram just happened to die accidentally. She wasn't there; she wasn't privy to the fatal biting. She especially didn't want to think Bane was capable of such a deed.

But one day at the farm, when she caught Bane with a rooster in his mouth, the rooster all slurpy, all wet, Janet came face-to-face with the facts. She yelled at Bane, and luckily he dropped the bird in time for it to live, so Janet felt vindicated. At least Bane was obeying her. As the rooster jumped up and ran off, she rationalized that Bane had only mauled the rooster slightly. There was no real harm done. Janet couldn't admit to herself that Bane had become a bad dog. In her mind, Bane was just a big lug who didn't know his own strength; he was like Lennie from *Of Mice and Men*. Bane wasn't the problem.

"Fury and Hera were the two that kept getting unleashed, they were the ones who thrashed the chickens everywhere," Janet insisted. "It was those two dogs who were always loose, and all my critters were dead, and there was blood on both those dogs."

As she came across more dead sheep and blood everywhere, Janet decided she wanted nothing more to do with those two females. She was sick over Fury and Hera killing her sheep. At least twelve were slaughtered, and Janet blamed herself for being unable to train the Presas correctly. She needed professional advice, but she was too ashamed to seek it.

Janet hated what was happening to her farm. She hated what the dogs had done, yet she didn't want to give up on them. They were her responsibility. She was still helping to nurse Isis's pups. She was extremely attached to Bane, and even if she hadn't bargained for Hera and Fury, she believed she could salvage them.

Finally, Janet spoke to Christine Whitcomb, a County Animal Care and Control officer, hoping the officer could give her some reasonable comfort. Janet had been friends with Whitcomb for years, but she didn't feel she needed to tell Whitcomb the extent of the trouble the Presas were causing. She didn't want to alarm the officer.

Janet was always rescuing animals, and Whitcomb knew her to be a true animal lover. Never in a million years would Whitcomb think Janet's livestock were being devoured by her dogs. Janet was not one to allow harm to come to any animal. Quite the opposite—she took in all types of strays. She was known to have a "special touch" with unruly animals.

When Janet talked to Whitcomb, she was vague about the Presa Canarios. The dogs were getting loose, Janet reported. One of them had eaten a few of her chickens. Of course Whitcomb wasn't being told the whole truth, so the ACC officer encouraged Janet to try to tame the dogs, offering a few basic suggestions that might help.

But as the calls and threats from Noel & Knoller flooded in, Janet finally decided she should consider washing her hands of the whole mess. She was tired of being badgered by Marjorie Knoller and Robert Noel, who insisted that the Presas be removed from her property immediately. They argued that if Janet felt the dogs were so dangerous, this would mean it wouldn't be her problem anymore.

Apparently, the attorneys had specific plans for the dogs. Knoller claimed that Brenda Storey had already arranged to sell Isis's four pups to a buyer in Southern California for $1,000 apiece. Janet didn't think the little pups were old enough yet, but Marjorie Knoller knew all the stats. According to her charts, the pups were eight weeks old—the right age to be transported.

Throughout the lawsuit and settlement process, Marjorie Knoller was condescending and rude to Janet Coumbs. The attorney had no reason to believe this mountain woman's tale about "big bad dogs." Because Coumbs had been writing Paul Schneider all along about how she loved the dogs and how much she cherished being a dog breeder, Knoller felt Coumbs was lying. Marjorie was under the impression that Janet was good at making things up, that she was willing to say anything just to hold on to her beloved animals.

Unbeknownst to Coumbs, Marjorie Knoller had been working for Brenda Storey and Paul Schneider all along. Marjorie and Robert knew Schneider intimately.

Schneider sent Knoller and Noel regular reports about how Coumbs was starving the animals, about how she was taking his money and then refusing to get the dogs' ears cropped, which was especially important for the sale of Roka and Menace, the offspring of Bane and Isis. Schneider believed Coumbs was cheating him, that her actions were placing the $20,000 investment he'd already put into the breeding at risk.

Although Marjorie and Robert had grown to think the world of Paul, considering all the nightmarish stories Janet had told about the Presa Canarios and their alleged bad behavior, Marjorie decided it might be best to send a photographer up to Hayfork to take pictures of the dogs and their surroundings. She wanted to see proof of what Coumbs was talking about.

Marjorie was shocked when the first rolls of film came back. Both she and Robert found the Hayfork situation quite alarming, and they wrote to Paul to inform him that they would do everything in their power to save his prized animals. It looked as if these champion purebreds were being chained, roped, and mistreated in every way. The conditions on the farm were deplorable. Bane's doghouse was all chewed up, just in shambles. The other Presas were all tied to stakes and living out in the open among old tires and junkyard garbage. As far as Noel and Knoller could tell, Schneider's dogs were being abused, kept in squalor, and being treated unfairly.

Clearly Bane and Isis were being favored, both dogs being grossly overweight, while Hera and Fury looked as if they were being starved to death. When Noel and Knoller studied the newest set of photos, they decided the circumstances in Hayfork were dire. They wanted to get a settlement as soon as possible. They needed to get up to Hayfork and rescue these poor animals. They promised Schneider that, if necessary, they would even house some of the dogs *themselves*.

By February 2000, Janet had found herself a pro bono attorney, out of Redding. He was a friend of the church, but the man seemed no match for the firm of Noel & Knoller. When the local lawyer advised Coumbs that she should accept the terms of the settlement, Janet balked. She had been telling Knoller about how dangerous these dogs were, she had recounted numerous incidents to her, but this woman still wanted to drive up from San Francisco and take possession of these dogs.

Repeatedly, Coumbs told Knoller that Hera had something "not right" about her. Hera had gotten to the point where she was beating up on Fury. Janet couldn't leave Hera alone for a minute. Hera would break the snaps on her chains; she was chewing up her doghouse and breaking out of her pen. It wasn't because she was hungry—Janet was feeding her plenty—it was just that Hera had become destructive.

"I kept telling Marjorie how Hera would get loose, and I don't know how many sheep we lost," Janet later reflected. "I think it was more than twelve we ended up losing. Then I told her we had all these dead chickens. I told her there was blood everywhere."

Janet finally got to the point where she was fed up arguing with Knoller. The woman seemed to be a know-it-all. No matter what Janet told her, Knoller had a counterargument. The attorney said she understood all about Prey Drive. The attorney claimed she was aware of a canine's natural instinct to kill, but that problem could be resolved with proper training.

Marjorie Knoller was so persistent and angry that Janet Coumbs became exasperated. Over the phone, Coumbs finally told her to "come and get them."

Of course Janet didn't want to sign the settlement papers. She didn't understand how these big-city lawyers could threaten her farm, her house, and her other animals. She didn't want to sign documents waiving any rights to the eight Presa Canarios.

Janet Coumbs told Knoller that Hera was a bad example for all the other Presas, that even Isis's pups were learning how to break open their dog kennels with their teeth. Joshua had ripped a chain-link fence apart. Janet couldn't believe that the pup could mangle such heavy metal. Coumbs tried to tell Knoller how powerful these dogs could be.

But Knoller only listened with half an ear. Coumbs realized she was getting nowhere over the phone, so she figured she'd just wait until the lawyers got to Hayfork. When Noel and Knoller got there, they'd see the difficulties these dogs presented, and they'd realize the dogs would be no good with people.

Nevertheless, Coumbs told her attorney she'd sign the settlement.

"Marjorie was nasty. She would call me two and three times a day," Janet reflected. "She would ask me information about this dog and that dog, and I told her they should be *shot* before they ever left my property. That's exactly what I said."

"Well, if you're having so much trouble with the dogs, you should be glad that we're taking the dogs away," Marjorie said.

"These dogs have bonded to us," Janet insisted, "and I don't know what would happen if they wound up with other people."

"It's not your worry, Ms. Coumbs," Marjorie assured her. "We will have all the arrangements finalized in a few days. And you should plan to see us there by the end of next week."

"Well, I hope you make sure you've got those professional trainers with you when you get here. Because you don't know how hard it is to get these dogs into crates. I had to work for eight hours with Fury—"

"You can expect us early," Knoller quipped, cutting Janet off. "We're early risers, and will probably arrive there at six A.M."

"Well," Janet warned her, "Bane and Hera hate each other, and the pups don't like Hera either. So if any of them get out of their crates while you're hauling them, God help you."

———

However, weeks passed and no one came to get the animals. When Janet called San Francisco, Robert and Marjorie would have excuses about why they couldn't make it to Hayfork. They had this problem, they had that problem. It was ridiculous.

"We can't find anyone to come up there," Marjorie finally told Janet. "So we think it's best if you haul the dogs. You bring them down to San Francisco and deliver them."

"Deliver them?" Janet asked. "Why should I deliver them?"

"Look, Ms. Coumbs. Either you do it this way, or when it goes to court, you'll be delivering them to the courthouse, to the Hall of Justice."

Janet couldn't believe that Knoller expected her to take eight giant dogs, and try to bring them into the big city. She told the attorney she had no means to do that. Knoller insisted it was Janet's responsibility, that Coumbs needed to hire someone to transport the animals, but Janet resented that. If the dogs legally belonged to Brenda Storey, Coumbs felt Mrs. Storey was the person who should deliver them.

"But you've signed an agreement to provide us with the dogs," Knoller argued.

"Well," Coumbs said, "there's no feasible way for me to do that."

Marjorie had her so upset that Janet considered driving the Presas to San Francisco. She talked to neighbors about borrowing trucks and finding crates, until a friend pointed out that if any of the dogs got loose or started fighting on the trip, these lawyers could claim that Janet was at fault and could threaten to sue her again.

Janet Coumbs held her ground. She wasn't about to play things their way. No matter how much Knoller pushed, Coumbs would not provide delivery. Yet as the days ticked by, the dogs were costing Coumbs a fortune to feed. Finally, Janet got the nerve to ask Noel & Knoller for a kennel services fee. Janet had called around, and had discovered the going rate for each dog was about ten dollars a day. Since Janet was stuck with eight dogs that didn't belong to her, she felt she was owed some serious cash.

Noel and Knoller balked at Janet's request, but behind the scenes, they had written to Paul, suggesting that he find some cash to placate Coumbs. After all, the lady was going to make nothing from the sale of the pups. She could cause them problems if he didn't compensate her slightly.

Schneider responded by writing an S.O.S. letter to his brother-in-law and his sister, Tammy. It was mid-March and Paul wanted to see if Tammy and Greg would help move the dogs. "We've gone through fuckin' hell to get these dogs, so *please* just get the shit done," Paul wrote. "No more delays, okay? Cause the bottom line is, we cannot afford to fuck this up, bro. If we don't get them moved this time, we can *lose* the 8 dogs."

When Paul didn't get an answer, his next letter to Greg and Tammy was more pushy. He mentioned Lucia, a family member of a Mexican drug cartel. Schneider reported that Lucia was unhappy about the problem with the pickup. She was the one who was paying top dollar for the pups; money was changing hands, Paul told them. There was other money unaccounted for, and the dogs had yet to be delivered. Brenda Storey was holding $4,800 in cash, she was getting all stressed out over the calls from Lucia, and bottom line: Paul wanted Greg and Tammy in the loop, just long enough to handle the transport. Schneider needed people he could trust. If Greg and Tammy didn't help him, he would have to start from scratch.

As it was, Paul had everything arranged. Lucia would get Fury and Hera, Rachel Hugez would get Scruffles and Joshua, and Carolyn Murphy, down in L.A., would deal with the remainder of the dogs: Bane, Isis, Roka, and Menace. Schneider begged his brother-in-law to do whatever was necessary to make the deal happen. He had the Hugez and Murphy families waiting for their dogs, and these were people he couldn't afford to screw over. Schneider owed these people their dogs, and he couldn't stall anymore.

Schneider gave Greg his word that he would make the trip to Hayfork worth his while. He promised he'd send Greg and Tammy at least a grand, just to cover the hassle. There were "years of sweat and bullshit on the line," Paul wanted Tammy to know, and all would be lost if they didn't do this one big favor for him.

He needed this done. He was desperate to save his dogs.

He used every trick in the book, flat out begging his sister to talk Greg into helping him. But this time, Paul's antics didn't work. If, at any time, Greg and Tammy had been considering the prospect of moving the dogs from Hayfork, once Paul mentioned the Mexican Mafia, it was all over.

Tammy wrote her brother back, telling him how sorry she was that she and Greg couldn't help. They just couldn't, with her bad health and all.

"The day they were taking our dogs away, the puppies, especially Roka, it was so hard," Janet admitted. "Roka really loved us. We knew one day we'd have to let him go, but he was just really special. And when he sat down next to me, he just wouldn't move. Roka was just a pawn, and he had to be carried into the truck."

Watching Bane and Isis and the rest get loaded up into their crates, Janet and Daisy were fighting back tears. They hadn't known what to expect from Marjorie Knoller and Robert Noel, but these two people didn't look anything like the slick attorneys they'd expected. Noel was a large man in his fifties. Quite eloquent, very personable, wearing jeans, a sweatshirt, and boat shoes, he looked like an old preppy. His wife, Knoller, who was much younger, was not as arrogant as she had been over the phone. In fact, she seemed to be trying hard to look "country," with her hair in pigtails, her tight jeans, and her old cowboy boots.

The attorneys had stopped by Janet's farm just before sunset, to take a peek at the dogs. Although Janet had specifically described the animals, had taken measurements and provided all of the dogs' dimensions, the attorneys obviously hadn't believed her. The Presas were much larger than they thought they'd be, and Noel and Knoller realized the crates they'd brought with them were too small. But the lawyers weren't worried about that. They were certain they'd find a way around the problem by the next morning, April Fool's Day, when they would be met at Janet's farm by a professional dog handler.

"They just didn't care. They just wanted to stuff the dogs into these crates and go," Janet reflected. "It was upsetting. I didn't feel like they were going to be caring for the dogs. The dogs were a commodity. I told them to put straw bedding in the crates, but they didn't want to do that. I think they set two or three of the pups on some shredded-up newspaper, but they really didn't want to do that either."

Noel and Knoller weren't completely unfeeling: they were somewhat compassionate with Janet Coumbs. They felt bad, watching Daisy's tears, and they made an offer to let Janet keep one of the pups. It was an offer they made over the phone, just once, and they wanted Janet to reconsider it. But Janet had made up her mind.

For one thing, one of the pups had bitten her, and Janet was frightened about how the pups would behave without their mother to guide them. Then there was the breeding business that Janet had hoped for. One pup would do her no good, and she sure couldn't afford to buy another purebred Presa Canario.

No. If Janet couldn't have Bane and Isis, there was no use in trying to hang on to a pup. Janet was just so disheartened, so downtrodden, by these strangers who invaded her life. Even though she knew they were lawyers and that they were using Brenda Storey to act on behalf of Paul Schneider, these two folks had landed on her doorstep without knowing a thing about animals.

After all the months of planning and hard work, this odd couple came and took her little family away. Janet thought it was despicable. Even if her dogs weren't the best behaved animals, she would have found someone to aid her, she would have managed to breed and sell the dogs and would have kept her promise to Schneider.

"If there had been honest, legitimate buyers, we would have sold them. We would have sold the puppies and gone into business the way it should have been done," Janet complained. "But it turned into a lot of headache and heartache, and I knew we had to let go and move on with our lives."

When they waved good-bye that cold April Fool's morning, Janet Coumbs thought everything was over. She thought she had seen the last of Noel and Knoller, and the last of her Presa Canario dogs.

Back in February Coumbs had been called to a meeting with Corrections Department Special Agents Devan Hawkes and Everett Fischer in Redding. This was right after she had received the first threatening letter from Paul Schneider. Coumbs told Hawkes that she wanted to wash her hands of Paul Schneider and that she was afraid for her life.

In all the shuffle and discombobulation with Noel and Knoller and the lawsuit, Coumbs had forgotten about the special agents and their investigation. She hadn't heard from them lately, and, with the dogs gone, she assumed they had lost interest in Schneider and his dog business.

But Hawkes was keeping tabs on everything. He knew Coumbs had been threatened with a lawsuit, he was still monitoring Schneider's mail, and he had correctional officers at Pelican Bay watching Schneider's every move, tracking the chain of Schneider's criminal dog scheme.

By running a dog-breeding ring, Schneider was violating the Department of Corrections rules, but there was no law on the book that could stop him from using "associates" on the outside to do his bidding. Even though Hawkes had proof that Schneider was selling the dogs to affiliates of the Mexican Mafia, as well as members of the Mexican drug cartel, there was no way to take that one step further—to show that these offspring of Bane and Isis would be used to guard methamphetamine labs and crack houses.

The only recourse Pelican Bay officials had was to slap penalties on Paul Schneider and Dale Bretches; but these guys were already in twenty-four-hour-a-day lockdown in the SHU. There was no stiffer punishment available. When Hawkes filed a report with the FBI office in San Francisco, the special agent there told Hawkes that nothing, unfortunately, could be done to prosecute the inmates. By having others raise dangerous dogs they had not violated any state or federal law.

Nonetheless, Hawkes followed up with Janet Coumbs. In late spring, he asked her what she knew about Noel and Knoller's involvement. Janet had no idea what the attorneys really planned to do with the dogs. They were shifty and seemed to change their stories all the time.

Hawkes kept trying to figure out the connection, but he only had partial knowledge of the relationship between the two lawyers and Schneider. Their correspondence with Schneider was confidential under attorney-client privilege. Hawkes could see the heavy volume of mail between the threesome, but their contents remained a mystery.

What Hawkes was able to put together—by reading other letters Schneider was writing to his "friends" and people on the outside, like his sister, Tammy—was that Schneider was pulling off a potentially violent Dog O' War breeding scheme. Even though his information was piecemeal, Hawkes suspected these fierce guard dogs would be sold to drug lords and gangsters. If these attorneys were involved, he felt they probably weren't clean. There were too many coincidences, and Noel and Knoller were making too many in-person visits to the private attorney-client visiting room at Pelican Bay. Somehow, Hawkes was determined to find a way to prove that these attorneys had their hands dirty.

CHAPTER ELEVEN

The day before Noel and Knoller went to Hayfork, they received this warning:

PEOPLE'S EXHIBIT
1A EV 181813-01

Dear Ms. Knoller,
Enclosed are rabies certificates and health certificates you requested on the eight dogs located at Janet Coumbs. I left the tranquilizers with Janet for use later. Physically, I found the dogs in great shape, with the exception of Roka, who had an infection in the left eye. It did not appear too bad and was probably due to an injury.

However, I would be professionally amiss if I did not mention the following, so that you can be prepared. These dogs are huge, probably weighing in the neighborhood of 100 pounds each. They have had no training or discipline of any sort. They were a problem to even get to, let alone vaccinate. You mentioned having a professional hauler gather them up and take them to La Puente. Usually this would be done in crates, but I doubt you could get them into anything short of a livestock trailer, and if let loose, they would have a battle.

To add to this, *these animals would be a liability in any household*, reminding me of the recent attack in Tehama County to a boy by large dogs. He lost his arm and disfigured his face. The historic romance of the warrior dog, the personal guard dog, the gaming dog, etc., may sound good but it hardly fits into life today. In any event, you'll do as you wish but at least I have given you my opinions.

This is my bill:

Travel and time	$20.00
4 rabies vaccines	$60.00
8 health certificates	$80.00
Tranquilizers	$20.00
Total:	$180.00

Yours very truly,
Donald B. Martin, DVM

Marjorie F. Knoller   *Robert E. Noel*

NOEL & KNOLLER
Attorneys at Law
San Francisco, CA 94147-2589
Telephone: (415) 441-7676
Facsimile: (415) 441-7009

March 29, 2000
Donald B. Martin, DVM
RE: Presa Canarios

Dear Dr. Martin,
Enclosed please find a check made payable to Donald B. Martin, DVM in the amount of one hundred eighty dollars ($180.00) to

cover the costs of the visit and treatment of the dogs. Sorry for the delay, but I did not receive your package until yesterday, Tuesday, March 28, 2000. The post office box number was missing the first two digits—47, and this delayed the delivery of the package.

Thank you for the letter, I will pass the information on to my client.

If you have any questions, please do not hesitate to contact me.

Sincerely,
Marjorie F. Knoller
Marjorie F. Knoller

CHAPTER TWELVE

"As to whether or not I believed Dr. Martin and his assessment of the dogs, at the time I received his letter, I did not believe anything he was saying," Noel reflected. "I had to see for myself. I wasn't going to take anything that anybody said at face value. I never do."

Robert Noel felt he had already become a bit of an expert on the subject, having spent months researching the Presa Canario, long before he and his wife made the trip to Hayfork. Robert found Web sites describing the general origin of the breed, stumbling across some materials from Show Stopper Kennels, and began subscribing to their newsletter, *The Gripper*.

By the time they picked up the eight Presas, Robert knew all about the warrior qualities of the "mutts," gobbling up every scrap of information he could. Robert was drawn to the rare and unusual. It was fitting that his client, Schneider, had discovered such an unheard-of breed.

From everything Robert read, the Presa Canario was the type of breed that would adapt easily to any circumstance, to any urban setting. There were stories about Presas living happily in big cities such as Barcelona and Madrid. Presas were characterized as dangerous and aggressive, but Robert felt he understood the unique value of the Presa as an adaptable guard dog. Robert liked the notion that the Presa would protect an owner from an attacker, guarding the owner with its life.

Robert especially relished that the Presa Canario seemed fiercer than the Rottweiler or the Doberman. If the aggressiveness of a Presa Canario outweighed that of a Rottweiler, so much the better for their dog-breeding business. Robert eagerly read downloads from a Web site called Perro de Presa Canario, which made the potential dangers of the breed abundantly clear: "This is a lot of dog. Your rollie-pollie puppy will grow into an uncontrollable overbearing and downright dangerous adult, if you do not invest the time necessary to raise this dog into a well-adjusted member of the society."

Robert was not only downloading these materials, he was making copies to send off to his buddies, Paul and Dale. Marjorie was busy sending photocopies of book chapters to their inmate buds as well. Unofficially, the attorneys had become Paul and Dale's partners. They agreed with Schneider's instincts about the Presa Canario becoming a *hot* guard dog, the next status symbol for dog owners, and they planned to share in the profits.

The Pacific Heights attorneys would not only retrieve the dogs from Hayfork, but would help arrange the further transport of the Presa Canarios to areas throughout California. It was Marjorie who solidified those plans, hiring dog trainer Jim O'Brien to take six of the dogs to the Los Angeles area, and the remaining two—Fury and Hera—to the Peninsula Pet Resort in San Carlos before being sent to Lucia.

At the Peninsula Pet Resort, just south of San Francisco, Fury and Hera were bathed and groomed, and treated to everything from hot-oil massage to nail trims. But it was a very expensive place to house the dogs, and after a month or so, since Lucia had refused to take delivery on two females together, Bob and Marj decided they would take Hera home with them.

Bob and Marj were excited about the prospect of being "doggy" foster parents for a few weeks. They bought all the accessories: the dog bed, the puppy toys, the chew bones, the special food. The couple never had any kids together, they never owned any pet, other than a parakeet, so they were thrilled at the idea of becoming a little family. The two of them were a soft touch for Hera, who was lavished with attention, turning into a spoiled brat.

Taking Hera to their home in Pacific Heights was a wonderful opportunity for Bob and Marj to bond anew. Not that their marriage wasn't strong; if anything, they were uniquely tied to each other. But the newness of having a big pup in the house, and all the shared responsibilities that Hera brought, made their lives even richer.

They fell in love with the regal animal. They couldn't understand how anyone might consider her problematic; they believed Hera had an easy disposition. Proud to show her off, they beamed when neighbors would stop to ask questions about what kind of dog Hera was. Always bragging about their magnificent animal, Bob and Marj were becoming overly attached to Hera. The three were inseparable.

"I could see that she was a really intelligent dog. She demanded a lot of attention," Robert recalled. "That was one of the things Marj and I committed to when Hera moved in with us. We decided we needed to spend a lot of time with her. Hera went everywhere with us, twenty-four hours a day, seven days a week."

After Hera was with them for about a month, Marjorie had become so comfortable and trusted Hera so completely that she would walk the dog off lead. In their posh neighborhood, Marjorie would *watch Hera roam* the few blocks over to nearby Lafayette Park.

"Hera was an off-lead dog. She would respond to my commands, and I didn't have any problem with her," Marjorie would later explain. "That's why we have off-lead dog parks. You train your dog to respond to you and you let them run while being able to see where they are. That's what an off-lead dog is."

Marjorie had her own special relationship with Hera. The two had grown extremely close. In fact, Marjorie always had Hera sleep by her side.

The development of the relationship between Robert Noel, Marjorie Knoller, and Paul Schneider crystallized in something they called "The Triad." As weird as it sounds, the two attorneys felt they could *psychi-*

cally inhabit Paul's body. The fact that they had his dog, Hera, who carried the name of an ancient Greek goddess, the wife and sister of Zeus, made their mythological relationship all the more poetic.

Long before they picked up the pack of Presas, Marjorie proclaimed her love for Paul in letters. She and Robert had been involved with Paul Schneider for years, having become interested in the notorious inmate through their fight against the Department of Corrections. In the mid-1990s, Noel & Knoller began representing allegedly corrupt prison guards, working with the highly powerful prison guard union, the CCPOA.

Noel & Knoller had many cases during their decade-long crusade against the California Department of Corrections. They represented not only unorthodox corrections officers but various inmates as well, including Paul John Schneider. But their working relationship with Schneider evolved into something else. As years of visits and letter writing to Schneider went from business to pleasure, Marjorie, with Robert's blessings, began having sexual fantasies about Paul. In early letters, Marjorie would hint at sex acts she wanted to perform on Paul. By the late 1990s, she would be blatant: Robert would perform the sex acts on her, but she would fantasize that it was Paul, not Robert, who was pleasuring her.

Marjorie and Robert were getting more than intimate with Paul. Marjorie saw him as her mythological Viking, as her hero from ancient times. The erotic letters she wrote included images of herself and Robert engaging in explicit sexual acts, acts she would one day want Paul to watch. Robert also wrote a few erotic suggestions to Paul, sending along full frontal photographs of his wife's most private parts.

In one of her many "confidential" pieces of legal mail to Schneider, Marjorie started off with information about the lawsuit filed against Janet Coumbs on behalf of Brenda Storey. That was the "cover" sheet. On page two, Marjorie explored having a three-way with Paul, telling him that it wasn't unusual for him to feel "somewhat strange about the idea" of watching her and Robert "make love to one another" while he was present.

Marjorie wanted Paul to feel a connection with her and Robert. She hoped Paul wouldn't mind voyeurism. She told Paul she planned to perform sex acts on herself, she hoped Robert would do the same, so Paul could watch from the other side of the Plexiglas wall. Allegedly this happened when Robert and Marjorie visited Paul in the attorney-client room in mid-January 2001, just days before Diane Whipple was killed.

Whatever the truth of the matter, according to Pelican Bay sources, Schneider's side of the attorney-client visiting room had to be washed down after Noel and Knoller's three-hour visit. It wasn't something they were doing for "cheap thrills," Marjorie would insist in her letters to Paul. It was an act she wanted them to share because she liked the idea of the three of them experiencing a "magnificent, mystical experience."

Even to Robert, Paul was a "find." He and Paul shared common interests in things other than corrupt prison guards and their "tigress," Marjorie. They were both obsessed with the Arthurian legend, they liked corresponding about Celtic history, and were each reading a new trilogy, writing notes back and forth about a book entitled *Enemy of God*.

Noel would sometimes call Paul "gorgeous." He seemed physically attracted to Schneider's thirty-six-inch waist and exceptionally wide shoulders. Perhaps it was sheer admiration for the male physique.

"Paul is the kind of person that if you put him in an Armani suit and take him home," Robert repeatedly said, "your mother wouldn't let him out the door."

Whatever it was Paul had, Robert and Marjorie wanted it. Perhaps Robert wanted to spice up his marriage. But Marjorie, unbeknownst to Robert, had become swept away. "Some things in life defy explanation. I crave and desire you to penetrate each of my orifices repeatedly," she wrote. "I cannot get enough of you and I cannot get enough of Robert, so I guess we are very well matched."

Marjorie told Paul she wanted to experience him "outside" prison. She wanted to be with him in the flesh. She wanted to taste him, to feel him, but until she and Robert could get Paul out, she would allow Robert to *explain* her taste, she would let Robert describe her passions for Paul.

As she became more and more immersed in the world of Paul Schneider, Marjorie began to take her fantasy life one step further. She wrote Paul about a recurring dream she had. It took place in medieval times, with a throne under a tent, carpets on a dirt floor, and a platform covered with fur skins and silk pillows. She described herself wearing battle attire—leather and metal armor—with sword, dagger, and mace in her hand, and called herself a "leader of a tribe." She wrote Paul an elegant tale about her being a queen, about her playing tribute to her king, by binding herself to his son.

The nature of the scene Marjorie described went from a portrait of an exquisite medieval kingdom to a pornographic ceremony between king, queen, and prince. She slowly removed her cape from her shoulders and stood in front of the prince naked, the king behind her. The king then asked the queen to make the prince her consort; Marjorie obliged, removing the prince's metal chest piece, the rest of his armor, and his undergarments, caressing and licking his legs, moving toward his groin.

Marjorie's letters were so graphic that anyone reading them could see the images just as clear as if watching a porno movie. She described licking the prince's shaft, teasing him with her flicking tongue . . . all this as the king watched, encouraging the prince to take the queen with "enthusiasm."

The intercourse Marjorie described involved both vaginal and anal penetration. As the prince exploded in her buttocks, she dreamed, the queen yelled in ecstasy. By being penetrated by the king and the prince at the same time, the queen would be bound to both men forever.

Using Robert and Marjorie's pornographic material, Paul began to draw medieval images of the three of them together. He crafted numerous elaborate works of art, some of which Marjorie posed for in the lobby of her Pacific Heights building. According to the corresponding letters and artwork found in Schneider's cell, the photos were probably taken Christmas Eve 2000. They were color photos of Marjorie, some half nude, wearing a black corset, sheer gloves, and high heels. In some of the corset photos, Marjorie added a blond wig, perhaps to appear more Aryan.

Even though she was too fat, honestly, to carry off that kind of Victoria's Secret garb, the photos really speak to who Marjorie thought she was. Her expressions, which looked severe and yet proud at the same time, were all the more ludicrous in light of the fact that she wore a crimson cape around her neck. That she bulged out of her corset and that her legs showed visible cellulite were of no concern to her.

And this was Paul's gothic queen.

But Schneider was smart enough to take the photos seriously. By the time things had become sexual for the three of them, Robert and Marjorie had already driven down to L.A. to rescue Bane, who was being poorly treated by one of Paul's Mexican Mafia affiliates. Bane was the kingpin of Paul's Dog O' War operation. Schneider couldn't afford to let anything happen to his warrior stud, and he wanted to be sure that Robert and Marjorie took special care of him. By reviewing the photos of Marjorie in the cape, and other photos of Marjorie with Bane and Hera at her side, Schneider formed a piece of artwork he entitled *Family of Three*.

The family included Attorney Noel, Paul Schneider, Attorney Knoller, and their Presa Canarios. In the drawing, Schneider depicted himself as a Christ-like martyr, his frame muscular, his face tortured, his waist shielded by swords, with the two massive Presa Canarios at his feet. Noel and Knoller were flanking Paul, their images transposed into gorgeous medieval characters, much thinner, much younger, a much more handsome couple than they ever could be in real life.

Along with the *Family of Three* drawing was an explanation of the runic symbols and ancient language Schneider embedded into his art. There was Marjorie as "Eihwaz: Protection, *central axis of the world.*" Then there was Robert as "Tiwaz: Justice, *attorney, self-sacrifice,*" which was supposed to signify world order. And finally there was Paul as "Othala: *inherited power, adoption.*" All together, the drawing represented a "three-fold mystery." And, according to the runic symbols, the three would use legal mail to travel to other realms, where they would unite in "justice, war, and personal love."

Schneider's drawing was detailed enough to include a depiction of Robert holding a sword with the letters N-O-E-L written in runes. Around Marjorie's neck was an amulet, described in runes as a thunderbolt, a destructive force necessary for battling enemies and *causing chaos.* Carved into the swords were symbols equating human lust and sexual love. On the throne, Dog O' War was written in English.

Marjorie so loved the drawing that she placed *Family of Three* in a prominent spot on her bookcase. On New Year's Eve 2000, four weeks before the fatal mauling, she posed next to it, wearing a white silk gown and blond wig. Her ring fingers dripping in diamonds, Marjorie leaned over to expose her cleavage fully, thrilled to pose as Paul's "bride-to-be."

Robert took the snapshot, then he and his wife toasted with three bubbling champagne glasses, to the three of them becoming "the dream of the Triad." Next to the glasses was a cork inscribed with the letters AB. Robert and Marjorie took a photo of the still-life toast, sending it to Paul with a note that explained how eager they were for the day when they could live with Paul "as one." When Noel and Knoller dined at their favorite pub, they often asked the waiters to set a third place setting—ordering an extra dish for Schneider.

The cleavage photo of Marjorie posing near the drawing of fierce fighting dogs was one of many they sent to Paul. It was a token of their love for him, and their appreciation for his great talent and art. Schneider drew a number of medieval representations of Marjorie and Robert, and he also drew portraits of Marjorie and warrior women with the Presas. Some depicted women in suggestive sexual poses with the massive dogs.

No doubt, Paul's drawings were becoming more twisted and sadistic. And Robert and Marjorie enjoyed them. Marjorie took a special liking to one image in particular—a fierce, scantily clad woman, legs spread, shield and dagger in her hands, flanked by two Presa guard dogs wearing metal coats of armor. Marjorie framed the unusual piece, displaying the likeness of herself, Bane, and Hera, in the apartment hallway; it was signed "Dog O' War 99."

It was just around the new year that Marjorie wrote Paul with big news. She and Robert had decided to make a lifelong commitment to Paul and they were willing to make it official. They had found a way to marry him through legal adoption. Until then, she and Robert would be there for Paul, as his durable power of attorney for his health care. They would help him as "family."

By then, Marjorie had become deeply concerned for Schneider's well-being. Noel & Knoller had been accusing the Department of Corrections of corruption for years, claiming department officials were turning California prisons into torture chambers. The firm represented inmates who said they were being chained to toilets and being Tasered (shot with Taser guns) just for kicks; other inmates maintained they were being burned with acid.

Because one of Paul's fellow inmates, Billy Boyd, had been stabbed to death by fellow inmates after testifying in a Noel & Knoller case involving "excessive use of force" at Pelican Bay State Prison, Knoller was concerned that Paul Schneider might be next. She was scared for Paul's life.

Marjorie told her husband they needed to protect Paul, and Robert fully agreed. Both of them viewed the Department of Corrections as the enemy. They felt the prison system could have inmates murdered at will, that it was violating inmates in every way possible. They wanted Schneider removed from the notorious Pelican Bay and would do everything in their power to that end.

Marjorie wrote Paul, insisting that she would work the prison system better than anyone, that no one could get the better of her. She promised Paul she would not call him to the witness stand in any of their upcoming cases against the California Department of Corrections. She vowed she would never put Paul into the kind of jeopardy Billy Boyd suffered. Knoller swore that she would get Paul out of the SHU at Pelican Bay, if it took all her strength and might.

Just like Brenda Moore, Marjorie Knoller felt she needed to prove to Schneider what a tough cookie she was, just what a badass she could be. She wanted to live up to Schneider's huge reputation, and she wrote down an expression she said she liked to use. She called herself "death incarnate." She said she told people that her face would be the last thing they were ever going to see before she kicked their "sorry ass" across the universe.

Secretly, Marjorie wanted Paul to know that she planned to be his woman in every way. There were notes written in French that made references to her being "only" for him. Marjorie had Paul studying French so they could communicate without Robert understanding everything. Paul had a handwritten dictionary of French-to-English that included the French words for "filth," the "stink of wild animal," and "fat slob." Those were just a few of their choice phrases.

Marjorie loved writing about sex to Paul, telling him anything that was in her heart. She felt like she was stealing time with him. She touched herself and sent him her *"essence,"* encouraging Paul to write to her in French and engage in her grotesque eroticism. She was happy to fuel his rage and fury about the prison system, and Paul clearly found Marjorie's erotic and perverse materials amusing.

For one thing, Paul loved the fact that he was getting over on prison officials, receiving all this graphic contraband in legal mail. More important, if he were ever to get out of Pelican Bay, Schneider needed to have strong attorneys doing his bidding. If Robert and Marjorie wanted to pretend he was their fantasy lover, Paul didn't mind. If they wanted to *experiment somehow* with his Presa Canarios, Paul didn't argue.

Schneider was allowing them to feel that he was comfortable with "going beyond all primary earthly bonds" as a threesome. He allowed them to think they had his blessings in the bedroom, that he was a part of them and was with them in spirit when they performed sex acts on each other—as Bane and Hera watched.

Paul received four letters from Robert that referred explicitly to certain happenings between Hera and Marjorie, and between Bane and Marjorie, but Robert's allegations could have just been pure imagination. There was no way for Paul, or anyone else, to know the real truth.

If the sex acts with the Presas went beyond fantasy, if sexual contact was occurring between human and animal, Paul treated it as if it were no big deal. He allegedly received only one photo that might serve as proof—it was of Marjorie, naked, bending over toward her laundry closet, with one of the dogs in the background.

CHAPTER THIRTEEN

From files redacted by Judge James Warren:

PEOPLE'S EXHIBIT
S-8 D 2257
CONFIDENTIAL LEGAL MAIL
December 27, 2000
Paul John Schneider / Re: "Triad"
and other various matters

Dear Paul,
    Well, as Marjorie told you in the letter she mailed out this evening, we have gotten clearance for visiting you all day 9–3 on Monday Jan 15, Dale from 12–3 on the 16, and you again from 12:30–3 on the 17. Got the call from visiting yesterday around 9:00 A.M. No one had a brain fart. Damn!!! Suffered through a detailed explanation about how they did not want you and Dale on the same chain, in the same boot, because you were SHU "inmates"—hate that fucking word when used in connection with you or Dale—"inmates neither of you are!"

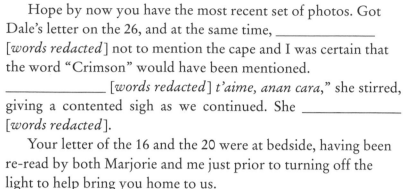

Hope by now you have the most recent set of photos. Got Dale's letter on the 26, and at the same time, _____ [*words redacted*] not to mention the cape and I was certain that the word "Crimson" would have been mentioned.

_____ [*words redacted*] *t'aime, anan cara,"* she stirred, giving a contented sigh as we continued. She _____ [*words redacted*].

Your letter of the 16 and the 20 were at bedside, having been re-read by both Marjorie and me just prior to turning off the light to help bring you home to us.

Later, _____ [*words redacted*] the canine duo, broke in doing their imitation of the prison break scene from the movie *Exodus*. Marjorie looked at me and said, *"So, this is what it's like to have kids?"* I told her, *"Yeah, that's why parents have locks on their bedroom doors."*

As Marjorie told you, we had been told by cops for a very long time, that *you had stabbed your own defense counsel.* Every time we were told that, my response was, *"If he did, he must have had a damned good reason and the schmuck probably deserved it!!!"* Couzins was an ass who deserved what he got for the disrespect shown you.

Given what Marjorie and I heard of you—especially the missing light switch plates and the air conditioning vent cover—I had no doubt that you were *carrying.* Neither Marjorie or I have any fear of you. If you went for the door and your route of travel was through the spot I was standing, I would get my ass out of the way so you would have a clear shot at the door or window.

When somebody early on in the Boyd case—made mention of wanting to depose you—Marjorie and I both agreed that we would have no problem with that. And I would just like to make it clear, that if I was not sitting between you and the door, and if you went for the door, all she or I would do is wave good bye and wish you good luck and god's speed.

Marjorie tells me she is getting ready to go to the box for

the 5:00 P.M. pick up, so I'm going to break off here. Keep yourselves and one another safe and watch your backs. Marjorie and I both look forward to being able to share *unsere Weibchen,* mine and your mate in person.

All the best, your *Leiber Freund,*

Robert

CHAPTER FOURTEEN

Robert Noel and Marjorie Knoller had come a long way from the time the two married in 1989. In the beginning, after just five dates together, they were so head-over-heels in love, the two moved in together in Robert's apartment on California Street. Back then, Marjorie was thrilled to be away from the suburbs, from the dullness of her second marriage in sleepy Benicia, a forty-minute drive away from downtown. Living with Robert in style, Marjorie had landed herself smack in the center of San Francisco's high society.

Knoller was quick to join the Little Jim Club, the oldest and most respected charity organization in the city. There, she became friendly with society people such as Mary Karen Fippinger, who would recall Marjorie and Robert as being "regulars" at the Davies Symphony Hall events. Fippinger would reflect that the couple always looked spectacular. Marjorie dressed in exclusive designer gowns with matching shoes and handbags. Robert always seemed debonair, wearing expensive suits and tuxedos. Magazines such as *Rolling Stone* would later show photos of the couple all dolled up, calling Noel and Knoller "fixtures of San Francisco society."

Robert and Marjorie seemed well suited to high-class living. They did well, hanging around the super rich, playing along with them. But most of the genuine upper-crust people could tell that they were social climbers. High-society people didn't give the couple very much thought.

Sure, Noel and Knoller could fit in with their neighbors in Pacific Heights. They walked the streets in Polo and Gucci, looking just like everyone else in the appropriate designer attire. But to anyone who got to know them, they seemed to be legal professionals trying to ride on the fringes of big money.

However, between Robert's political connections and Marjorie's networking, the pair would manage to get themselves invited to a number of the important San Francisco society functions. They'd attend the Mardi Gras Ball every year, they'd receive the occasional invitation to events at Ann and Gordon Getty's house, and they'd purchase invitations to less-expensive black-tie affairs. Life was good to Noel and Knoller in those days, when they enjoyed the pretenses of the wealthy.

Though Robert could become obnoxious and quite condescending at times, he was, after all, a litigator with an impressive résumé; and he had done stints at two blue-chip Republican law firms in San Diego. Noel was considered a competent and diligent attorney, so people put up with his arrogance. For her part, Knoller would act as Noel's buffer, always toning her husband down.

In reality, Robert Noel had very little money to his name. He'd been wiped out financially by two costly divorces, and suffered further when he was fired from a prominent law firm and lost his $100,000 annual salary. So it was Marjorie who had all the cash. The recipient of a small trust fund, Marjorie had enough money stashed away to get them through any rough patches.

Marjorie's nest egg allowed Robert to worry less about having *paying* clients; he could become a hero, in his mind, as he did more and more work for the poor, handling pro bono cases. Marjorie was all for that. She worked diligently with Robert in his efforts to help people in public housing. In fact, in 1992, for its efforts to help the needy, the county bar association named Noel & Knoller "Volunteers of the Month." In their view, the fact that they helped the poor made them seem all the more rich.

Robert Noel was an imposing figure, and he carried himself well. Robert was someone Marjorie could be proud of. At black-tie events, especially, when he was in his silk bow tie, cummerbund, and gold cuff links, Robert was a charmer. He knew how to engage people. He was well versed in many subjects, had a phenomenal memory, and was good at banter.

Around Robert, Marjorie seemed more refined as well. Gone were her out-of-style hairdos, her polyester dresses, and her introverted nature. Suddenly, with Noel at her side, Knoller's voice became more haughty, she wore her hair swept up like a beauty queen, and she became clever enough to place just the right piece of jewelry, just the right Hermès scarf, to give herself the appearance of substance.

Even though they fraternized with the wealthy, for the most part, Robert and Marjorie were basically loners. They had no real close friends, and many people thought they were an enigma. Around their society acquaintances, they were polite and gracious, but the couple worked hard to pull the carpet out from under the feet of rich folks. For instance, Robert recalled an incident where he and Marjorie were seated next to a noted society couple at a black-tie dinner at the Mark Hopkins Hotel. After an hour of general chitchat, the society couple realized that Robert and Marjorie were the attorneys, Noel & Knoller, who were *suing them* to block them from building a high-rise development. They were infuriated by the audacity of Noel and Knoller's phony behavior. But Robert and Marjorie were like that. They thought they could double-cross people and still remain friendly.

"When this couple realized who we were, they actually got up from the table and walked out of the ballroom," Robert recalled, laughing. "They were having such a fine time with us, until they found out we were the ones costing them hundreds of thousands of dollars."

Robert and Marjorie loved stirring up trouble. They saw themselves as the last hope for every underdog: the poor, the homeless, the incarcerated. In their minds, they were paragons of virtue, fighting City Hall and corporate greed. They felt they knew all the answers, and anyone who didn't agree with them was an idiot, a moron, a *cretin*.

Because they were smarter than everyone else and more righteous, they thought they could outwit anyone and talk circles around people. Being particularly good in that arena, Robert was a master at making any crazy scheme seem possible. He was brilliant at twisting facts around and readjusting the truth to suit his argument.

Of course, in reality, Noel and Knoller saw the world through an upside-down looking glass. They lived in a false wonderland, and thus whatever good they did always seemed to backfire. Whatever deeds they accomplished would later get flushed down the toilet. The low-cost housing building they spent years trying to save was ultimately torn down. Of the various homeless clients they represented, none ever obtained any monetary relief. Noel and Knoller's anger at the world didn't seem to serve anyone. But still they deluded themselves, believing that they were going about things with truth and justice on their side.

Robert liked to think of himself as Dudley Doright, the cartoon character on *The Bullwinkle Show* who would march in to save the day, even when he had no idea how to do that. Marjorie was more like Natasha, who pulled the strings from behind, always letting her husband, Boris, take the heat for her scheming ways.

Of the two, Marjorie was perhaps more deluded, thinking she could have everything her way. She and Robert both felt they could use their legal prowess to bully people, believing that none of their actions would have consequences. These attorneys thought they could get away with anything.

With that type of attitude, Noel and Knoller would step on people's toes. They would often bite the hands of the people who fed them. It was a bad habit of theirs. Robert and Marjorie liked to attack people. Robert, in particular, had trouble maintaining relationships with anyone, including his own children. He had difficulty keeping up his professional relationships, and as he became more and more deluded, his career started to fail.

When he met Knoller, Robert Noel was at the top of his game. But after years of self-aggrandizement and years of Marjorie's backing him in all his misguided thoughts and efforts, he lived in complete and utter denial. Instead of humbling himself or trying to develop business, Robert Noel remained pretentious. He walked around puffed up like a peacock, thinking he was a pillar of the legal community.

With all the insults that Noel uttered and the bad manners he openly displayed, his career began slipping further every day. But Knoller would justify and rationalize everything he did. Noel and Knoller were still doing business, and clients were knocking at the door, but fewer friends were offering them referrals.

As public incidents piled up, the cracks in the façade of Noel and Knoller began to emerge. Robert and Marjorie were acting in ways that were unacceptable. At some point, they seemed to lose touch with social etiquette. Volunteers from the charitable organizations began to keep their distance, but the couple was so self-centered that they didn't even know what was happening. They were oblivious to the fact that their circle of acquaintances was beginning to dwindle.

One starry evening, while hobnobbing at Ann and Gordon Getty's, with everyone drinking, eating, and making small talk around the ice sculptures, Noel mumbled an attack on their hostess.

"Why doesn't Ann just turn her mansion into a house for the homeless," he said under his breath, "you know, since she cares so much about them. Donating her big fat house here could probably solve the whole problem."

Knowing all the power the Gettys wielded and that they donated so much money to charity, Knoller was stunned. Generally immune to her husband's awkward comments, she quieted him down. She didn't let anyone hear this outrage. In public, Marjorie's feelings toward Robert were always adoring. At home, Marjorie was his follower, especially during the early part of their marriage; and in return, Robert worshiped the ground she walked on.

Up until their troubles in the mid-1990s, Robert had given Marjorie the moon. He turned his paychecks over to her every week, gave her full rein over their finances, and had even signed a pre-nup waiving any rights to her own property and income for the duration of their marriage. He insisted that she keep her own separate bank account. He wanted Marjorie to feel like an equal partner in every way. Even before Knoller passed the state bar, when she was technically a paralegal, Noel wanted her to have half of whatever profits they earned as a team.

The couple who had started off well, who had honeymooned in Paris, staying at the Hotel de Crillon on the Right Bank next to the American embassy, where they dined at the world's finest restaurants, always seemed to live in a fantasy world.

During the early days of their marriage—in exotic places like Paris, Cairo, Athens, and Rome—Robert showered Marjorie with expensive gifts. Madly in love with her, he spoiled Marjorie, and had even converted to Judaism just to satisfy her. Robert liked to make it known that he idolized his wife. Even though he was the one with all kinds of lofty law credentials and she was still a law student, Noel treated Knoller as if she would be the next Sandra Day O'Connor. Noel was becoming Knoller's Svengali. He would help mold her into the great attorney she always wanted to be.

But Robert's heavy influence over Marjorie would slowly begin to change. By the time Knoller became a member of the California State Bar in 1992, she had become more certain of herself, and, taking a cue from her own hard-assed husband, she began to develop her own set of *cojones*.

Like her husband, Knoller became the type of attorney who had no compunction about threatening people with lawsuits. In her verbose letters and complaints to her landlord in Pacific Heights, for instance, Marjorie threatened to file suit over any petty issue.

Whatever circumstances Noel and Knoller didn't agree with, whatever person stood in their way, they would concoct a lawsuit. There was one suit they filed based on a showerhead that needed repairing. Noel and Knoller were seeking damages in the amount of $50,000 because one of the repairmen, who spoke to them with a German accent, gave them a military salute when waving good-bye. Even though the repairman was an immigrant from Germany, Noel charged that the guy intentionally used the accent and the salute to offend his Jewish faith. Although Noel was raised Catholic and had been an avid Irishman when married to his first wife, he loved to accuse people of being Nazis. In the court papers, Noel & Knoller claimed "intentional infliction of emotional distress." They stated that the salute made them think of the Holocaust, which made them both very upset.

"We thought this was really kooky, really crazy," an attorney who represented the German repairman later told a reporter. No one in their

Pacific Heights building could believe that the *massive six-foot-three* Robert Noel would be distressed over a *humble plumber* fixing a leak.

But Noel and Knoller saw themselves as being in the right. They were fighters. More than just left-wing liberals, they were people on a mission to have the world see things their way. The couple always had a cause: they had huge complaints about the U.S. government and had major concerns about the corrupt ways of corporate America.

They were the type of lawyers who gave all lawyers a bad name, and as their practice continued to go down the tubes, they were compelled to take down the shingle they had once used on Sansome Street. People didn't know it, but by the mid-1990s, their law office was being run out of a converted closet in their Pacific Heights apartment.

The firm of Noel & Knoller used an answering machine to hide behind. They made their own stationery. Their business cards made them look respectable, but essentially, they were a two-person show. Without even an assistant or a paralegal, the pair did all their own photocopying, typing, and legal research. Noel's career, which had started on the most dignified path, including six years as an attorney at the Department of Justice's Tax Division in Washington, D.C., had come almost to a screeching halt. Noel & Knoller's practice had become murky and vague. Their reputation in San Francisco was basically shot.

Perhaps that was why, in 1994, when Noel & Knoller were offered the opportunity to handle their first case for a Pelican Bay guard, they were eager to file a federal civil rights action. Prison guard John Cox claimed Pelican Bay officials were retaliating against him for testifying in a landmark case, *Madrid v. Gomez*. The *Madrid* decision, which eventually came down in 1995, was based on a federal class action suit filed on behalf of inmates, claiming that excessive force was used by guards at the super-max facility. In his decision, U.S. District Judge Thelton Henderson expressed outrage at the corrupt conditions at Pelican Bay prison and ordered an overhaul of its policies. This paved the way for numerous inmate accusations about corrupt prison guards, such as John Cox, and later, for an array of countersuits from inmates and guards alike.

With Noel & Knoller at the helm of Officer John Cox's case against the Department of Corrections, the court threw out the suit on summary judgment, pointing to evidence that Cox had been disciplined for legitimate reasons—for instance, numerous sexual harassment allegations were on file from Cox's co-workers. Just after the judgment, John Cox was charged and jailed for alleged sexual assault. Days later, he was found hung in his cell.

When they learned of Cox's death, Noel and Knoller were sure the system had conspired against them. The attorneys loved to dabble in conspiracy theories, and they believed that Cox was actually killed in his jail cell, that someone from the Department of Corrections made it look like a hanging. This bizarre theory fueled the two attorneys, who were hell-bent on fighting the Department of Corrections even more.

Before Cox killed himself, Lieutenant Bob Trujillo, a correctional officer in the California penal system for more than twenty years, gave a deposition in the case. He remembers being insulted by Noel and Knoller—he was condescended to, talked down to, and angered by their audacity.

At issue was Noel and Knoller's theory that Officer Trujillo was working in stealth with the Department of Corrections, secretly threatening John Cox so that Cox would drop his case.

"Do you own a pellet gun?" Noel bluntly asked. "Or a slingshot?"

"Well, yeah, I have those at home," Trujillo admitted.

"Have you ever gone by John Cox's house and fired at his house with your pellet gun?"

"No," Trujillo said.

"Do you know of anyone who might have fired bullets at Officer Cox's home?"

"I don't even know where John Cox lives," Trujillo said, disgusted by the unfounded accusations.

But no matter what Trujillo told them, under oath, it was Noel & Knoller's belief that he and other California Department of Corrections officials were on a witch-hunt, conspiring against their client, John Cox.

When Cox turned up dead, it gave Noel & Knoller reason to take on other injustices against prison guards who were "trying to do the right thing" by turning against their co-workers, siding with inmates who felt confident that they could legally badger prison guards.

For the guards working at Pelican Bay, this situation became outrageous. Inmates would use homemade weapons, they would create riots, battles, and attacks, but if a guard used "excessive force" in dealing with the problems, the person could wind up facing a lawsuit and possible criminal charges.

Noel & Knoller, who liked to work both sides of every fence, found the fight for inmates' rights to be a noble cause; at the same time, they also wanted to fight on behalf of allegedly corrupt prison guards. They knew if they could win one case, there would be endless cases and CCPOA union money to follow. In the summer of 1997, they landed a higher-stakes assignment to represent Officer Jose Garcia. Garcia was the first Pelican Bay guard to face criminal charges for allegedly conspiring with inmates to attack two convicted child molesters.

Garcia's trial, which began in the fall of 1997, was the longest trial ever held in Del Norte County, lasting three months and featuring ninety-three witnesses. Noel handled all courtroom appearances. Knoller was present every day, and she sat listening to the testimony, writing notes, and whispering comments during the proceedings.

Moving up to Crescent City for the duration of the trial, Noel and Knoller were brilliant at acting the part of slick city attorneys, and the locals trusted them. It didn't take long for a number of accused Pelican Bay prison guards to sign up for the firm's services. Disgruntled Pelican Bay guards thought they were lucky to have savvy San Francisco attorneys at their disposal. Robert and Marjorie were very convincing, making accused prison guards think they could win millions from the California Department of Corrections. They had the egos to make people believe in them.

Throughout the Garcia trial, Marjorie Knoller was a standout. Not only was she impeccably dressed, not only did she get the jury's attention with short skirts and flashy outfits, she knew how to flirt. During breaks, Knoller worked the men in the gallery and courtroom, getting the dirt on every new witness so Noel could then bring up all kinds of inappropriate allegations in court.

Based on Knoller's input, Noel stood before the Del Norte judge, making irrelevant sexual accusations against Department of Corrections witnesses. He made out-of-this-world statements, accusing District Attorney Jim Fallman of being a co-conspirator in illegal sexual activities. Noel was making so many weird comments, accusing the prosecu-

tion of anything and everything; at one point, he told the judge that prosecution witnesses were on a witch-hunt, that, like their predecessors in
Salem, these officials probably believed that "pigs could fly."

Of course, the jury, the judge, and the people in the courtroom were
all flabbergasted by this accusation. The "Noel & Knoller act" was so out
there and was so insulting and bawdy and grotesque, it would have been
comedic were it not costing the people of Del Norte County hundreds of
thousands of dollars.

As the weeks passed, certain people began to notice that Marjorie
Knoller was a rather mean-spirited woman. Courtroom observers
reported that Knoller was always taking cheap shots at the opposition,
especially at attorney Barbara Sheldon, who represented the Department
of Corrections. Knoller insulted Sheldon under her breath, so that only
people at the counsel tables could hear. But Knoller's nasty remarks didn't
escape the ears of Mike Shine, the Del Norte bailiff, who remembered
them quite well. "Marjorie would do anything she could to irritate somebody. She basically smart-mouthed, she was very sassy," Deputy Shine
confided. "Marjorie would make little comments that you normally
don't put up with in a court of law. She would push the envelope almost
to the point of being held in contempt. She was right there on the edge all
the time."

Deputy Shine watched as Knoller repeatedly pushed Sheldon's but-
tons. Apparently, Knoller was threatened by other women, by their
beauty, by their intelligence, and she looked at Barbara Sheldon as com-
petition. Under her breath, Knoller would call Sheldon a bitch; she
would mumble things in court, making fun of Sheldon's dress or suit.
Knoller was continually doing unnerving things—muttering, rolling her
eyes, and making faces in the courtroom.

Knoller was the type who liked to quietly boss people around, treating strangers as her personal assistants. She wasn't the stereotypical loud-
mouth—far from it. But in her own sneaky way, she'd do things to hurt
people. Knoller enjoyed seeing people cringe, yet she was a smooth
manipulator, operating in stealth.

Knoller knew how to get people to bend the rules for her. She did all
the background work for Noel and apparently enjoyed that role. In the
courtroom, she would play the part of the little woman, standing by her

man. But as she waited in the wings, she was working her own kind of magic. She did whatever she could to unnerve Fallman and Sheldon. Ultimately, however, her contribution didn't seem to matter—Noel & Knoller lost the case and Officer Garcia was taken away in shackles.

Still, Marjorie looked up to Robert as a god, and in return, Robert put her on the highest pedestal. Robert liked to parade Marjorie, especially in the courtroom, where he wanted her to don shorter skirts and higher heels. He enjoyed watching men ogle his wife, and he encouraged her flirtations, knowing that it was a good way to pry information. Under his breath, Robert would brag about Marjorie's great ass. To anyone who would listen, Robert would gloat about what a male magnet his wife was, and would make quirky comments about her sexual appetite.

It was through the Jose Garcia case that Paul John Schneider first entered Noel and Knoller's lives. Schneider was one of a number of inmates called to testify, but he refused to talk when he took the stand. This impressed Noel and Knoller, who immediately decided that he was a "stand-up guy."

Schneider was followed on the stand by inmate Billy Boyd, who was serving time for second-degree murder. Boyd was killed by fellow inmates in March 1998, just months after his testimony. The Boyd murder was rumored to be a gang retaliation, and Noel & Knoller believed the killing was related to his testimony.

Following Boyd's murder, Robert Noel filed a jury trial demand on behalf of Boyd's widow, Kim. It claimed that, because Billy Boyd was the only inmate to testify against Garcia and because the thirty-six-year-old inmate was left "in the open" on the mainline at Pelican Bay, the Del Norte County Prosecutor Jim Fallman and California Department of Corrections officials were responsible for his death.

On behalf of the stabbing of convicted murderer Billy Boyd, the firm of Noel & Knoller were seeking the following: $50 million for the widow and heirs; $50 million for exemplary damages; and $20 million for compensatory damages.

Thus, for the alleged Gladiator "set-up" of William "Billy" Boyd, in which Boyd was allegedly stabbed to death by Aryan Brotherhood gang members, Noel & Knoller were asking for a $120 million in damages,

he Pacific Heights apartment building where Diane Whipple, Robert Noel, and Marjorie noller lived prior to the fatal dog mauling that ended Whipple's life.

All photographs courtesy of the author unless otherwise noted.

Diane Alexis Whipple. *(Corbis-Bettmann)*

The hallway on the sixth floor with bloody handprints, groceries, and Diane Whipple's shredded clothing. People's Exhibit 75 N EV. *(Public Exhibit)*

Entryway to Diane Whipple's apartment 606, her keys in the door as she struggled to get inside. People's Exhibit 75 G EV. *(Public Exhibit)*

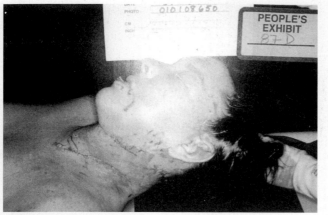

Profile of victim Diane Whipple, who suffered seventy-seven bite wounds from the tip of her head to the soles of her feet. People's Exhibit 87 D. *(Public Exhibit)*

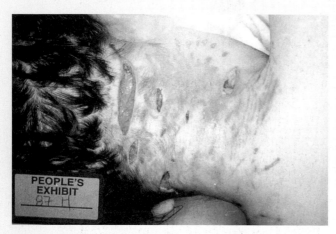

Fatal wound on the back of Diane Whipple's neck. People's Exhibit 87 H. *(Public Exhibit)*

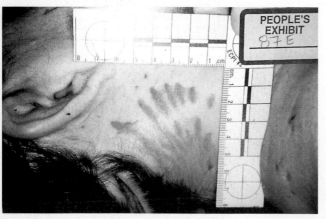

Graphic example of 5.5-centimeter wound. Bane went for Whipple's jugular. People's Exhibit 87 E. *(Public Exhibit)*

Bane, a Presa Canario, at the farm where he was raised in Hayfork, California. Bane was allowed to roam freely and was caught killing animal livestock. *(Courtesy of Janet Coumbs)*

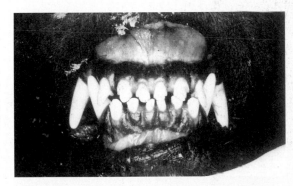

Bane bares his teeth. *(Courtesy of Animal Care and Control Department, San Francisco)*

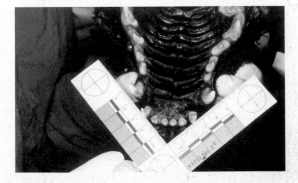

Whipple was slaughtered by the jaws of Bane. *(Courtesy of Animal Care and Control Department, San Francisco)*

Isis, a Presa Canario and the birth mother of Roka, Bane's offspring. Here Isis is playing wit kittens at the farm in Hayfork, the "Appalachia" of California. *(Courtesy of Janet Coumb*

Noel and Knoller's dog, Hera, participated in the fatal mauling of Diane Whipple. Shredded clothing was found in her feces. *(AP Worldwide)*

Marjorie Knoller poses with Bane in her Pacific Heights apartment. Letters by Robert Noel suggest that Knoller "experimented" sexually with her pet. *(Public Exhibit)*

PEOPLE'S
EXHIBIT
35A EV
181813-01/181813-02

Bane being led away on come-along poles by San Francisco Police Department and Animal Care and Control officers.

The Hall of Justice in San Francisco, where Robert Noel and Marjorie Knoller faced their day of judgment.

A media throng in the San Francisco Hall of Justice.

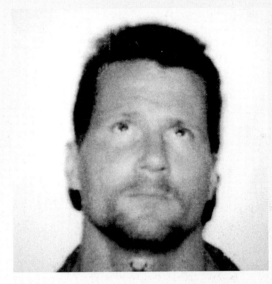

Inmate Paul John Schneider, aka "Cornfed": the Hannibal Lecter of Pelican Bay State Prison. Schneider ran an "illegal" dog ring, the Dog O' War. Schneider was responsible for arranging to import the rare Presa Canario breed from the Canary Islands. *(Public Exhibit)*

Inmate Dale Bretches, who shared a cell with Paul John Schneider. Bretches is still involved in a Presa Canario dog-breeding operation, which he has extended to include Africa, South America, and Great Britain. *(Public Exhibit)*

Hera was held at the Animal Care and Control center in San Francisco as evidence for more than a year. She was destroyed on January 30, 2002.

Ana Aureoles, animal activist, with her constant companion, Henry Miller. Aureoles represented the court of public opinion that wished to save Hera.

Animal lover Captain Vicky Guldbech of Animal Care and Control in San Francisco. She presented the dangerous dog hearing regarding the Presa Canario Hera to Sergeant Bill Herndon.

Sergeant Bill Herndon of Animal Care and Control was at the center of a swirling controversy regarding the fate of Hera. *(Courtesy of Animal Care and Control Department, San Francisco)*

Marjorie Knoller's defense attorney, Nedra Ruiz, faces the media. Ruiz's unusual courtroom tactics (she reenacted the mauling on all fours) drew ire from fellow attorneys.

Sharon Smith, Diane Whipple's same-sex partner, addresses the media backed up by her attorney Michael Cardoza, who handled her civil case. Smith would become a gay activist, fighting for legislation to give rights to same-sex partners.

ADA Kimberly Guilfoyle-Newsom, aka "Victoria's Secret model," in her office at the Hall of Justice. Guilfoyle-Newsom was the second-chair prosecutor in the case against Knoller.

Gavin Newsom, high-profile husband of Kimberly Guilfoyle-Newsom and partner with the Getty family in the ownership of the high-end Plump Jack Winery, Restaurant, and Lounge. Newsom has announced plans to run for mayor of San Francisco.

The two lead investigators in the case: San Francisco Police Department inspectors Rich Daniele *(left)* and Michael Becker at the General Works Department in the Hall of Justice.

Sergeant Inspector Stephen Murphy of the San Francisco Police Department. The "Murph" discovered key evidence in the case such as nude photos, bizarre drawings of man and animal, and letters with sexual connotations.

Lieutenant Henry Hunter of the San Francisco Police Department, General Works Department. Hunter handled all media requests regarding the case.

ADA Jim Hammer comforts Sharon Smith, the partner of Diane Whipple, after Marjorie Knoller's second-degree murder conviction is overturned by Judge James Warren.

Controversial figure Terence "Kayo" Hallinan addresses the media as Jim Hammer shows anguish over Judge Warren's decision to throw out Marjorie Knoller's murder conviction.

Robert Noel awaiting sentencing in the San Francisco County Jail.

Roka, the offspring of Bane and Isis, was rescued in the Los Angeles airport area and now lives happily in the San Fernando valley. Some of Bane's other offspring were put into the hands of Mexican Mafia associates.

California Department of Corrections Special Agent Devan Hawkes. Hawkes was the key figure who linked "illegal" Presa Canario dog-breeding operations to the notorious Aryan Brotherhood prison gang and the Mexican Mafia. Dog owners Noel and Knoller were obsessed with a conspiracy theory involving the California Department of Corrections.

as well as reasonable attorneys' fees, to be paid for by the People of California.

The case would remain on the docket of Judge Thelton Henderson for roughly three and a half years. Among the delays was a pre-trial continuance at the request of Robert Noel due to a hand injury. Apparently, Noel had a finger severed during an attack involving his Presa Canario dog.

Noel and Knoller seemed undeterred by their setbacks in the Garcia case. Throughout the trial, Noel would openly make accusations against the Department of Corrections, ranting and raving, never actually backing anything up. He would insist that he and his wife were being followed, that their motel rooms were broken into, that their computers and files were tampered with. Noel would later confide that he felt compelled to rent a variety of cars to keep the Department of Corrections "spies" off his trail.

"We did not want the Department of Corrections to know what kind of car we were driving," Noel explained to a reporter. "The administration at Pelican Bay is an absolute cesspool, and even though a lot of good, conscientious people work there, the rest of the place smells like a whorehouse."

They appealed Garcia's criminal conviction, alleging an elaborate conspiracy between the Department of Corrections and the Del Norte DA. In numerous filings, Robert Noel continued his diatribe against the government agencies, likening them to the archenemy, managing to somehow drag *Adolf Hitler* into the equation. "I am requesting that all your tapes and files on Garcia be turned over, but please do not jeopardize the case by giving any confidential data to Garcia's civil attorneys," Noel wrote to Pelican Bay officials. "That would endanger witnesses before you move them. . . . When Hitler opened a second front in Russia, the result was to lose on both sides!"

That Noel had grandiose views of his role in fighting the Department of Corrections, and had unusual perceptions about the government agency, was further evidenced by his claim that "inmate workers are given free rein over the program officers." In his legal filings, Noel would insist that "with the knowing and tacit approval of the administration at Pelican Bay," inmates were causing "exactly the assaults on other inmates that Defendant Garcia was wrongly accused of doing."

"There's a tactic that defense attorneys use where they just throw in everything they can to confuse the jury," a source from the Department of Justice explained, "but I'm not sure Noel had a strategy. He was just flying by the seat of his pants. I was actually astounded at all the junk he was presenting. It shows just how sick he is."

Other sources from the Department of Justice would later comment about how difficult it was dealing with Noel & Knoller. Sources revealed a Jekyll and Hyde persona behind Noel, explaining that in his letters, Robert Noel was "bombastic, outrageous, sometimes insane," but face-to-face he was quite "courteous and professional."

Apparently it was Marjorie Knoller who was much more angry, much more outrageous in person. "She was vindictive, always spewing personal attacks on people," the government source noted. "She would make crazy statements, accusing the warden at Pelican Bay of killing some inmate, or getting an inmate killed."

After they met Schneider in 1997, Noel and Knoller filed more than twenty-one federal lawsuits on behalf of prison guards, other employees, and inmates, targeting the California Department of Corrections and its officials. In his numerous legal claims, Noel would pontificate about "inmate issues" and "internal affairs" investigations at Pelican Bay. But Noel's claims were almost always dismissed, and his appeal on Garcia would be thrown out by the appellate court, which had trouble believing a word of Robert Noel's conspiracy theory. An appellate judge wrote, "These are serious allegations, indeed, and we question whether even the most charitable reading of the record would support such events occurred."

Officials at the Justice Department and the CDC would handle Noel & Knoller's written claims in the most professional ways possible, responding with comments such as "if you have evidence of that allegation, we urge you to go to the FBI and the District Attorney." But it was all a game to Noel & Knoller. The Department of Justice would tell them to report the information to the appropriate authorities, then Noel &

Knoller would make further accusations, and the cycle would start all over again.

Noel & Knoller made insane threats in the Garcia case, saying they were "going to the Mexican Consulate" if things didn't get handled more efficiently, that there would be "an international incident" if certain paperwork wasn't filed in a timely fashion.

"We just all sat around and shook our heads," one government source explained, "particularly with Noel, who had been at the DOJ's Tax Division in D.C., which is a prestigious section within that organization. At one time Bob was well thought of. But the legal work we saw from him now was horrible. He didn't have a good understanding or analysis of the law."

The insanity of it all was that it was their own client, Garcia, who was at the center of the corrupt prison guard activity at Pelican Bay. After his conviction in Del Norte County, Jose Garcia and fellow guard Mike Powers would wind up the targets of a RICO (federal racketeering) investigation.

These convictions came after U.S. attorneys divulged taped statements that Garcia made to FBI agents in which he admitted to disliking child molesters, offering weapons to inmates, and discussing "how to kill a person." The two guards were eventually convicted by a jury in a federal court, being held accountable for "setting up" inmate stabbings.

Along with a small clique of guards who cooperated with inmates at Pelican Bay, Garcia wanted to play good cop/bad cop. Violating all the rules, these unorthodox guards hoped that by setting up child molesters, they would curry favor with the higher ranks of gang leaders (people like Paul Schneider). Garcia wanted to win Schneider over, hoping to discover where Aryan Brotherhood members were keeping their stockpile of weapons. If Garcia could discover weapons, he thought, he would earn brownie points with internal investigators at Pelican Bay, thereby justifying a promotion.

Garcia didn't care about civil rights, human rights, or anything else at Pelican Bay. A radical officer who liked to do things his way, he admitted to FBI Agent Stan Walker that his methods were unorthodox; on videotape, he even told the FBI that he supplied inmates with extra food and expensive liquor. A man who chose to live in the woods sleeping in a tree, Garcia bathed in the ice-cold Smith River. He was over-the-top when it came to being unusual, and according to Noel and other Garcia attorneys, the man was so nutty that he once drove his car twenty-five miles in reverse because the gearshift was stuck. In depositions, Officer Garcia would admit that he gave inmates cold-remedy drugs, sewing kits, shaving items, and even silk boxer shorts.

Garcia also admitted that he sometimes took inmates' so-called C-Files, listing inmates' offenses, from the Gang Unit Office. After signing out the files, he would hand over detailed information to gang leaders, encouraging "white boys" to kill Mexican inmates because, in Garcia's words, "any Mexican who's a child molester should know better."

Garcia ran the inmate kitchen/dining hall facility, where he discussed bringing in items such as ice picks and homemade knives with his inmate kitchen staff. Being a karate expert who ran his own dojo, Garcia evaluated methods of killing and taught his hand-chosen thugs the moves that would enable them to "whack any fucking dude" who Garcia felt deserved it.

According to a sworn statement by Kenny Costa, an inmate who later became one of Schneider's prime enemies (he was then transferred out of Pelican Bay because of Schneider's death threats), Garcia often held meetings in his dining hall office. Inmate Costa would recall discussing the beating up of other inmates, the stabbing of other inmates, the killing of other inmates. Internal investigators would learn that at one point, Garcia was so adamant about having an inmate beaten to death that the guard had to be told to "cool down" by the inmates inside the dining office. Most of the inmates who were a part of Garcia's insider "ring" reported the same details to Department of Corrections special agents and FBI agents working the case. This was highly unusual; in fact, it was unheard of (typically, prisoners would tell fifteen variations of any given story).

The fact that Jose Garcia was convicted, largely on the testimony of inmates—people who traditionally don't have any credibility—was a landmark step in efforts to curb abuses at Pelican Bay and other prisons. That Garcia's conviction pointed internal investigators to a wider federal probe was even more incredible. At Pelican Bay, for example, internal investigators suddenly had proof about a specific group of guards who were setting up child molesters, who were pulling C-Files, passing along information to gang leaders, then helping them arrange lethal attacks. Because of internal informants, investigators were noting that "bad apples" were turning up on staff at other prisons around California as well.

For the record, Jose Garcia's conviction was affirmed, and Garcia served more than two years in state prison, coming out of his shell only after Diane Whipple was killed, when he wished to report to San Francisco investigators the evildoings of Noel & Knoller and the firm's association with Paul Schneider.

As Robert Noel became more steeped in the ways of the prison "pecking order," he took it upon himself to track down the location of Kenny Costa. Noel then told Schneider that Costa was in a federal facility in Colorado, thus making it possible for the Aryan Brotherhood to place a hit on its enemy. It wouldn't be the only time that Noel would supply Schneider with the name and address of a person on the inmate's hit list. The attorney had no problem giving names and locations of people to Schneider. Noel insists that "everyone in the prison system knew" where Schneider's enemies were housed, and that his letter to Schneider, guised in "confidential legal mail," was just confirmation of the enemy's whereabouts . . . nothing more.

Although Paul Schneider was known to have ordered two dozen hits on AB enemies from behind prison walls, and there was existing proof that Schneider could get people whacked, both inside prison and out, Noel's attitude regarding Schneider remained cavalier. Perhaps Noel liked being considered an Aryan Brotherhood associate, even as he laughed at the notion, heartily making fun of the Department of Corrections for getting the facts wrong.

Maybe Noel provided Schneider with names and addresses of AB enemies because he liked the idea of *getting even*. If strangers wound up getting killed by Schneider and his people, well . . .

CHAPTER FIFTEEN

CRIME/INCIDENT REPORT: Battery on inmate with serious bodily injury/C.O. Frank Clemann
State of California/Department of Corrections
Pelican Bay State Prison/Security Housing Unit D,C Pod

On April 5, 1997, at approximately 1450 hours, while performing my duties as D-8 Control Officer, I had locked inmate Cabrera in the upper shower and inmate Perez in the lower shower. After changing showers in the other pods, I went back to C Pod and let inmate Schneider and inmate Bretches out to come down and use the nail clippers by the pod door. After they exited their cell, I shut the door.

Schneider went down the stairs and was headed towards the pod door. Bretches was still on the upper tier, so I opened the shower doors, thinking they were going to shower. Before I realized I had made a mistake, I saw Perez step out of the lower shower and Schneider started towards Perez. They started exchanging punches. At the same time, Bretches rushed into the upper shower and started fighting with Cabrera. I immediately yelled to get down and sounded the unit alarm. I grabbed the Federal Gas Gun serial number 052805, loaded with one

264R round. I also grabbed an additional round and ran up to C Pod window.

I saw Schneider and Perez rolling around on the floor, still fighting. Bretches and Cabrera were still fighting in the upper shower. I could see blood on Schneider and Perez. I again ordered them to stop fighting and get down. They did not comply with my orders, so I fired one 264R round from the Federal Gas Gun, aiming it directly in front of Schneider and Perez so as to skip it off the floor. I again ordered them to stop, with no response. It was obvious they were not going to stop, so I fired a second 264R round, ricocheting it off the wall next to Perez and Schneider.

Bretches and Cabrera continued fighting on the second tier shower, so I fired a third 264R round into the shower, ricocheting the round off the wall, but they were still not complying to my orders and continued to fight. . . .

The reporting employee, Correctional Officer Clemann, continued to order the inmates to stop fighting, with negative results. At that point, he fired a fourth round, skipping it off the floor in front of Perez and Schneider, and both inmates finally broke it up, with Schneider remaining about 250 feet away from the pod door, and Perez crawling to the right of the pod door.

With Bretches and Cabrera continuing to fight in the second-tier shower, Officer Clemann fired a fifth 264R round (it went into the shower), giving orders to stop fighting and get out into the corridor. With the fifth round, Cabrera came out of the shower and assumed a prone position. Officer Clemann immediately closed the second-tier shower door, securing Bretches inside. Four other correctional officers appeared at the scene, and a sergeant ordered Schneider to get into the first-tier shower, where the inmate was secured.

Minutes later, all four inmates were handcuffed, taken off to holding cells, and examined by a medical technical assistant. Inmate Perez had an abrasion to the left side of the neck and redness to his chest. Cabrera had an upper and lower lip bite, abrasions to his right shoulder and left triceps, scratches to the left side of his face approximately six inches long, a contusion to the right knee, and a contusion to the left eye. Bretches had scratches and abrasions on his chest, and a laceration on his left hand between the ring and little finger. Schneider had a laceration down the center of the top of his head.

All four inmates refused treatment, but Bretches and Cabrera were bleeding profusely and were transported to the infirmary. Cabrera was the only man with severe injuries, requiring three sutures to his right upper lip, which Bretches had partially bitten off.

Eventually, the four inmates were medically cleared and returned to their assigned cells; no other injuries were reported to staff as a result of the incident. However, a full year later, Dale Bretches, acting on his own behalf, filed an official complaint against the Department of Corrections, citing "staff misconduct." Bretches was asking for an appeal of the "use of force" policy, stating that his complaint was being filed as a prerequisite to a pending lawsuit.

"This prison and CDC as a whole had engaged in a practice which continues to this day of orchestrating, setting up, and encouraging altercations between SHU prisoners," Bretches wrote. "Then the staff, responsible for staging these cock fights, use 37mm's or 9mm's or other types of force upon the prisoners, to allegedly quell the very altercations they themselves contrived. As a recent example, on 4-5-97, Gunner Clemann, D-control booth officer, let myself and my cellie Schneider out of the tier, with two Northern Mexican inmates."

Dale Bretches went on to describe his version of the incident in detail, requesting that formal action be taken against Clemann and the other correctional officers at the scene.

"I want 1.5 million dollars in damages, for damages I incurred during the incident and shooting of 4-5-97," Bretches wrote in his complaint, "and injunctive relief in the form of better training and disciplining of Correctional Officers to avoid further incidents."

The complaint was rejected just weeks after Bretches filed it. But with the help of an attorney friend, Herman Franck, Paul Schneider and Dale Bretches filed a lawsuit against Warden Steven Cambra and others regarding this incident.

On March 16, 1999, the two inmates were deposed at Pelican Bay State Prison. The depositions took place on prison grounds because both men were considered too dangerous to transport.

Paul Schneider was questioned by Susan Myster, a Department of Justice attorney. In his hand, Schneider held what Myster called a "cheat sheet," a handwritten note from Robert Noel that was scribbled over a declaration from the Jose Garcia case. Noel had supplied Schneider with the confidential information, Schneider explained, but Schneider was reluctant to let the government attorney see it.

The cheat sheet made reference to "some stuff about Janet's dogs," Schneider told Myster, including directions to Janet's house and her phone number. Still, Myster wanted Schneider to make it available. But Schneider refused.

"What documents are those?" Myster asked, looking at the rest of the paperwork Schneider had brought along.

"A letter I got from an attorney named Noel and Knoller and transcripts he sent me off *People v. Garcia*," Schneider said. "It was a case involving an officer here who was convicted, sent to prison, for shooting somebody three times with a .37 millimeter."

"Okay."

"And I received transcripts of expert testimony used in the Garcia case," Schneider explained, "about the effects of a .37 millimeter round hitting anybody. Even bouncing it, ricocheting it, like they're supposed to. This statement by the Garcia expert, a former police officer, says he's seen it knock people's eyes out and peel back their scalps."

"Now, how do you spell the Noel?" Myster wondered.

"N-o-e-l and K-n o l l e r. They're a San Francisco firm. Noel got a copy of my complaint and sent me several documents, including the Garcia court transcripts."

"Well, let's get along with the reason we're here."

"All right."

Schneider told Myster the details of his life in Pelican Bay SHU. He'd been housed in that lockdown since 1984, living in a little section of the C Pod, a self-contained housing unit with eight cells on the top tier, four on the bottom, with two showers, and one enclosed exercise yard. The control officers would pop open an inmate's cell door according to who signed up for exercise or showers, and inmates' doors would open in the order in which people signed up.

Unlike other mainline areas of the prison, the SHU was so security-tight that the inmates could walk down to the end of the pod unescorted. Whether the men were going for exercise or showers, there were no escorts needed because SHU inmates were confined to this corridor—it led only to the enclosed yard and shower facility on one end and the control booth on the other.

"So what happened on the day of the incident?" Myster asked.

"Okay. They opened up our cell. It was like that kind of thing where we're just so used to it. They open the door and you just mosey on down the tier. And, you know, you're not supposed to be stopping and talking to people too much," Schneider explained. "But Dale, Mr. Bretches, had taken something over to one of the other cells in the upper tier. He was talking to someone in cell 209, which is right next to the showers."

"What did he take over there?"

"I don't know. It's pretty common to take either a reading book or something, you know, and just slide it under their door real quick."

"You're not supposed to pass stuff, are you?" Myster interrupted.

"I don't know."

"You don't *know* the rules?"

"No, they change monthly. You know, it's like, nobody sweats it, but to tell you the truth, I don't remember what reason he was on the upper tier," Schneider claimed. "I don't know if he was talking to somebody, passing a book or some food. I wasn't really paying attention to where he was going. I knew that we were both going out to use the nail clippers, and sometimes, it's pretty common that one of us will stop at somebody's cell and say hello, and the other one might head over to the nail clippers or the shower yard, whatever."

"So you went downstairs?"

"Yeah, and when I seen the little cup with the nail clippers, I'm looking at the cells that are on my right and I'm just saying hello to people as I walk by their cells. Out of politeness, you know, just trying to keep a little humanity in the darn chaos of this place," Schneider told the attorney. "And then all of a sudden, I don't remember when I noticed the other inmate was out on the tier, but I knew this guy was a Northern Mexican inmate."

"And when you saw him, what happened?" Myster asked. "You ran toward him?"

"No. When I seen the door opened, when I seen it open simultaneously, I knew what would happen. I know, it's on. So I just do it."

"Let me stop you," Myster interrupted. "When you say it was *on*, you mean you guys knew that you were going to fight?"

"Oh, yeah, we know that's inevitable," Schneider told her.

"Well, why didn't you turn around and go back upstairs or yell to the guy in the control booth?"

"You don't turn around when a guy . . ." Schneider paused. "I can tell you one person right now that was in A Pod who turned around and ran upstairs and he ended up dead in his cell and a sergeant had to come in and revive him."

"Okay, let's try and stick to this case right now," Myster demanded.

"Okay. Even if it's a perceived threat, if somebody is advancing, it's like you don't have no option," Schneider said. "That's just how it goes. Not only would that have subjected me to possibly getting chased down and shot anyway, it also subjected me to getting killed by everyone else in the prison for doing so."

"Why?"

"Why? Because it's going to happen anyway," Schneider insisted. "There's going to be an altercation and there's going to be shots fired, regardless. Now if I'm going to run away from that and then just delay it for a few seconds, and end up getting worse treatment by laying on the ground and getting kicked like a dog or something, or getting my head smashed against the wall, laying on the ground, then I'm also going to get killed in prison for running and doing that kind of stuff. It's just not accepted in this environment."

"So if the other inmates think you're chicken," Myster wondered, "they'll beat up on you?"

"No. They don't beat up on you. They kill you," Schneider stated matter-of-factly. "That's just the frame of mind. That's just this environment. I cannot retreat from stuff like that. I know that gunner up there, Clemann—he's been up here a few years. I don't think he's one of them sadistic types that's just going to go looking for a reason to shoot me. I don't believe he's sadistic or nothing. You know, the fact is, I've seen it happen so many times, on flukes. Your head could just get banged against a wall. Somebody could come out with a knife."

"So that's the sort of inmate's code of honor, that you have to be brave?"

"That's just how life is in the SHU. There's no getting around it," Schneider said. "Dead bodies are popping up and it's because of reasons like this that it happens.

"You know, I just try to keep from being listed as one of the deceased. That's the bottom line. It's all about just trying to survive. I wasn't going out there trying to kill nobody or nothing."

During his deposition, Dale Bretches had facial expressions that were hard to read. The man seemed to be hiding behind his thick black mustache. He appeared to be shy (or at least he was acting coy), requesting that the high-powered attorney be a little patient with him. Bretches said he wasn't used to doing this much talking. But Myster didn't care about that. She wanted to know if Bretches met with anybody to prepare for the deposition, such as Paul Schneider, but Bretches said no, he'd only met with his attorney, who was there with him.

As far as coordinating a story with Schneider, Bretches denied that. He said the two of them talked every day, naturally, being in the cell with each other, and since the case involved both of them, they had discussed the incident. However, Bretches claimed he couldn't remember anything they talked about because, as he put it, "being in the hole for twenty years, your memory goes south real quick." By "the hole," Bretches meant the Security Housing Unit.

Bretches had viewed the incident report from April 5, 1997, and made some notes for himself, to remind him of key points. He offered to let Myster copy them, if she could make them out. He said he really didn't know much about the law. Bretches let Schneider handle all the legal aspects of their different cases, since Paul was more literate than he was, when it came to that kind of thing. Bretches talked about life in the SHU: having to fight to stay alive, and guards setting up gladiator fights for their viewing enjoyment. After about a half hour, Myster was able to get down to business, having Bretches give her the up-close details of the bloody shower scene.

"So you guys started to fight?" Myster asked, trying to get Bretches to focus.

"Yeah."

"Inside the shower?"

"Well, it started right at the door, the doorway of the shower," Bretches told her. "And I guess the other guy didn't want to get shot, and I didn't either, so we let it proceed in the shower."

"Were you guys punching each other?"

"Yes."

"Any kicking?"

"Not that I remember."

"Biting?"

"No."

"Scratching?" Myster asked.

"No. At least, I wasn't."

Bretches didn't remember much. He didn't know if the Northern Mexican inmate even hit him at all. He said they were just throwing punches at each other. Bretches argued that he was in the heat of the moment, and all he could think about was defending himself. He didn't even feel what was happening, Bretches asserted—he was just reacting.

Myster had done her homework and knew Bretches had a lot of experience as a fighter. In fact, Dale Bretches had once been a welterweight boxing champion in Hawaii. Bretches couldn't believe it when the attorney pulled that tidbit out of a hat. When she questioned him about it, he could no longer play dumb and deny that he was a good fighter. As the deposition progressed, Bretches couldn't deny a lot of things, such as having been convicted for second-degree murder and having been cited for possessing inmate-manufactured weapons at Pelican Bay.

Myster also had information regarding a specific tattoo on Bretches's left biceps: a skull within the shape of a cross, beneath it a rose and the words "Dago Southern California."

" 'Dago Southern California,' is that from when you used to be in the Hell's Angels gang?" she asked.

"I was never in Hell's Angels," Bretches said, clearly annoyed.

"Where are you getting this? I'm in prison for . . . you know. I'm not even going to get into it."

"Haven't you seen reference in your records to you belonging in Hell's Angels?"

"Yeah, but it was thrown out of court by the judge."

"So you're denying that you were—"

"I was never in the Hell's Angels," Bretches raged, cutting her off. "Never an associate of the Hell's Angels."

"How about the Aryan Brotherhood?"

"Never them either."

"You're not in that gang?"

"No."

"Does Schneider know about this?"

"He's not either."

"Really?" Myster asked. "Then what are those tattoos that say 'AB' all over him?"

"American bulldog for all I know," Bretches grunted.

Unlike Schneider, who had Aryan Brotherhood tattoos everywhere, large representations of the sign of the shamrock and the number 666, Bretches had only what he called "regular" prison tattoos. He had skulls, flowers, spiderwebs, and, next to his eye, a teardrop, which was a universal symbol for people doing life without parole.

As Susan Myster went through the shower incident with Bretches one more time, having heard Schneider's version and comparing notes, she discovered that Bretches *thought* he'd been shot a few times with a pellet gun. He wasn't sure if they were rubber pellets or what, but he recalled washing the blood off himself after being hit in the shower. He claimed he had cuts all over his face and body, cuts that were not evident in the photos.

Myster showed Bretches three photos of Inmate Cabrera's injuries, Cabrera's right and left profile, and full frontal view.

"Is that the inmate you beat up?" she asked.

"Yes, the one that I had the altercation with."

"Well," Myster asked, "doesn't it look like *he* lost the fight?"

"You can't see all the blood I had all over me too," Bretches argued, "before I took the shower."

"His blood?"

"My blood and his blood. Did you read the incident report? You'll see that I had cuts all over me. You can't see it in the photos because I washed the blood off."

"After you showered, were you still bleeding?" Myster wondered.

"On my face, arms, and chest, yeah. Before they took them photos right there," Bretches said, pointing, "you can see the stuff on my hand, the stuff they put on to clean up my wounds."

"Something like iodine?"

"Yeah, it might have been. Because where my hand got cut from his teeth."

"Is that because you punched him in the mouth?"

"It might have been because he bit me. I don't know."

"Do you remember whether he bit you or not?"

"I don't remember him biting me."

For Myster, talking to Bretches was futile. The inmate was taking zero responsibility for his actions, lying over and over, claiming the fight wasn't his fault. According to Bretches, Officer Clemann was responsible, Clemann was the one who set the fight up on purpose. Although he couldn't offer proof, Bretches claimed Clemann had set up a similar fight in the past, that the guard didn't care if his actions could "cost people their lives."

Myster wanted to know why Bretches was asking for more than $1 million in damages, wondering how he came up with that large sum. Bretches insisted that that was the amount he needed to get the lawsuit going. When further pressed, Bretches finally admitted that he thought his pain and suffering was worth something, maybe $20,000.

Myster also wondered how the yearlong suffering Bretches said he had been "experiencing" was possible. She wanted to get a sense of why he felt he should get $20,000 for the minimal injuries he suffered due to the incident. Bretches told the attorney he deserved that amount because he'd been "put on the spot" so many times by prison guards.

Bretches became upset when Myster smirked at him. He didn't like the fact that Myster found his claims funny, that Myster was becoming more and more sarcastic through the deposition. The Aryan Brotherhood member tried to play the poor-me act, telling Myster it had been so long since he'd been with a person face-to-face that it was hard to talk to somebody without having to look at them through bars. But Myster didn't fall for Bretches's sympathy routine. She still wanted to know why Bretches thought the government should pay him thousands of dollars for a fight he'd been in a year before.

After tossing it around in his head for a minute, Bretches told the attorney he deserved $20,000 because he'd become "anxious" about living in the SHU.

"When I come out on the tier and conduct business—not conduct business," he corrected himself, "but whenever I come out on the tier and I talk to people or, in my everyday actions, people will want to talk to me, and I get this heightened sense of anxiety. And my immediate reaction is to get on the offensive."

"Isn't that more a result of one being in the SHU for twenty years, than this particular incident?" the attorney suggested.

"Like, it's bad enough in here, to have to deal with long-term isolation," Bretches complained, "but we have to deal with like, shell shock, and always expecting to get shot."

As people would later note, Paul and Dale's dog Hera had an unusual gait. It was something folks noticed around the streets of Pacific Heights. She made stop-motion actions, like one sees in animations. Ron Bosia, a professional dog walker, said that Hera moved "a little bit different than real creatures do."

Perhaps the dog walker remembered Hera's being strange because he'd been through a frightening encounter with her in June 2000. Hera attacked Bogie, a large poodle that Bosia was walking in an off-leash dog area in beautiful Alta Plaza Park.

On the kind of glorious summer afternoon that San Franciscans rarely see, with blue skies and white puffy clouds, Ron Bosia struck up a conversation with Noel and Knoller, the three of them having a friendly chat about the fabulous weather. Bosia was curious about their unusual dog. Noel explained how he and Marjorie "rescued" Hera. The dog walker had never heard of a Presa Canario before; he thought she was perhaps a cross between a Rottweiler and a pit bull. As they continued to chitchat, Bosia and Noel decided the dogs should get to know each other, so they took Hera and Bogie off leash.

Seconds later, when Bogie approached Hera and playfully put his paw on her, Hera immediately locked onto Bogie's neck. She had latched onto the large poodle and was vigorously shaking him back and forth, relentlessly tearing through his skin. Instantaneously, Bosia jumped in and got a headlock on Hera, keeping her from doing any more damage to the poodle.

Using all his might, the dog walker was able to get Hera to calm down a bit and to stop moving from side to side. As Bosia let go of her head, he placed his thumbs behind Hera's jaws, knowing exactly where to apply intense pressure to get her to release her grip. It took Bosia a full five minutes, but the dog walker kept adding pressure to the muscle at the back of Hera's jaw, and she ultimately released Bogie.

Bosia couldn't help noticing that neither Noel nor Knoller made any attempt to jump in or intercede. The two of them just watched the incident as though they were watching live theater and were fascinated by the whole thing.

When the dogs were separated, there was a lot of blood on Bogie. Bosia realized Hera had bitten deeply through the poodle's skin. Bogie had a flap of skin off and a seven-inch diagonal cut behind his left ear. Bosia rushed the poodle over to Pets Unlimited, a pet hospital on Fillmore Street, where Bogie required five sutures.

The dog walker took Noel's card and had written down his home address, telling Noel that Bogie's owner might want compensation for the medical bills. Noel offered his apology, but didn't offer to pay for any vet bills.

In the end, Bogie's owner didn't bother calling about the expenses. However, Robert and Marjorie had learned something. They found the incident to be quite informative. They had been reading books about the Presa Canario's ability to grip and its aggressive nature, but now they'd witnessed proof. Noel wrote Schneider about it, happy to tell Paul and Dale that their dog, Hera, had a truly intimidating presence.

Around the same time, when Hera was still new to the neighborhood, David Moser, who lived in Noel and Knoller's building, had an even more disturbing experience with them one evening.

Moser was in the process of moving out and had a box of clothing in his hands. When the elevator reached the lobby and Moser opened up the old-fashioned elevator door, he was hard-pressed to get by Noel, Knoller, and Hera, who were standing there, taking up every bit of space at the elevator entrance. Moser felt like they were pushy, as if they wanted to get on the elevator before he could get off, so Moser decided he would try to go around them.

As Moser was managing to slide by, the large box in his hands blocking his view, suddenly Hera lunged and grabbed him by the pants, her teeth going right through his jeans into his right buttock.

"Your dog just bit me!" Moser yelled, turning around to look to see if he was bleeding, if his skin had been broken.

"Hmmm," Noel said, pausing. "Interesting."

Moser stood there stunned, watching as Noel walked into the elevator with his wife and dog, closing the gate, starting the elevator mechanism. Noel never reprimanded his dog or said another word. For a few moments, Moser stayed in the lobby, shaken up. It was hard for Moser to believe that the dog owners hadn't even acknowledged what their pet had done.

After composing himself in the lobby for a few minutes, Moser went upstairs and showed his wife the painful welt on his right cheek. Moser realized it wasn't severe enough to require medical treatment, so he and his wife decided not to pursue the matter further. They were moving out of the building in a few days, and it just wasn't worth the bother.

But perhaps they should have reported the bite, because as it happened, Hera was causing trouble all over Pacific Heights. Of course, according to Noel and Knoller, all incidents that involved Hera were other people's fault. They claimed that the elevator squabble with Moser was his own imagination—their neighbor had "charged" Marjorie as he was coming out of the elevator and Moser hadn't been bitten—he had *bumped himself* on the elevator door.

No matter what the incident was between Hera and others, Noel and Knoller would contend that *Hera* was the victim. The *other* people or the *other* dogs caused the problem. That fit in with Noel and Knoller's us-against-the-world mentality. Hera was now becoming an integral part of their "triad." In their minds, she could do no wrong.

There was at least one other incident that summer. One evening around 7:00 P.M., Neil Bardack, a Pacific Heights resident, was walking Meryl, his Shetland sheepdog. Bardack had taken his Shelty, a three-legged cancer survivor, beyond their usual range.

Bardack and Meryl were about six feet from the corner of Pacific Avenue when he saw a woman with a large dog walking toward him. As the woman got closer, her dog started to pull toward Meryl. At the time, Bardack wasn't frightened. He figured the dogs were going to make a quick acquaintance.

Then out of nowhere, the other dog—it was Hera, of course—lunged at Meryl, simultaneously pulling Marjorie Knoller to the ground. Bardack watched as the dog's owner lay *prostrate*, holding on to her dog's leash while being dragged several feet along the sidewalk. Without any advance warning or growl, Hera had pounced on the three-legged Shelty, and Bardack watched in horror as Hera's giant jaw grasped the spine of his timid dog. The yelping Hera caused was "just ungodly," he recalled. All the while, Marjorie lay on the ground trying to keep hold of Hera's leash.

"Get control of your dog!" Bardack yelled.

But the woman didn't do anything. She was lying on the ground, flat on her stomach. Realizing that he'd have to get on top of Hera to save his Shelty, Bardack summoned the strength to lift the hundred-pound Presa by her collar. He raised her just enough so his Shelty could scoot out from underneath and run to the other side of the street.

During the attack, the prone woman was yelling something at Hera, but Bardack couldn't remember what it was. He recalled helping Knoller off the ground—she was a large woman, not particularly attractive, and she looked rumpled, her sweat suit all dirty from having been dragged down the sidewalk.

"Are you okay?" Bardack asked, seeing that the woman was scraped up.

"Yes, I'm fine," she told him. "I don't know what happened. My dog has never done anything like this before. I don't know what got into her. . . ."

The woman was making some form of an apology, a contrite statement, but Bardack didn't have time to stand around listening at that moment. His Shelty had already run down Pacific Avenue, and Bardack ran after her. When he retrieved her, Bardack quickly looked Meryl over to make sure she wasn't hurt. Once he put her back on her leash, he turned around, but the woman and her large dog were gone. They were nowhere in sight.

The incident was frightening for Bardack, a longtime dog owner. He'd seen what he called "dog dust-ups" before, but this was a much rougher and scarier encounter. Because he didn't see any blood on Meryl, Bardack felt his dog dodged a bullet and took her home.

But the next morning Meryl was lethargic. Bardack took Meryl to the vet, where he discovered that the dog had a large swelling on the side of her rib cage. The vet shaved Meryl and found a puncture wound the size of a pinkie finger between her ribs. The bite was drained, she was put on medications for two weeks, and Bardack vowed he would never take her back near that street corner. He stayed angry for a while, taking his dog to the vet for checkups, but once Meryl recovered, that seemed to be the end of it.

Like most people who had encounters with Hera, Bardack hoped never to see that dog again. When Bardack discussed the attack with his friends, people were appalled to hear that a woman would just flee, that she seemed to disappear like a hit-and-run driver. But there was nothing anyone could really do about it.

CHAPTER SIXTEEN

By the end of the summer of 2000, Hera had been diagnosed with a heart murmur by the cardiology staff at the UC Davis Veterinary Hospital. Noel and Knoller discovered this as part of a routine checkup on Hera, who was still being primed for their dog-breeding business. When they were informed of the potential implications of Hera's heart defects, including the small chance of sudden death, Noel and Knoller were troubled. When it was further determined that Hera's heart condition was congenital, Noel and Knoller were at a loss.

It was bad news for Hera: she had a diminished and sluggish arterial pulse, and her heart defect was compounded by valve leakage. To make matters worse, the staff at UC Davis told Noel and Knoller that they should not breed her. Schneider would be unhappy about that, but the lawyers decided they were meant to keep Hera, and they spent Schneider's dollars to pay for Hera's medical tests. They would worry about finding other breeding options, thinking Hera might possibly be salvageable with surgery. They would find out in time.

From the moment they brought Hera to Pacific Heights, Noel and Knoller took the dog on a three-mile walk every day. They treated her like a queen, feeding her chicken, roast beef, and boiled ground chuck.

They hadn't noticed anything wrong with her. Now they were worried sick over their baby; Hera wasn't expected to have a full life.

From that point on, Hera became a constant source of concern for Noel and Knoller, who brought the dog to Pets Unlimited for numerous office visits. She had cardiac ultrasounds and regular cardiology consults, and ultimately it was decided that she needed surgery. Hera was infused with catheters; she needed nursing, special care, and monitoring services. The bills were exorbitant.

All along, Noel and Knoller were taking the money out of the Dog O' War bank account they had established for Schneider. They knew Schneider wouldn't really be thrilled that his dollars were being wasted on a defective dog, but they had fallen in love with her and couldn't bear the thought of letting her go.

On September 6, 2000, Noel and Knoller drove down to Los Angeles to add a second Presa to their household. "El Supremo Bane" was being kept in the backyard of a Mexican family, where, according to Paul Schneider, he was in poor condition. His coat was being eaten up by flies and his weight was down. Schneider insisted that Bane be taken away from the Mexicans, and Noel and Knoller were the perfect people to accomplish that.

Without having to threaten a lawsuit, and without much of a fight at all, Noel convinced the Mexican family that it would be in their best interest to stay in good standing with Paul Schneider. Noel loaded Bane into his rented Jeep, heading back home with Marjorie to their tiny place in Pacific Heights.

Again, their housing the Presa was as a favor to Schneider; it was supposed to be only temporary. There was no plan for Noel and Knoller to keep Bane as a family pet. But since Bane was the center of the breeding scheme, having the champion bloodlines and all the documentation to prove it, the lawyers agreed that they would keep Bane as long as necessary. Schneider didn't want to chance placing Bane with the wrong family again. With the kind of money Bane's champion pups would fetch, they all agreed it just wasn't worth the risk.

Noel recalled the first few days with Bane in San Francisco as being quite amazing. Bane was a "babe" magnet. Noel said that when he first met Marjorie, Bane's "big red arrow" popped out. Bane had an eye for the ladies. Robert would take him out very early every morning, well before 6:00 A.M., and they would walk down Fillmore Street to the Marina Green, where they would stop at a Safeway. Robert got himself a cup of coffee and a few water bottles; Bane got a little chewy snack.

Robert wanted to get the dog used to city living, so he'd then take Bane on a Muni bus for the short ride back up the steep hill to Pacific Heights. This was the same procedure that Hera had gone through. Having been a dog owner from way back, Robert knew how to "break in" a dog. He would take both Bane and Hera on city buses at the crack of dawn, when there were very few people around, then slowly acclimate them to the point where they could ride the bus during rush hour. By the time Bane arrived in town, Hera had already become a pro at it, and Bane caught on quickly.

Everything being new to him, Bane was fascinated by the many attractions of city life. He would sit at his apartment window, staring out at the streets for hours, amused by passing buses, taxis, and taillights. Bane had never been exposed to anything like that before, and Robert and Marjorie could feel his rush of excitement whenever they would get ready to go out. They began taking Bane and Hera everywhere, happy to parade their rare-breed large dogs.

Noel and Knoller loved the attention the dogs brought them. Everyone seemed to stop and stare on the streets. Soon, they started getting Bane and Hera familiar with some well-known North Beach establishments, like the San Francisco Brewing Company, where Bane and Hera were much welcomed outdoor guests.

The Presas were enjoying the good life. They went walking on the beach at Crissy Field and strutting around the Palace of Fine Arts. They were in circulation, being shown off all around town—even being taken to the big tourist spots such as Fisherman's Wharf, where the dogs attended public street festivals and other large outdoor events with their guardians.

However, the transition to city life wasn't a completely smooth one for Bane. Just four days after he got to San Francisco, on Sunday, September 10, he was involved in an attack. It happened around 6:45 A.M. in one of the most beautiful off-leash-dog areas in the city, over at Crissy Field.

According to Noel, the attack was the fault of a Belgian Malinois, who he claimed was "set up" to attack Bane. Only Noel and Knoller could know who caused the fight for sure, since the Malinois owner ran off after the fight broke up. But for what it was worth, Noel wrote a paranoid statement in a declaration to a judge, explaining that the dog attack occurred in "what appeared to be a deliberate manner."

"A large Malinois dog, who was with its owner, had pursued us for over a hundred and fifty yards down the beach, and was repeatedly being told to stay away from us and our dogs," Noel wrote. "The Malinois first struck me in the right hand and then struck the large male Presa Canario in the face and head. I was astride the large male at the time of the attack in order to constrain and control him.

"In rapid succession I wound up on the ground with the two males and my right hand completely in one dog's mouth, between its back jaws," Noel explained. "When I was successful in getting the dogs parted, and retrieved my right hand, I found that I had sustained a crushing of the index finger at the knuckle, with lacerations almost completely severing the finger from the hand."

Marjorie rushed Robert to San Francisco General, where he was admitted for emergency surgery. Noel's medical examination revealed that the bone had been completely crushed and the major arteries to the finger had been severed, as had the nerves and tendons in the finger. Noel underwent six hours of surgery to have his finger reattached, and because there was concern that the finger might have to be amputated, remained hospitalized for five days in intensive care.

Noel didn't return to work for over a month. During that period, he was on painkillers, antibiotics, and blood thinners. Noel wrote excuses to a judge about why he wasn't able to appear in court, including odd details about being unable to attend to matters such as "zippering my fly, using the lavatory, opening doors, and the like." Noel was fatigued and uncomfortable, and he suffered from continual swelling of his right hand, as well as an open wound incision, which continued to drain for several weeks.

It would be two months before the surgical pins setting Noel's finger in place could be removed. All throughout his recovery, Noel would receive occupational therapy at the hospital twice weekly, but the bone in that finger never did quite heal. Noel was permanently disfigured.

"What happened was, Hera was walking off the lead, Bane was on the lead," Noel claimed. "We decided to go to the western end of the beach over by the new lagoon because that area is pretty well deserted at that time of morning, and we wanted a stretch of beach where we could test Bane and see how he would do."

Noel claimed they had seen a woman with a Belgian Malinois who looked suspicious to them, having allegedly walked over from a government employee parking lot. Noel and Knoller wondered if she was a special agent, someone from the Department of Corrections who was looking to cause a skirmish. Noel figured it was a plot, a scheme to start a fight, to get the Aryan Brotherhood dogs locked up into Animal Control, or worse, to get them put to sleep. It was a theory Robert had, one that Marjorie agreed with, both of them convinced that Special Service Unit agents from the California Department of Corrections were capable of anything.

"We were about thirty yards away from the surf and Marjorie yells at me, 'Watch out, it's coming!' I turned and the Malinois was charging right for me, snarling and barking," Noel reflected. "The Malinois dropped down, sinking an upper tooth over Bane's right eye and lower tooth into the other side of Bane's jaw."

When later questioned before a grand jury, Noel testified that Hera stayed out of the fight. He wasn't sure which dog actually bit his finger off. Noel thought it was probably Bane, because Noel had put his hand down Bane's throat. In any case, Noel didn't consider what happened to be a dog bite. It was simply a case of Noel's finger getting stuck in a dog's mouth.

According to Noel, the dogs were biting each other, and he stuck himself in the middle to try to break it up. When pressed to give a direct answer about who bit him, Noel admitted it *was* his dog Bane who inadvertently bit off the index finger.

CHAPTER SEVENTEEN

PELICAN BAY STATE PRISON REPORT
CONFISCATED FROM CELL OF AB ASSOCIATE/
ADMITTED SKINHEAD

Drawings containing runic codes for Skinhead; Swastika; Celtic Cross; Death's head.

Explanation of runic alphabet; codes for Supreme White Power.

Photos of Skinhead Tattoos: Supreme White Power.

White Supremacist Code written in runic; 14 words = We Must Secure the Existence of Our People and the Future for White Children; 5 words = I Have Nothing to Say (Code of Silence).

S&M Drawing of Female about to be anally assaulted with an ax, with Presa Canario in foreground.

Drawing of Hooded Knight and Female = Schneider and Knoller.

References to the Dog O' War Bane.

Overt Drawing of Animal Carnage, with animal claws dripping blood.

CHAPTER EIGHTEEN

"You know, I really don't appreciate encountering these dogs in the hallway," Knoller's next-door neighbor complained.

"Don't worry," Knoller assured. "They won't harm you."

"Well, I think it's irresponsible," the woman insisted. "Especially the way you let them walk around without leashes."

It was obvious that Noel and Knoller's neighbor was intimidated by the presence of the large dogs, but Knoller made no further attempt to calm her. She walked away from the woman without saying another word.

"My first impression, being introduced to Hera by Robert Noel, I was taken aback by the huge size of this powerfully built dog," the next-door neighbor reflected. "I thought it wasn't suitable to keep such a dog in an apartment. And Hera's demeanor, the way she gazed at me, told me to be aware of this unpredictable animal."

For a while, no one realized that Hera had been joined by another Presa. Noel and Knoller had been successful in hiding Bane, hoping people would think Hera and Bane were one and the same dog. They didn't want to be questioned about keeping two large Presas in their tiny apartment. However, as more neighbors began to see that Noel and Knoller actually had two distinct but similar-looking dogs, they began to worry. Some of the neighbors were making noise about approaching the landlord, even though everyone knew that Noel and Knoller had successfully bullied their landlord with lawsuit on top of lawsuit. Ultimately, the neighbors felt that there was nothing anyone could do to rid the building of the animals. Many of them believed that the landlord couldn't stop the attorneys from doing anything they damn-well pleased.

Over the years, the attorneys had developed a bad reputation, and people in their building were afraid to say anything that might offend them, even in the slightest way. Neighbors preferred to be insulted and downright intimidated, rather than face the grim reality of Noel and Knoller's spurious legal actions. In the eleven years that Noel and Knoller resided there, the two attorneys had actually run one landlord out of the building. Apparently the previous landlord wanted out so badly, the guy sold his beautiful gothic structure dirt-cheap, just happy to be rid of their legal hassles.

Noel & Knoller borrowed trouble, they reveled in it, and the fact that their dogs were scaring people was funny to them. They really believed people were just overreacting about their animals. Marjorie, in particular, laughed in people's faces when they acted frightened. She thought it was absolutely ridiculous that anyone would be afraid of Bane and Hera.

Of course it hadn't started off like that. When Hera arrived, when Noel and Knoller had no idea what kind of effect the Presa would have on people, they were concerned about the unsocialized dog's being out in public. They tried to keep their dog under control.

Diana Curtis, a resident of 2398 Pacific Avenue, never had any problem with her toy poodle and her German shepherd until Noel and Knoller acquired the first Presa Canario. As soon as Hera arrived, Curtis found herself afraid to go downstairs, afraid to go through the lobby.

Having lived in the building for six years, Curtis knew most of the residents. Many of her neighbors, including Diane Whipple, were animal lovers. Whipple had once talked to Curtis about helping her find a cat sitter for her two cats, and Curtis thought Whipple had a kind heart and a good spirit. It was clear that Whipple loved dogs; the young woman was always friendly and loving toward Curtis's tame pets.

But Noel and Knoller's Presa Canarios were a different story. No one in the building liked them, and some people, especially Diane Whipple, were becoming truly afraid of them. For her part, Diana Curtis felt the two attorneys had crossed a line by bringing these giant animals into an apartment building. Not only were Bane and Hera poorly behaved animals, they were too large to be cooped up in the small apartment.

By the time Bane and Hera felt fully comfortable in their new home, in late autumn 2000, Curtis noticed that the energy of the building had changed. People were more tense; people seemed more anxious when they stood waiting for the elevator, when they retrieved their mail. Bane and Hera seemed to bother everyone around them, and Curtis wished there was some way to get the big dogs out.

Diana Curtis was kind of foggy on the exact time of year she first encountered either of the Presas, but one day she got trapped in the elevator as the door opened. Out of nowhere, Bane had lunged at her, full on, and Noel couldn't control him. Bane was up on his hind legs and charging right at her. Curtis could feel his paws just a few inches from her face.

Bane's bark was ferocious. Curtis's heart was palpitating.

"Whoa, big fella!" Noel told Bane, trying to make it seem as if his dog was just being overly friendly.

But Curtis was scared to death. When she was able to jump out at the fourth floor, she shuddered as the elevator door closed. As she went over the incident in her mind, her heart still racing, she recalled how Bane stood on his hind legs, almost as tall as a full-grown man. Curtis was shocked by how much force Noel was using to hold the animal from chomping at her neck.

Noel was a really huge guy—six feet three, *weighing more than 300 pounds*, yet he had a hard time holding on to Bane.

Diana Curtis, in a sense, had become the eyes of the building, having ample opportunity to stare outside and watch both Robert and Marjorie mishandle their dogs. A few weeks later, Curtis was looking out her apartment window when she noticed Noel walking with Hera and Bane. Curtis was sure she saw both the dogs *off leash*, and she held her breath as she watched Noel and his dogs bump into a little boy and his grandfather.

"The grandfather was talking to Noel about the dogs," Curtis recalled. "The little boy approached the dogs, and one of them lunged at this boy. The boy pulled his arm back." Noel grabbed one of the dogs by the collar, pulling the animal away from the little boy. Even from her fourth-floor window, Curtis could hear Robert Noel yelling, "No!"

On two further occasions, when she ran into Noel and Hera in the lobby, the Presa Canario went bonkers, lunging and barking furiously at Diana's German shepherd and toy poodle. Both times, Curtis was able to get her dogs to back off, and she shook her head in disbelief as Noel walked off like nothing happened.

As bad as Noel was with animals, his wife was even worse. Never having owned a dog in her life, it was an understatement to say Knoller was ill equipped to take charge of two giant guard dogs. There were at least a half-dozen instances where Curtis saw Knoller walking one or both of the Presas, and, to Curtis, it looked as if the dogs were walking Knoller rather than the other way around.

Even at five feet five, and 150 pounds, Knoller wasn't strong enough for the two Presa Canarios. Together, Bane and Hera were 230 pounds of dog.

"They would pull her, tug her, and pull her down the street," Curtis reflected. "She would kind of try to yell at them but she just couldn't keep them under control."

A newer resident in the building, Jill Davis was eight months pregnant when she left her apartment one day. As Davis was coming off the elevator at 6:45 A.M., Noel and Knoller were trying to get around her with their dogs. Without warning, one of the Presas lunged directly at her stomach, its paws leaving the ground and its mouth open. Jill Davis grabbed at her unborn baby, holding her belly for dear life. The dog was showing its teeth, the dog was growling, and it was six inches from her baby. Davis stepped back and Noel pulled on the leash, able to pull the Presa back in its place, and Jill Davis ran out of the building. The couple didn't bother to look at her in the eye or ask if she was all right.

"I was surprised that they didn't say anything," Davis recalled, "but I was also in a hurry to get out of the door and away from the dogs. I was afraid. I was half asleep at the time, but I was definitely awake after the dog jumped up."

After her child was born, Davis was even more worried about the dogs, especially if she was headed into the garage with her infant in a carrier. She always walked into the lobby looking back over her shoulder. Whenever she saw Noel or Knoller walking one of their dogs, her pace would quicken.

As winter descended, Bane and Hera were becoming more ferocious and more territorial. Not only did they seem to be controlling both of their owners, the dogs were now treating the entire apartment building as if it was their personal property.

Mary Willard had lived in 2398 Pacific for three years before moving just directly across the street. One day she observed both dogs standing on the sidewalk in front of the entrance to her old building; Bane and Hera looked like they were guarding the front gate of a castle. Another time, Willard was sitting in her car when she saw Noel and one of the dogs. As Willard recalled, "the dog pulled Noel to the ground on his knees, and then pulled him down on his side, and dragged him across Fillmore Street. Noel was able to get up only after he crossed the street all the way, on his side. He got up, looked around, and yelled at the dog."

Noel was already wearing some sort of cast on his wrist, but other than that, Willard could see Noel wasn't really hurt or scraped up. She wasn't sure what made this giant dog run off like that, but having dealt with Noel in the past, she didn't want to confront him with any questions.

But there were others who did confront Robert Noel: dog walkers, curious onlookers, and dog trainers who were concerned about how the dogs ran amok. Mario Montepeque, a trainer who spent every day in Alta Plaza Park working with dogs, made it his business to go up to Noel and suggest some basic training techniques. Mario had already been warned about Bane and Hera by his friends Stephen and Aimee West, who had expressed fears about letting their dog interact with the Presas.

When Mario went up to Robert, offering to give Noel a business card, Robert accepted it. The dog trainer warned Noel that his Presas shouldn't be held by just harness alone, that they should be held by collars with heavy chains which would allow Noel to "choke hold" the animals. Then, as he chatted with Robert, Mario noticed Bane was

179

becoming aggressive with another male dog, so he offered to take Bane's leash and demonstrate a technique.

Mario pulled Bane by the harness in a different way, and Bane stopped his bad behavior immediately. When the trainer tried showing Robert the little correction, Noel didn't pay attention. Mario offered to train Bane and Hera together at a discount price, but Robert wasn't interested, later calling Mario "the local gigolo who bills himself as a dog psychologist."

"Mario had absolutely no experience with Presa Canarios or he would realize that a choke collar wouldn't work with a Presa," Noel later insisted. "Presas have very rough skin and fur around their necks, you can grab handfuls of it and wave it around," Noel asserted. "They have an extremely high threshold."

Noel would insist that Bane was immune to anything such as a choke hold, citing the fight Bane had with the Belgian Malinois at Crissy Field. Bane, he said, had never made a peep, never barked or whined, even though he'd allegedly been bitten in the throat by the Malinois. And Noel claimed Hera was the same way, that Hera "never had a pain threshold."

As time passed, and Mario continued to watch Noel and Knoller together with their two big dogs, he could see that Bane and Hera were becoming more aggressive. Again, Mario approached Robert Noel, offering to train the dogs at a reasonable price, but Noel didn't want any part of it. Mario tried to explain that if Noel and Knoller didn't curb their dogs' aggressive behavior, if they didn't do anything about Bane and Hera's barking and lunging, it would just encourage their bad behavior, and their dogs would go further and further down that path. But Noel and Knoller made it clear that they weren't interested in Mario's services.

The dog trainer felt the couple was being completely irresponsible; he could see they lacked experience, but there was nothing more he could do. He tried to point out to Noel and Knoller that their dogs were running away from them, that Bane and Hera were getting into "bad situations" with other dogs in the park, but they just nodded their heads, eyeing the trainer suspiciously, offering him platitudes.

"They knew what they had," the dog trainer later said. "Noel and Knoller knew exactly what they were dealing with. Their dogs would bite me all over the hand. Their dogs were getting in a posture, not mixing with other dogs, and they admitted that they never did anything about it."

"Is your dog fixed?" Mario asked Robert.

"No, we're not going to fix her. We actually plan to breed her," Noel said.

"Well, there's nothing wrong with that, but you should learn how to train the dogs," Mario warned. "They need to know what they're allowed and not allowed to do."

Robert Noel was put off by Mario's comment. He was annoyed by Mario's questions, but he restrained himself and was polite. Mario asked about Noel's arm being in a sling and discovered that the injury had been caused by a serious dogfight.

"They would listen to me. They seemed like nice people," Mario reflected, "but their dogs were being openly aggressive, and they decided not to do anything about it. They didn't care."

Mario repeatedly tried to explain that by using harnesses on the dogs, Robert was actually giving Bane and Hera more opportunity to pull away from him. But Robert made it clear that the care of the dogs was *his* decision to make. He thought what Mario was saying was all well and good, but his dogs were none of Mario's business. Robert wasn't sold on Mario's training program, not in the least, and Noel gave the trainer some lip service, just trying to shut the guy up.

"Mario didn't think a harness was the way to go," Robert recalled, "but from my point of view, with respect to these dogs, especially the fact that they were kept on collars and chains for over a year, and had suffered some injuries as a result of collars, collars weren't the way to go."

According to Robert Noel, dog collars only served *decorative* purposes. . . .

One afternoon in the park, when Mario was training a large female mutt, Hera came over and placed her chin on top of the other dog's shoulder. Hera was picking a fight, and Mario immediately grabbed Hera by the back of her harness and Hera stopped. To Mario, it was clear that Hera's need to show dominance was extreme. Mario told Robert he would *have to* become hardened about curbing his dog's aggression, saying it might be necessary for Robert to kick the dog if she was causing a fight.

But it was futile to talk about curbing Hera or Bane. Mario had pretty much resigned himself to the idea that these two large dogs would be a constant thorn in his side at Alta Plaza Park. Still, it bothered Mario that these dogs were causing problems to himself and other people, and he thought Noel and Knoller were crazy to let Hera run around off leash.

"There was an incident at the park when our dog was playing with Hera," Stephen West would recall. "They were kind of jumping on top of each other. A third dog named Bacus was involved, who had jumped and mounted Hera."

In West's opinion, the male dog mounted Hera playfully, not in any sexual way. West and his wife, Aimee, considered the behavior normal dog interaction. As Bacus approached Hera, Hera turned and grabbed Bacus by the head. Having become viciously aggressive, Hera was clenched onto the large male dog; she had a serious grip on him.

With Noel and Knoller standing there, Aimee West grabbed her set of keys and threw them at the dog. Aimee had been told that in an emergency, throwing a set of keys could startle an animal, and thank God, it worked. Hera's jaw disengaged and the dogs separated.

Rather than discuss the incident or reprimand Hera at all, Noel and Knoller acted as if it had been a false alarm. As they quickly went their separate ways, the Wests and the other dog owners were left in shock. Bacus's owner was just happy that his animal wasn't badly hurt.

"Marjorie and I were together for the two incidents where male dogs tried to mount Hera, when she refused to be mounted," Noel recalled. "They attacked her and she drove them off. One involved a dog named Brodie, that his handler euphemistically described as pushy, which in my mind is a euphemism for aggression."

Robert never spoke about the Bacus incident, but he recounted his version of what happened with Brodie. He claimed that Hera was happily playing with two female Rottweilers she had befriended, when Brodie decided to come over and place himself in the middle of the group. Brodie played "fairly well" with the females for about fifteen minutes and then tried to mount Hera. "Hera warned him off with kind of a ruff," Noel recalled. "Brodie stopped for a second and then tried again, and when she ruffed at him the second time, he nailed her in the throat. He wound up giving her a six-inch laceration and puncture wound. In response, she turned and bit him, and he let go, after his handler and I pulled them apart."

Interesting that there were no medical records produced to indicate that Hera was treated for any wounds from that skirmish.

In the other "similar incident" Noel would recall, a male Labrador tried to mount her. Afterward, Hera's bite wound was treated for an infection . . . but again no medical records support that.

Noel's response to these incidents: he and his wife ordered large *decorative* collars for Bane and Hera. They were specifically designed collars, made of green leather and covered with dozens of sharp pointed metal spikes. They were harsh-looking and could have passed for S&M accessories.

Of course, there were other unusual doggy items that Noel and Knoller had around the house: creepy drawings, the Gladiator-Dog books, growth supplements, the prescription doggy painkillers . . . but then there were also the regular things, the fetch balls, the stuffed toys, the rope-toys. Hera even had a little blond doll she chomped on and played with.

Noel had nicknamed the dogs "the muttleys." Knoller called them "the kids." In their letters to Schneider, they would refer to Bane as "the Banester" and describe what they called "Hera Happenings." At their front door, they placed a doormat reading, "Ask Not for Whom the Dog Barks, It Barks for Thee."

A former prison guard who occasionally socialized with Noel and Knoller became concerned that Noel was too obsessed with the Presa Canarios. It was obvious from Noel's strange comments that the attorney's connection to his dogs "just wasn't right." The guard said that the couple didn't even notice that the dogs had turned their once charming little apartment into a "piss pot."

"All Bob did was talk about how big Bane's balls were," the guard later confided to a reporter. "And when I went to visit them, Bob had to bring the dogs out, introducing them one at a time, because he couldn't control them."

But weird and irresponsible as everyone else thought they were, Noel and Knoller felt everything in their life was running along smoothly.

They had their lawsuits mounting against the Department of Corrections, and they were expecting their big payday soon. The Dog O' War operation seemed to be going well, with the pups of Bane and Isis being bred to produce more Presas, most of them housed in Southern California.

Robert and Marjorie continued to send regular reports to Paul, usually including new digital photos. They wanted Paul to know just how well Bane and Hera were being taken care of—with Marjorie cooking them bacon and hamburgers, and Robert buying $10.99 lb. roast beef for them at the swank Mayflower Market.

Whenever he received new pictures, Paul Schneider would arrange to get the pictures posted on the Dog O' War Web site. Schneider liked to come up with the captions, and he said breeding the Presas made him feel "alive again," almost as if he were "back out on the street." Paul was particularly fond of his stud, for whom he came up with the caption "El Supremo Bane. Born to Raise Hell!"

The fact that Bane and Hera were scaring the hell out of people in Pacific Heights was something folks didn't compare notes on. Because many of the Presa encounters occurred with strangers out on the streets, it was impossible for these victims to connect the dots.

Of course, after the Whipple mauling, people in Pacific Heights would report that Bane and Hera had attacked three neighborhood dogs, nearly killing a German shepherd. But nobody had ever filed a report with the authorities at Animal Care and Control.

Even more unfortunate was the fact that no neighbor in the Noel & Knoller building had compared stories either. Sure, a few people made rumbles at first, and one couple, the Cooleys, wrote Noel a letter to complain about the loud barking at night. But for the most part, the residents at 2398 Pacific were keeping their fears to themselves.

The fact that their dogs were hurting other animals was something that Noel and Knoller would deny forever. That Bane and Hera were frightening people, however, was something they seemed to somewhat enjoy. From the tenor of their letters to Bretches and Schneider, the attorneys clearly reveled in their reports about just how fierce the dogs were becoming. Noel did most of the bragging. He once referred to "a timorous little mousy blond" who weighed less then Hera and who "almost had a coronary" when the elevator door opened and she was confronted by the "Dynamic Duo."

Noel never said who the blond was. Apparently Robert didn't know his next-door neighbor, Diane Whipple. In all the years that Whipple lived just a few yards away, Noel would claim he never uttered a word to the striking blond. . . .

Alex de Laszlo, a dog lover who knew Noel and Knoller casually, was intrigued by their beautiful rare-breed dogs, bumping into them at Tully's Coffee Shop. He thought it was incredible that these animals looked like giant pit bulls, yet they seemed so calm and reserved. De Laszlo had never seen dogs like that.

But one day, just as de Laszlo was approaching Tully's, Bane made a break for it, running straight at him. "He was moving toward me in a way that had a curious body language," de Laszlo recalled. "It seemed like he had designs on me, other than to say hello, and in fact, my reaction was so strong that I moved back three or four feet.

"Ms. Knoller was standing stationary, and she laughed at the idea that I was actually frightened by the dog. It was just so extraordinary, I couldn't forget it."

The fact that there was nothing funny about the incident really made de Laszlo wonder just what kind of person Knoller was. She thought it was ridiculous that de Laszlo, who was over six feet, would be scared. She would never *dream* that her dog was capable of an attack, and Knoller was smirking as she came over to Bane as he waited for her. Knoller was so calm and cool with Bane that suddenly de Laszlo felt kind of awkward. The man studied the situation for a second, wondering what to say.

"Would it be okay to pet the dog?" he asked.

"Sure, you can pet him," Knoller said, "he loves that."

But when de Laszlo put his hand on Bane's head, he got a very distinct sensation from the dog. Bane generated an incredible tension, a strange energy.

"If there's something called an intuition or a vibe, there was something very strong and dark about this animal," de Laszlo reflected. "And it wasn't going away."

As he tried to analyze the scene, de Laszlo said he felt like he was having an out-of-body experience. Things were happening so quickly. This big powerful dog still looked like he wanted to attack, while Knoller just stood there laughing. "I actually was so frightened of the dog that I decided that the only thing I could do was try to make myself familiar to it by offering up a scent," de Laszlo recalled. "I was offering some consolation, in a sense, because I knew that if I moved abruptly, there was potential that the dog would attack me."

The fact that Knoller didn't apologize in any way, the fact that she laughed, resonated with de Laszlo. But at the same time, he wasn't about to show that he was annoyed or angry with her. He decided to remain friendly and pleasant. He didn't dare do anything that would make Bane react.

"Gee, it looks like that dog could really do some damage," he told her, ducking away as he headed into Tully's.

"Oh no, not at all," she said, smiling, "he's a pussycat."

According to medical reports, Bane was put on pain medications after a bad fall he had in the early winter. Noel said Bane was "trying to show off for the ladies" on a basketball court when he suddenly ruptured his ligament. The cost of Bane's surgery was an issue, and Noel and Knoller were discussing making payments and other ways to be eligible for a discount on the surgical repair of Bane's left rear leg.

The vets over at Pets Unlimited were certain that Bane would not heal without it. They promised to work something out to help Noel and Knoller, and a consult with a surgeon was scheduled. In the interim, Bane was put on strict exercise restriction, allowed only to take short, slow walks to relieve himself.

PEOPLE'S EXHIBIT
12 EV 181813-01
Confidential Legal Mail

Dear Paul,   January 8, 2001
    Okay, you asked about "Banester blurbs." You asked why we're giving him Ascriptin. Dr. Sams suggested it when he heard

Banester had problems with the Rimydal. He said the Ascriptin would have to be discontinued two weeks prior to the surgery, and we give him the Ascriptin only when he seems to need it. It's cheaper and seems to do the trick, and no doggie diarrhea. Big help!

As for Hera, she weighed in on Monday, January 8, at 116 lbs. It seems that's going to be her weight for the winter. I'm not going to cut back any further on her dry food portions, but I don't give her as many snacks as I used to, due to her weight gain. She still looks buff, not fat.

Yeah, I agree that Menace and Roka eat like pigs, but their appetites and weight can also depend on how much exercise they get during the day. It may just be that they have such ravenous appetites from all the exercise they get. I was feeding Pupness more and she was thinner when we had her running around the park more than she does now. Don't fuss about the statistical norms, as long as the kids are healthy and happy!

Robert wrote another letter to Stygian Kennel today, as they haven't returned Robert's two (2) additional phone calls. We'll see how stand-up the guy really is and if he wants to make right about the Banester. If he doesn't, there is always e-mail on the Web on the Showstopper site to tell people the Banester's story. (We can use someone else's e-mail to post the story.) Stygian should be able to handle the inquiries and publicity the story generaton. As it is, the guarantee the guy gives is so ambiguous, stating both two (2) years and three (3) years, any attorney worth a damn could drive a bus through the agreement.

I've enclosed an article on a house I thought you'd get a kick out of, especially in the light of the contents of your letter received today. I think the bark-on-cedar columns are interesting, don't think I could live with them though, but like the look of the walkway, with its stone fireplace, stone walls, and stone floor. I like them. Definitely need fur rugs though, in strategic areas.

Take care, stay well, watch your back and give my fondest regards to Mr. Bretches. I am always happier when I receive a letter from you. Really makes the rest of my day all that more enjoyable.

> Sincerely, Marjorie *ta vrai amie.*
> *Je t'aime beaucoup, mon amour. Je suis pour toi.*
> *ANEM CARA*

CHAPTER NINETEEN

THE VOICE OF ROBERT NOEL

"There's a line from a poem: 'Young without lovers, old without friends,' and I wouldn't want Marjorie to be old without friends. What a poor monument to the love I held for Marjorie, to expect that she never had anybody, or any love interest after me. . . .

"If you haven't seen the correspondence between us and Paul, it wasn't like he became instant family. It wasn't any different than it would have been if we were corresponding with anyone else over a period of time. You become more and more familiar with people. It takes a lot more effort, a lot more thought. There's a lot more of yourself that goes into writing a letter than just an offhand comment. . . .

"There's also the aspect that Marjorie's family consists of her mom, dad, and me. Her folks are in their eighties. They're going to be gone. At some point in the future, I'm going to be gone. . . . So if Paul is inside forever, because we developed this friendship with him, there would be somebody for Marjorie to focus on after I was gone. And she would have a purpose. . . .

"One of the things we were kicking around was whether we could get *any of Paul's convictions set aside, and spring him legally. It wasn't a game. I don't know what would have happened down the road if we were successful in getting Paul on the outside. . . .*

"In her correspondence, Marjorie does refer to herself as Paul's mom. That's part of the protective aspect of what we were focusing on with Paul. As for being jealous, in a younger day, I may have been more bothered by it, but I got to the point where I knew who Marjorie was, I knew how the two of us were together. I knew where Marjorie was sleeping, and she knew where I was sleeping. . . .

"Paul has charisma. I mean, you just talk to the guy, and you like him. You know, he's honest. I mean, it's a strange thing to say about a guy who is doing life without parole in prison. He was an armed robber, but he's honest. . . .

"There's a story that the cops tell about him. It's not a story that I've confirmed with Paul, but I've been told this by cops who say they were there to see it, when Paul was charged with assault on Couzins, the lawyer, and Paul turns around and says he'll plead guilty if the warden gives him two pizzas and two quart bottles of Pepsi-Cola. And the DAs are jumping up and down, saying they can do that, so Paul says, 'Okay, I plead guilty.' . . .

"At the Sacramento trial where Couzins was stabbed, the warden at Folsom had ordered that Paul be given full-body X rays before he went to court. And I've seen Paul's medical records. They were doing full-body X rays on him, and I seriously doubt that the guy smuggled that weapon out of his ass. It's clear from the size of Couzins's wound, there was really no way to put any weapon that size up there. . . .

"Paul's an extremely bright guy. And the stories we had heard about Paul, I wouldn't be surprised if he had been carrying weapons. Paul was able to strip enough metal out of doors of his SHU—and this isn't from Paul, this comes from cops—Paul stripped enough metal out of his SHU cell so the door wouldn't work. So, you know, this is what happens when you keep a guy locked up twenty-two and a half hours a day, with nothing to do but think . . .

"Like I said, the guy is honest. If you asked me if Paul is a member of the Aryan Brotherhood, I can't say that he is or not. But I can tell you this: in a videotaped deposition, he did admit that he was a member of the

Aryan Brotherhood. He was asked that question under oath, and he answered it. . . .

"You know, Paul's smarter than the average guy. The Department of Corrections declared war on him back in 1987, and I mean, the CDC killed two guys they said were Aryan Brotherhood members, and they beat the shit out of Paul. They put Paul in what's called dog status. That's where, in the cold of winter, they throw you in an unheated concrete box, with a hole in the floor as the only sanitary facility. You're there with no running water, naked, with no blankets, no mattresses, no nothing. They leave you there for three days, and the only thing they would slip through in the way of food was a tray with a pile of, literally, frozen dog shit on it. Yes, that's the kind of treatment they were subjecting Paul to. . . .

"And on top of that, Paul was getting death threats. And this stuff about Paul stabbing a correctional officer. I read his trial transcripts. He was tried twice in Sacramento. The first time the jury hung. They wouldn't convict him. Paul's defense was self-defense, that he'd been beaten, and had bones broken. . . .

"His friends had been shot and killed, and he was getting written death threats from the correctional staff. When he'd go out on the exercise yard, they'd throw Ping-Pong balls down that said Corndead *instead of* Cornfed. *And when he stabbed that cop, he thought the cop was coming to kill him. . . .*

"Paul is a ward of the state, okay? No matter what Paul had done to get himself in prison, the state has obligations to him. The state cannot operate lawlessly against him. But you will find a whole group of people, and I've talked to some of them, who go to jail and then they're treated like scum. The cops say fuck you. The cops beat you, and who gives a shit?

"Schneider put a lawsuit together for his buddy Todd Ashker. Todd had been shot in the arm at Pelican Bay. He's one of the white boys the Department of Corrections shot, and then they didn't give him adequate medical attention. So Paul put Todd's lawsuit together, and out of appreciation, when Todd got a settlement, Schneider got $27,000 out of the pot of about $275,000. . . .

"Paul is a kind of righteous outlaw, okay? And I mean, I think Paul was born a hundred years later than he should have been. It's legal to be a jailhouse lawyer, it's perfectly legal. And, like I said, Paul is bright. He's

got a $20 million lawsuit *going against the Department of Corrections right now. The suit is based on the inmates' trust funds....*

"Paul figured out the Department of Corrections never credited any interest on all the millions of dollars the inmates maintain on deposit in their trust fund accounts, so Schneider put together another lawsuit, and there's a reported decision on it in the Ninth Circuit, that says the Department of Corrections will have to pay interest on all those inmates' accounts. Then they sent it back to the U.S. District Court for further proceedings, and I think it's back up in the Ninth District now, waiting....

"You ever read any of Louis L'Amour's stuff? I've read one or two of his books, and that's how I would characterize Paul, as an outlaw hero. You know, you hear the name Cornfed, and you think you're going to see a guy in bib overalls with all sorts of facial hair, right? But instead you've got a guy who comes in, he's very courteous and well spoken in person, and if he was wearing a designer suit, he wouldn't look bad at all. The guy is drop-dead gorgeous...."

CHAPTER TWENTY

From the *San Francisco Chronicle*, January 27, 2001:
**POWERFUL DOGS MAUL WOMAN, KILL HER; S.F.
NEIGHBORS' PETS LUNGED DOWN HALLWAY**
A San Francisco woman died last night after being attacked
inside her apartment building by two bullmastiffs as the dog's
horrified owner struggled to pull them away. . . .

From the *San Francisco Chronicle*, January 28, 2001:
**S.F. NEIGHBORS SAY DOG WAS AGGRESSIVE; "THIS
WOMAN DIED FROM OUR NEGLIGENCE"**
"None of us ever filed a complaint, and that's what makes me sick
now," said Cyndee Dubrof, a dog owner who lives a few doors
down from Noel and his wife, Marjorie Knoller.
"Marjorie just about had the dogs completely in the apartment
when the elevator door opened and our neighbor came out," said
Noel, who arrived home shortly after the attack. "Bane sort of
perked up and headed down to the end of the hall. The woman had
the apartment door open, and was just standing there."

From the Associated Press, January 28, 2001:
COACH KILLED BY DOGS MOURNED
Diane Whipple, 33, was just putting her keys in her front door about 4:00 P.M. when two large dogs bounded toward her. One latched onto Whipple's neck while the other tore at her clothes. . . . Neighbors who heard the screaming said they thought a mugging or rape was taking place.

On Saturday, well-wishers left bouquets at the doorstep of Whipple's Pacific Heights apartment building. Some urged that the dogs' owners, Marjorie Knoller and attorney, Robert Noel, be held accountable for Whipple's death.

From the *San Francisco Chronicle*, January 29, 2001:
CASE OF KILLER DOG IS PROBED
San Francisco police are trying to determine if the owners of the dogs involved in Friday's deadly attack on Diane Whipple should face criminal charges.

The male dog, Bane, was put to sleep following the attack. The female is in custody at Animal Control, where officers are calling for a hearing to find out what role the second dog played in the attack and whether it should be put to sleep, or returned to the owners.

From the *San Francisco Chronicle*, January 30, 2001:
SAN FRANCISCANS OUTRAGED AS THEY
MOURN DOG ATTACK VICTIM
People called the district attorney's office, demanding that authorities throw the book at the couple who owned Bane—a 123-lb. cross-breed who charged Diane Whipple Friday in an attack so gruesome that police at the scene needed counseling.

From the *Contra Costa Times*, January 31, 2001:
UPDATE: SF WOMAN KILLED BY DOG HAD
BEEN BIT BEFORE
SFPD Lt. Henry Hunter said that about two weeks before the

deadly attack, Whipple told her roommate she had been bitten by one of the dogs. He said Whipple also showed her wounds to colleagues at St. Mary's College, where she was varsity lacrosse coach, including broken skin on her hand.

San Francisco District Attorney Terence Hallinan said his office received a bulletin from the state Attorney General's Office saying authorities discovered that Pelican Bay convicts, who were not specifically named, were raising fighting dogs and using middlemen.

From the *San Francisco Chronicle*, January 31, 2001:

S.F. LAWYERS ADOPT CONVICT WHO BRED KILLER DOG; ACTION BY ANIMAL'S KEEPERS STUNS STATE CORRECTION OFFICIALS

In a bizarre twist, the attorneys whose Presa Canario dogs mauled a San Franciscan woman to death have adopted the Pelican Bay inmate that prison officials say bred the dogs as attack animals.

Robert Noel, 59, and Marjorie Knoller, 45, were granted adoption decree Monday by the San Francisco family court. The decree makes them the parents of 39-year-old inmate Paul John "Cornfed" Schneider, who is serving time for aggravated assault and attempted murder.

"Our decision was based on Mr. Schneider as a person, and our feelings toward him and his feelings toward us," Noel said in an interview with Chronicle columnists Phil Matier and Andrew Ross, adding, "It was not an action taken lightly."

From the *San Francisco Chronicle*, January 31, 2001:

PRESA CANARIOS ALL THE RAGE WITH SHADY CHARACTERS; INMATE IN S.F. CASE PRESSED BREEDER TO SELL

The imprisoned owner of the Presa Canario dog that killed a San Francisco woman had bombarded a Canadian dog breeder with requests to buy more of the animals, the kennel's owner said yesterday. . . . [Angelika] Morwald, proprietor of WereWolf Kennels in Ontario, decided against doing business with Dale Bretches after learning that he was imprisoned.

Bretches inquiries show how the powerful animals, recently saved from the brink of extinction, have become increasingly popular among prison inmates, fighting-dog owners, and operators of methamphetamine labs.

From the Associated Press, January 31, 2001:

PRISON GANG DUO LINKED TO DOG THAT KILLED WOMAN
The dog that killed a San Francisco woman had a long history of viciousness and was secretly owned by two Aryan Brotherhood prison gang members as part of an underground scheme to breed and sell the animals. . . . The Presa Canario is not one of the 150 breeds recognized by the American Kennel Club. The AKC lists the Presa as one of 42 "foundation stock" breeds, a lesser category.

Authorities say Paul "Cornfed" Schneider and Dale Bretches were investigated by state prison authorities last year, and were found guilty in February 2000 of running a dog-breeding scheme, using third parties and attorneys to do the work on the outside.

From an editorial in the *Los Angeles Times*, February 2, 2001:

LESSONS OF CANINE KILLING
The death of a slight San Francisco woman mauled by two massive dogs teaches us such obvious lessons: Killer dogs bred for size and ferocity have no practical purpose and should be banned. Why does it take a nightmare attack for this message to be heard?

CHAPTER TWENTY-ONE

THE VOICE OF ROBERT NOEL

"Regarding the allegation that Bane bit Diane Whipple on the wrist two weeks prior to her death, I was there. It didn't happen. And I'll tell you why. If you look at the empirical evidence, when people say this was supposed to have happened just prior, sometime in December, Bane was in surgery that day. Nothing like that ever happened.

"There was never any complaint by anybody about these dogs. Yeah, we got a letter of complaint from Skip and Andrea Cooley about the barking, and Hera was barking that afternoon, but what they were actually hearing was mostly me. I was trying to teach Hera to play. She never had playful interaction with any other dogs, so I got down on the floor with one of Hera's toys, and I started barking at Hera.

"And I start throwing the toy around with my mouth. And then I start moving toward Hera, like I'm chasing her, and then I back away, and I'm barking. Finally, Hera gets the idea that she's supposed to bark. She's supposed to throw the toy around, she's supposed to run when I chase her, and chase me when I go the other way. I've played with other dogs the same way.

"Poor Andrea Cooley. She's a very blond person, blond-brained. She sees me with Bane and asks me how Hera is. I mean, the coloration of the dog is the same, but Bane has this large penis and these huge balls, and Andrea never picked up on it. I always wondered how she was with Skip, if she couldn't tell the difference.

"To tell you how quiet these dog were: nobody in the building even knew we had two dogs in the apartment. Nobody other than Hank Putek. And Hank knew because he let us use his car a number of times to transport them. But other people didn't know because the dogs looked enough like each other, and that helped.

"As far as apartment living goes, the dogs were great. They were very quiet, they were not hyperactive. They didn't run around barking and yapping like little dogs do. Janet Coumbs says that Bane and Hera didn't get along. But if you look at the photographs, the dogs are sleeping together, you know, they're wrapped around each other.

"If you look at the statement Janet gave to the cops, Janet, at one point, says that Bane and Fury killed a sheep. That's a story I heard after all this happened. But it turns out when she's further questioned by police, the cops ask her specifically if she saw that. And she says, no, she didn't. She says that when she came home, the sheep was already dead. Bane is standing next to the sheep, kind of pushing it with his nose, like he was saying, 'Come on, come on, get up.'

"It's perfectly possible that a bear, coyote, or any of the other animals that were killing her sheep before did it. There was nobody home to witness this. Or it's possible that Fury is the one that killed it. As a matter of fact, Janet told Devan Hawkes that one of the dogs was killing her livestock, and when Janet and I talked the first time, she told me that it was Fury that was doing the killing. She never mentioned Hera at all. It was always Fury that was the one killing her livestock.

"You know, when all this happened, when Animal Care opened the bathroom door, Bane was pacing back and forth, but Bane was described by Officer Scott and at least one other Animal Control officer as being docile and friendly. You know, kind of wagging his tail when they got him out of there. I'm not saying they weren't afraid of him, but keep in mind that they shoot him in the ass three times with a dart gun, and he doesn't react, he doesn't yelp.

"If I were in Marjorie's position that afternoon, quite frankly, I would have never done what she did, getting in between them. I mean, I might have been standing there fighting Bane off, for all I was worth, but I don't think I would have gotten in between. I don't think there's another person alive who would have done what Marjorie did. Marjorie's the kind of person I want in my corner.

"The DA has maintained all along, you know, that Marjorie wasn't down on the floor. He's fanned the media. He says Marjorie wasn't down there, that Marjorie didn't get any injuries that day, that Marjorie didn't do anything. But Marjorie says she did, and the last fucking witness the DA puts on admits that the evidence is consistent with Marjorie's version of the events. She was down on the floor between Whipple and the dog. She was taking bites from the dog.

"You know, if you play this as a tragic accident, you're going to get one news story at ten o'clock in the evening and you're going to get one news article in the paper the next day. And that's going to be it. But play it as a battle between the forces of good and evil, and you see what you get. A whole circus."

CHAPTER TWENTY-TWO

Excerpts from Robert Noel's eighteen-page letter to DA Terence Hallinan, in which he detailed his version of the mauling, were published in the *San Francisco Chronicle*. In the letter, Noel went on the offensive, telling the DA that Diane Whipple brought the attack on herself by putting herself in harm's way. Viewed as the rambling of a madman, the letter was Noel's attempt to exonerate his wife.

According to Noel, Diane Whipple stood facing her apartment door, staring over at Marjorie, when she had come down from the roof with Bane. With Bane by the lead, Marjorie dumped his excrement down the trash chute, and then was pushing the dog into her apartment. As Marjorie struggled to get Bane into her own door, Diane Whipple was standing a few yards down the hall at her open doorway, allegedly for an entire minute "making no effort to move inside and close the door." Then Bane began moving down the hall, dragging Marjorie to her knees.

"With his gimpy rear leg and the resistance from Marjorie, Bane moved slowly down the hall," Noel wrote, claiming that after even more time had passed, Bane jumped up and put his paws on the wall, on either side of Whipple's head.

As Noel's wife held Bane with one hand, she used her free hand to push Whipple into her own apartment. With that, Marjorie and Diane fell on the floor of Whipple's apartment, and Marjorie got on top of Diane, trying to protect her. Noel asserted that Marjorie told Whipple to stay down, not to move, claiming that Marjorie had Bane by his harness, and was backing him out of the apartment.

But Whipple got to her knees somehow. She managed to crawl back out into the hallway, going after Marjorie and Bane. Noel's letter claimed that Marjorie had no idea why Whipple, "rather than remaining in her apartment and closing the door," would come back out into the hallway. But when Whipple moved toward Marjorie and Bane once again, crawling down the hallway, Marjorie fell on Whipple again, putting her arms and body on top of Whipple. As Marjorie began backing Bane away for the second or third time, Whipple, rather than stay still, continued to crawl toward Marjorie and Bane, at which point, Bane began to bite. "Ms. Whipple forcibly struck Marjorie in the right eye," Noel wrote. "When Ms. Whipple struck Marjorie in the face, Bane moved forward and made contact with Ms. Whipple's neck and throat."

Robert Noel's letter was not only incredibly detailed, it was overtly insulting. He implied that Diane Whipple might have used a certain perfume or steroid that produced a pheromone that provoked Bane's attack.

In response, Hallinan made a statement to the media, saying he was considering filing homicide charges.

With the Bay Area public outraged, calling for justice, Noel's eighteen-page missive had provided the DA with the information he needed to up the ante. This was no longer a tragic accident. Instead of charging people for owning "vicious and dangerous dogs," the case was bordering on manslaughter—and SFPD Inspectors Becker and Daniele were piling up witnesses to prove it.

Noel's letter also provided confirmation about previous "doggy incidents." For instance, Noel mentioned Stephen and Aimee West, describing the details of Hera's aggressive moves as a reaction to another dog's aggression. Noel also provided details about the adoption of Paul John Schneider, a blueprint of Paul Schneider's dog-breeding ring, mentioning enough names and places for Terence Hallinan to order a raid on the Santa Rosa house of Russ Stanton, an Aryan Brotherhood affiliate.

The raid on the Stanton home produced stacks of evidence, including address books, phone numbers, letters from Paul Schneider regarding the history and genealogy of Bane and Fury, as well as Hera's pedigrees. The mobile phone records of Russ Stanton showed contact with Noel and Knoller. Also found in Santa Rosa were twisted drawings of man, woman, and animal—including a copy of a drawing police saw hanging in the Noel/Knoller hallway on the night of the attack: the half-naked woman, legs spread, with the two Presa Canarios.

THE VOICE OF ROBERT NOEL

"I mean, the reason my eighteen-page letter was written was that Hallinan's office and the Department of Corrections were throwing all this shit out there. And it set off a firestorm. The Department of Corrections came running down here and started spreading all these lies and bullshit, saying that Bane and Hera were intended to be used to guard Aryan Brotherhood and Mexican Mafia drug labs.

"Listen, our local District Attorney and the Department of Corrections, on January 30, announced that they were allowing into discovery that we adopted Paul Schneider, and that this was a break in the case. And I mean, the reasons behind the adoption are really just kind of a side issue that doesn't relate to what we're trying to do. We made a determination, long before we got personally involved with Paul, that we were going to protect him.

"And you know, within a day, Marjorie and I got out of town. From January 30 through the morning of February 1, Marjorie and I got over three hundred calls, a lot of them threatening, a lot of them very explicit death threats. Our voicemail at the office was continually filled. You couldn't keep it empty. And I'm dead serious when I say there were at least thirty explicit death threats, really vile stuff. The machine at our home was continually filled; a lot of them were saying things like 'You fucking Nazi bitch—we know who you are and we're going to get you.'

"I can't remember too many specifically, but there were really really vile things said like, 'Knoller, you cunt, we're going to get your ass, you Nazi bitch. We're going to come up and put a gun to the back of your

head and walk you down the street and put a bullet through your brain.'
And all this shit was set off because the Department of Corrections said
the dogs were being raised to kill.

"On February 1 we got out of Dodge, and we didn't let anybody
know where we were staying after that. We never went back to live in the
apartment. We went up to Eureka for a trial. We were suing the city of
Eureka over a kid who'd been beaten up by a cop. It was a four-day trial
and the jury came back with a verdict for the defense, so we lost. The jury
decided that the city wasn't responsible for the damages this kid received
in the beating. The beating happened just after the kid finished serving
prison time. We felt the cop and the city should have been held accountable. It was kind of like a Rodney King incident, but the jury didn't agree.
Then after the verdict, we went up and we visited Pelican Bay.

"You know, the big thing about how we were blaming the victim.
That was Hallinan's office, that was the press screaming that. I had gotten
a call from a guy who had experience in training large dogs, it was on the
morning of January 30, I can't remember his name. But the guy calls and
says he's had experience in training large dogs, and he says he wants to
make a suggestion. He says we should check to see if Whipple was on steroids because she was a long-distance runner. And the reason he was suggesting it is because a by-product of steroids is a hormonelike substance
that is sexually attractive to dogs.

"And another thing. I was told to check on whether or not Whipple
was wearing a certain perfume that had a pheromone base, because that
could explain it. And the guy who called me pointed out that an animal
expert who was cited on Who Wants to Be a Millionaire had done a study
on ocelots and the response of male ocelots to pheromones in the Calvin
Klein perfume Obsession. So I wrote Hallinan a letter.

"It was not that I said she was using steroids. I was asking Hallinan to
check it out and take steps to preserve any physical evidence that might
relate to steroids, and that's all I said. And then the press picks it up, and it
becomes, you know, that we're blaming the victim.

"This gal Jill Mako, I think that's her name, talks about how Diane
loved dogs, how Diane was going to get a big dog. And I heard from
somebody who was sitting next to Diane's mother at the trial, I think it
was Sharon talking about how afraid Diane was of big dogs, and her

mother basically commented that that was bullshit. That Diane loved big dogs. And I don't believe Diane was afraid of Bane and Hera, not for a minute.

"I had one reporter ask a question, if I knew Whipple was gay, and I was really offended by that question. What relevance is that? And the answer is no. No, I didn't know she was gay.

"You know, Smith and that crowd tried to make it out that this was sort of a hetero versus gay issue, and that didn't get them anywhere, because if you look at our wedding photos, the photos taken at our wedding, at least half of the non-family members at our wedding were gay men. So for us, that antigay charge was so much bullshit.

"As a matter of fact, it was Sharon Smith who outed her. I understand from people who saw the first interview Whipple's mother gave, that her mother supposedly didn't know that Whipple was gay until Smith made the announcement.

"This gal, Jill, in her statement to the cops, in her recorded statement, says that Diane was talking about getting a dog, about living out in the country, and it said somewhere that Diane had a boyfriend *at one time. And I saw that, and I thought, hmmm, okay.*

"Because in Smith's answers to the interrogatories we served in the civil case, she was claiming she and Whipple had this seven-year relationship, that neither one of them had sexual relations with anyone else during that seven-year period. And I thought it was interesting that we find there's a boyfriend out there."

Key aspects of Noel's eighteen-page letter and his public comments to the media contradicted the statement Marjorie Knoller had given to Inspector Becker the night of the mauling. The San Francisco Police Department alerted the press that in her brief recorded statement, Knoller said that both of her dogs bolted toward Whipple, that Hera started barking and then Bane attacked. At the scene of the crime, Knoller mentioned nothing about being struck by Whipple, and in fact hadn't even realized that there was an abrasion over her eye.

Lieutenant Henry Hunter, head of the General Works Department handling the case, would later tell media that in contrast to Noel's claims, witnesses had come forward to report that Whipple was terribly afraid of her next-door neighbor's dogs, that her friends and colleagues had indeed seen evidence that Whipple had recently been bitten on the wrist.

SFPD Inspectors Becker and Daniele were overwhelmed by the horror stories, collecting data from more than forty people who had come forward to report incidents with Bane and Hera. At the same time, the DA's office was dealing with the Department of Corrections, getting leads from Devan Hawkes. Special Agent Hawkes called Pelican Bay officials the Monday after the mauling to have all evidence confiscated from Schneider and Bretches's cell. The Whipple case now had three sets of investigative teams working in tandem: San Francisco police, the District Attorney's investigators, and the California Department of Corrections. Moreover, the three agencies were compelled to use a legally appointed "special master," Mike Osborne, to assist in sorting through anything that was marked "confidential."

While SFPD began collecting evidence for search warrants, Carlos Sanchez and Dave Parenti, the investigators from the DA's office, flew to Pelican Bay to work with CDC officials and Special Master Osborne as they undertook the daunting task of reading all of Paul Schneider's supposed *"Confidential legal mail."* Most of the mail was unrelated to any legal proceeding whatsoever.

What investigators found was that Noel and Knoller had violated the constitutional attorney-client privilege, using their status as attorneys to discuss matters of guard dog ownership, Aryan Brotherhood activities, bizarre sexual fantasies involving a love triangle between themselves and Schneider, and hints of a love triangle between Knoller and her Presa Canario dogs.

When hearings were set before San Francisco Judge Leonard Louie, and later before Judge James Warren, the most damning and incriminating evidence (anything hinting at bestiality) was sealed. Only the District Attorney investigators, Department of Corrections investigators, and San Francisco police were privy to the actual letters and diagrams that exposed the blurring of the lines between humans and animals.

As headlines on the mauling continued, more witnesses came out of the woodwork, recognizing Noel and Knoller on TV. Inspectors Becker and Daniele continued to link previous dog attacks to Bane and Hera, and they called in SFPD Sergeant Inspector Stephen Murphy to prepare search warrants for the Noel/Knoller apartment.

In the weeks following the mauling, as evidence continued to mount, Robert Noel foolishly basked in the limelight of the media, making snide remarks to newpaper reporters, holding a televised press conference at the gates of Pelican Bay State Prison, and appearing on *Good Morning America* and *Prime Time Live*.

DA Hallinan had assigned Kimberly Guilfoyle to the Whipple case in the early days of the investigation, before authorities had evidence that pointed to homicide, but now he enlisted Jim Hammer to handle what was becoming a high-priority murder investigation.

Guilfoyle, meanwhile, was inundated with media requests, and in the first days after the mauling, she provided interviews via satellite to *Geraldo Live!* at CNBC, to *The Point* with Greta Van Susteren at CNN, and did taped interviews with *Dateline NBC, Inside Edition*, and *Extra*. The cameras loved her, and Guilfoyle had suddenly become a media maven. At the time, she was dating Gavin Newsom, a rising political star in San Francisco with connections to the Getty family, so Guilfoyle was attracting heavy local press almost daily.

"Blaming the victim, talking about the pheromones, all the things Noel had said, made people ask a lot of questions in the beginning," Guilfoyle reflected. "Then there was the adoption, the Aryan Brotherhood, and Diane Whipple and Sharon Smith, a really attractive dynamic couple living in Pacific Heights, and I'm sure I was of interest, since I was dating Gavin at the time. So there were all these nuances that just made it a bright shining star of attraction for everyone to focus the camera on."

Throughout the scandalous reports, Noel was denying any responsibility for the actions of his dogs. He was also denying ownership of the dogs, and he took every opportunity to attack DA Terence Hallinan and the California Department of Corrections. When Robert Noel met with a media throng at the gates of Pelican Bay, he told reporters that his reading of the case indicated that there would be "no basis for criminal charges to be filed" against him or his wife.

"Noel and Knoller were on the news a lot," Guilfoyle recalled, "and though he spoke more to the press than she did, I would say Knoller's interview on *Good Morning America* further fanned the flames by attacking Diane Whipple and saying Whipple provoked the dogs to bring about her demise."

District Attorney Hallinan and ADA Jim Hammer were looking at previous cases where dogs mauled humans. Of particular interest was a case in Santa Clara County. Because the prosecutors knew that murder charges would be difficult and almost impossible to prove, they reviewed a case where Michael Berry had been charged in 1987 with second-degree murder after Berry's pit bull, Willy, fatally mauled a two-year-old boy who had wandered into Berry's backyard. Berry had trained Willy to fight, using the dog to guard a marijuana patch. Berry was found guilty of the lesser charge of involuntary manslaughter. That conviction, believed to be the first of its kind in California, was later upheld by the State Court of Appeal.

DA Hallinan was considering filing *both* second-degree murder and involuntary manslaughter charges against Marjorie Knoller. There were only two cases in American history of a murder conviction resulting from a dog mauling: one in Ohio, where a man was convicted of murder in the mauling of his wife by his dog; and the other in Kansas, where a woman was convicted of murder after her three Rottweilers killed an eleven-year-old boy.

Both these cases were strong. There was proof that the Ohio man *ordered* his dog to kill his wife. In Kansas there was evidence that the woman had engaged her dogs in *Schutzhund*, a German dog-training sport that teaches dogs how to bite.

Still, dog-bite related fatalities had risen dramatically in the United States from 1979–1994, and dog attacks caused 279 human deaths in that period. Diane Whipple's death was the first such fatal dog attack of an adult in San Francisco, and if Hallinan and his team could persuade a jury to convict Knoller of murder in the second degree, it would be a history-making case in California. The verdict would have a tremendous impact on vicious-dog owners.

Sharon Smith had been forced into the headlines as "the partner" of the mauled woman. As she began reading the newspapers and watching the

TV appearances of Noel and Knoller, she became convinced that the attorneys were trying to "spin" their way out of trouble.

"I want to see Noel and Knoller locked up," Smith repeatedly told print journalists. "This wasn't just an accident. I believe they knew exactly what the dogs were capable of, and they let this happen."

Sharon was publicly grappling with the heartbreak and sadness of Diane's death amid a lot of hoopla. For instance, people drove by her building nightly, honking their horns and yelling "Justice for Diane!" Smith decided to hire her own attorney to monitor the developments of the case. It was highly unusual for a victim to hire a private counsel in a criminal matter, but Smith felt strongly that her partner's death was not being taken seriously—she had never been personally visited by anyone at the DA's office. Smith was worried that Noel and Knoller would not be prosecuted to the full extent of the law. It turned out that her attorney, Michael Cardoza, a publicity-savvy former prosecutor with a great track record, thoroughly shared that opinion.

"Sharon came in here, her sister was with her, and we talked," Cardoza reflected. "I asked her if she thought about filing a civil case, but she wasn't thinking about that. It was as if she were hidden behind a pane of glass. I remember she was just sort of sitting there with a vacant look—devastated."

Sharon Smith didn't regard herself as being vengeful, but as she saw Noel and Knoller acting so irresponsibly, she wanted to be sure that the criminal justice system would do its work. She wanted the two of them locked up for murder. At first Smith didn't care about making the couple pay through filing a civil action. Then Cardoza filled her in about the law, letting Smith know that she had *no legal civil rights* to file for wrongful death, being that she was gay. When Smith discovered a same-sex partner couldn't file a wrongful death suit after a loved one had been killed, the tenor of their meeting changed. Smith was suddenly becoming a gay activist.

"You have to wake up to the issue that same-sex partners do not have the right to file for wrongful death," the lawyer explained.

"I don't understand that," Smith said. "That's not fair."

"There's no law that will enable you to do that," Cardoza told her. "That's it . . . that's the law."

"Well then, we should just change the law," Smith said.

"Hmmm. Maybe we should change the law," the attorney told her. "You know, maybe you're right!"

Thus the fight for the legal rights of gay partners of murder victims began. But that was really a sideline for Smith, at least at that moment. In Smith's mind, the wrongful death suit was to take a backseat to the criminal proceedings. Cardoza also felt that the San Francisco DA wasn't paying much attention to the case. "They don't have their homicide people on it," he told Smith, "and that worries me."

As Smith began to realize what Cardoza was implying, she wanted the attorney to get in there and start fighting for her. She hired him to monitor the criminal case, and to handle any civil case as well.

After his meeting with Smith, Cardoza told media that he was "optimistic" that Noel and Knoller would eventually face criminal prosecution, calling their actions "wanton and willful" and their dogs "as lethal as a loaded gun." But behind the scenes, Cardoza wasn't convinced that Hallinan's office was doing everything it could to secure a second-degree murder indictment.

The next day, Cardoza set up a meeting with DA Hallinan. ADA Jim Hammer was not officially on board at that point, and Cardoza was skeptical about ADA Guilfoyle.

"I didn't call Guilfoyle. I wasn't being disrespectful, but I didn't want to talk to her," Cardoza confided. "I wanted to talk to Hallinan, or his second in command, Paul Cummins."

Cardoza had no problem getting Paul Cummins on the phone. He and Cummins went back many years together, old buddies from their college football days. Nonetheless, the conversation became somewhat heated when Cummins, with all his diplomacy and skill, couldn't convince Cardoza that the DA's office was on top of things.

"Hey, Paul, I'm representing Sharon Smith and nobody from your office has talked to her. *What's going on over there?*"

"Well, I wasn't aware of that. Why don't we set up an appointment," Cummins said.

"You know, I'm not telling you how to run your office," Cardoza said, "but you've got somebody who's never tried a homicide before. So you don't even have a homicide team on this."

"We'll set up a meeting this week and you and Ms. Smith can come on in and we'll sit down and have a talk."

A few days later, when Sharon Smith and Michael Cardoza arrived at the DA's office, they were greeted by Kimberly Guilfoyle. Jim Hammer had just been assigned to the case, and the role of lead counsel was still not yet clearly defined. Before they began their meeting with the group—Hallinan, Cummins, Hammer, and Guilfoyle—Cardoza asked to speak with Guilfoyle privately.

"I understand that you are the lead on this case right now, and I'm going to suggest that you not be," Cardoza said bluntly.

"Why?" Guilfoyle wondered, taken completely off guard.

"Because you don't have the experience. You have not tried a homicide case."

"But I *have*, when I was down in Los Angeles, and I never lost a case."

"If you've never lost a case, that tells me you're picking and choosing your cases," Cardoza told her. "Either you're cherry picking, or you're not telling me the truth."

"I've tried difficult cases," Guilfoyle argued, "and I haven't lost because I'm *good*, not because I pick and choose."

"Kimberly, you and I know that the cases you tried down in Los Angeles were in front of juvenile court. You've never tried a case to a *jury*. When you're only in front of a judge, you can make rookie mistakes, and judges are very forgiving. But in front of a jury, it's a whole different ball game. And this is not a case to practice on."

"I've been here over six months, trying tons of animal abuse cases in front of juries," Guilfoyle argued, but her voice was drowned out.

"I'm just telling you, Kimberly, I'm warning you," Cardoza said. "Whatever you tell Hallinan, I don't care. *I have a client and I'm going to protect her.* And my opinion is that you shouldn't be lead prosecutor on this case. You can be second chair, third chair, but you don't have the experience to be lead prosecutor. I don't care how good you are."

Smith and her attorney then met with the prosecutorial team, but nothing much was said about what role Jim Hammer would play, or what might happen if Kimberly Guilfoyle continued on as co-counsel. After the meeting, Cardoza took Hallinan aside and made it clear that he and his client expected a seasoned person such as Jim Hammer to take over the case. Cardoza went so far as to suggest that Kimberly Guilfoyle be removed from the case altogether.

"It's not unusual among DAs to work together," Hallinan later confided, "but in a big case, everybody is fighting over who is getting credit for it. I mean the celebrityhood makes a difference to people, but in reality, Guilfoyle's problem was that she was not recognizing her inexperience. She wanted to bite off more than she was really capable of handling."

"If you remember O.J. Simpson," Hallinan reflected, "there was F. Lee Bailey and Robert Shapiro and all these guys fighting over who was in charge, and then the prosecutors got in the same sort of fix. I think the O.J. case would have gone better if it was clear who was the lead counsel. And I felt the same way with this case."

The Whipple case, as it turned out, required Hallinan's intervention on more than one occasion. Because there was much behind-the-scenes squawking going on, the DA wanted to make sure everyone *understood* their relationships and their roles on the team. Hammer was lead prosecutor, Guilfoyle was second chair. Hallinan wanted to avoid warring lawyers, à la the O.J. Simpson case. Often Guilfoyle would argue about which witnesses she would be allowed to question, trying to expand her role in the trial and sometimes hinting to colleagues that she was being treated unfairly.

Because of her extreme beauty and her high-profile super wealthy boyfriend, Kimberly Guilfoyle was attracting the attention of local political pundits. Many of them were in her corner. Then local newspapers reported that she was a former Victoria's Secret model. In reality, Guilfoyle had modeled for Macy's catalogues, not Victoria's Secret, but readers and viewers didn't care about the truth. Many people of the Bay Area, men and women alike, loved looking at Guilfoyle. Reporters loved to write juicy gossip about her, and the public didn't care what kind of underwear model she was. Guilfoyle's was a Cinderella story—half Irish, half Puerto Rican, she was a girl from the poor side of town who had made it big. She had beauty and brains, had even dated one of the Getty sons, and now rumor had it that she was going to be marrying the most eligible bachelor in town.

There were gossip columnists out there who would print anything new about Guilfoyle—she had become a fixation—and she and Gavin Newsom were being dubbed "the Kennedys of San Francisco" even before they were wed. Some political pundits who were on to the backstage power play between Guilfoyle and Hammer even implied on local TV that the DA's office was being antifeminist by taking Guilfoyle out of the lead.

But, in fact, nothing could have been further from the truth. DA Hallinan's first choice for lead counsel had been Murlene Randle, an African American who was the head of his homicide unit. When she said no, already busy with a heavy caseload, Randle was one of the people who suggested Jim Hammer for the job.

As the criminal case progressed with Hammer at the wheel, Sharon Smith did indeed file a wrongful death suit against Robert Noel and Marjorie Knoller. At a press conference, she said she felt hopeful that progay legislation would be passed. If she won, it would mean any gay man or woman in America might gain a new status as a recognized partner in a wrongful death case. Smith also let the media know that any payout from the wrongful death lawsuit would go to the Diane Alexis Whipple Foundation to fund scholarships for female lacrosse players.

Smith had never met Noel or Knoller, the couple who lived just next door, but she certainly had seen their two giant dogs. When Diane was bitten on the wrist by Bane, early in December 2000, she called Sharon in a panic: "It's those dogs—one of them bit me!"

Diane wanted Sharon to rush home right away. But when Sharon arrived to comfort her girlfriend, she looked at the marks on Diane's wrist, and there wasn't much to see. Apparently, Bane had bitten the band on Diane's rubber sports watch and the watch had protected her from any real injury. Still, Diane was freaked out over these dogs next door.

Because Diane had no real puncture wounds, Sharon decided to calm her partner down, thinking it would be best if they just let the matter drop. Later, Noel would make much of the fact that Smith, with her high-powered position at Charles Schwab, hadn't said anything to the building manager, the landlord, or any of her neighbors about the "alleged" incident. Noel would further remind reporters that neither Whipple nor Smith filed any complaint to Animal Care and Control, insisting that the bite never happened, that he had bumped into Ms. Whipple exactly three times in their apartment building, and on each occasion Diane Whipple was polite and quiet, and she seemed to like his dog, Bane.

THE VOICE OF ROBERT NOEL

"Sharon Smith claims that she's maintaining her civil lawsuit for the Diane Whipple Foundation. But she hasn't executed any documents that require her to turn over any proceeds from any lawsuit to the foundation. I forced her to say that under oath in the interrogatories.

"And when you look at the lawsuit, it's maintained, not in the name of the Whipple Foundation, but in her name, individually. So she can keep the money. And on top of that, as a matter of law, Smith cannot commit to turn over the proceeds of a wrongful death lawsuit, because a wrongful death action is brought on behalf of all the people who would inherit, or who are entitled to make claims from a wrongful death. So Whipple's mom and everyone else has got a share in the recovery. So I mean, she's full of shit.

"But Sharon Smith is a stockbroker. She sells Enron stock, for Christ sake. How many little old ladies got screwed out of their retirements because she sold Enron stock? I know what these people do for a living. I used to defend them. I did securities fraud defense work, okay?

"I'm not saying that people didn't have encounters with brindle dogs. But they weren't ours, and they weren't Marjorie and me. Smith says Diane says Bane bit her. It's hearsay. It shouldn't have been admitted into trial, but it was. The people that the cops talked to at St. Mary's were people Sharon Smith contacted before the cops took their statements. And if you look at their statements, you'll see that their stories aren't straight.

"The one gal, Whipple's friend from St. Mary's, Sara Miller, says that the bite occurred in the afternoon. And we're talking in the afternoon,

213

after Whipple got home from work that day. But then Smith says she got a call from Whipple around noon, okay? So the time is off.

"And they say it was the first week in December. But Bane went in for surgery on December 5, and supposedly Whipple related this to people at a coach's convention that starts on December 6. Now Smith is absolutely specific about that December date, but when she's asked in interrogatories about trips Whipple took in December, Smith says Whipple never left town in December. Then she later gets on the stand and testifies at a hearing that Whipple did in fact go out of town on December 6.

"I don't recall seeing Whipple until January. In the discovery, it shows Whipple living somewhere down in the Peninsula in April of 1999. So to me, I think you can look at that and speculate that Smith and Whipple may have broken up in April 1999, and that what was happening in January was an attempt to reestablish the relationship, maybe.

"The first time I remember seeing Whipple was January the 11, 2001. In one of her statements, Esther described Whipple as a recent resident of the building. Sharon Smith moved into that apartment in April of 1999, but Smith is the only one whose name is on the lease. Smith is the only legal resident of that apartment. And like I said, looking at Esther's police statement, she thought she saw Whipple in October of 2000 for the first time. Esther had seen her on her roof, when the Blue Angels were flying over in October.

"You know, one of Diane Whipple's girlfriends, Jennifer Morris, says that when Diane talked about her encounter with the dogs, she was kind of lighthearted and laughing about it. So, no, she wasn't afraid of the dogs.

"When I encountered people with these mutts, especially when I had the two of them, my left hand would be clamped down on their leads, so there was absolutely no slack, and the dogs would be standing shoulder to shoulder. And I would move them to the curb, or if there was a driveway there, I would move them into the street, with my body in between them and anybody who was walking by. I would wait for the people coming by me to pass.

"Why? Because I'm walking two big dogs—not that they're vicious, but you know, they are going to be moving around a lot on leads, and I don't want them tripping somebody or biting. And quite frankly, they both had the tendency, although Hera had it more, to want to herd people.

214

"*They've got a herding instinct. You see it in the pictures of these pups. They look like a sheepdog trying to herd sheep. And Hera would put her body up against you and push you the way she wants you to go. I mean, she'd herd you. And she would herd Bane.*

"*As a matter of fact, Hera was a really confident female. She wasn't confident when we got her, but by the time we'd gotten her healthy and had her out playing with other dogs, she really became sort of an alpha male, up to the point where she would urinate by cocking her leg back up. That's one of the indications that a dog thinks she's an alpha.*

"*One day, Hera went over and pissed on Bane's head. Bane was sniffing a bush and had his head down in the ground and Hera walked over, cocked her leg, and pissed right on his head. And when Marjorie goes to pet Bane on the head, I tell her not to touch him, but she didn't listen, and then she wanted to know why her hand was all wet and sticky. I had to wash him up.*

"*See, the thing that was happening, initially, when the cops and the DA were getting stories about all these people who encountered our animals, I mean, they had stories of encountering us in places we'd never been. They got a statement from a gal who works for Petco, a gal named Jennifer who supposedly encounters me and Marjorie with Bane and Hera in the store one day. She describes this horrifying event. She says in her statement, which I've seen, that she knew Marjorie and Hera very well because Marjorie would always come in and buy food called Nutro in a forty-pound bag. But she also says Marjorie was in there with a guy who she couldn't identify as me.*

"*The gal identifies some guy other than me, okay? She didn't recognize my photograph as the guy who was there with Marjorie. And I knew that Marjorie would never drive over by herself—she had a driver's license, but I was always the one to drive. And Marjorie never took the dogs—absolutely never took either of the dogs—in the car without me. And we never bought food in a forty-pound bag, and we never bought that brand, Nutro.*

"*And then you have Hank Putek going around getting people to write statements in our building. I can understand why Hank was upset, because the cops initially told him they thought it was his wife, Ginger, who was dead on the floor, okay? I can understand where he's coming*

215

from. And Hank's got the added burden that he was cooperating with us in keeping the dogs there. We were using his car to take them everyplace. So Hank was trying to draw some distance between him and us. As a matter of fact, we've got a cross-complaint against Hank for indemnification for helping facilitate the keeping of the animals there at 2398 Pacific.

"Then you look at the outrageous statements Hank was making to Kat Brown at Animal Care and Control. About how he was living in fear of the dogs. I mean, the dogs are riding in his car. And he's riding in the elevator with the dogs, his wife is riding in the elevator with the dogs. And if you look at our photos, you'll see a white Jeep Wagoneer with simulated wood panels on it, and that's Hank's car. It's his car!

"You have to understand the mind-set of the neighbors. Here we are fighting to keep Hera alive. They didn't want this dog back in there, and they're rightfully terrified, I can understand that. But then at that point, they all start talking to one another, and it becomes a confabulation, and the lunging and barking gets described out of proportion and the dogs become twelve feet tall, that kind of thing."

CHAPTER TWENTY-THREE

Around the same time Robert Noel and Marjorie Knoller were talking with Elizabeth Vargas on *Good Morning America*, via satellite from Eureka, California, San Francisco Sergeant Inspector Stephen Murphy was executing a search warrant to seize the following property from the Noel/Knoller apartment:

1. Any bloodstained clothing and/or towels; any clothing worn by Marjorie F. Knoller on January 26, 2001.

2. Dog leashes or harnesses; restraint or control devices for the dogs; any documentation related to the ownership of the two dogs known as Bane and Hera.

3. Photos or drawings of the two dogs, Bane and Hera; any and all videotapes including VHS and 8-mm. format depicting Bane and Hera.

4. Documentation relating to the training of the two dogs, Bane and Hera; any veterinary bills or invoices regarding Bane and

Hera; any diet supplements or medications relating to Bane and Hera; any lineage documentation of Bane and Hera or the dog breed Presa Canario.

5. Any and all correspondences from Pelican Bay State Prison, Janet Coumbs, and/or Brenda Storey relating to Bane and Hera, to include electronic messages, computers, hard drives, as well as any Web site information relating to either Bane, Hera, or the dog breed Presa Canario.

6. Receipts relating to the dog attacks by either Bane or Hera; records showing payment for medical treatment for any dog bite to Robert Noel, Marjorie Knoller, or any other person.

7. Financial records and any personal property tending to establish the identity of the persons in control of the premises, including rent receipts, utility bills, and addressed mail/envelopes.

Stephen Murphy, a street-smart law enforcement man who operated in shadow, was backing up Becker and Daniele in every step of the mauling case, without asking for credit. During his lengthy career, Murphy earned a Bronze Medal of Valor and more than one hundred commendations from his captains. "The Murph" was, as DA Paul Cummins once put it, "a cop's cop." Cummins claimed that Murphy could "take a quarter in his hand and bend it in half, and then bend it in half again."

Throughout the Noel/Knoller case, Murphy acted as a liaison between the SFPD and the District Attorney's office, working in tandem with Becker and Daniele, often pulling fifteen-hour days and splitting his time between the Hall of Justice and the San Francisco Federal Building, where he'd been assigned as a Special Federal Officer working on the FBI's Joint Terrorism Task Force. He was *not* a guy to mess with. When he accompanied the team of SFPD inspectors to the Pacific Avenue apartment to conduct the sweep, Murphy took the front door off with a crowbar, speaking loudly, *"Police, search warrant . . ."*

That day, Inspectors Becker, Daniele, and Murphy were assisted by Inspector Dominick Celeya and Special Master Mike Osborne. The five men were very methodical in their search. Their first order of business was to be sure no persons were hiding in the dwelling and to secure the scene.

They made certain that Special Master Osborne was the only person to go through any legal papers. There were all kinds of documents piled up mile-high in the lawyers' "office," their large converted closet.

"As we walked into the house, the place smelled like dogs. It was a real old dog smell—absolutely horrible," Murphy confided. "After our initial sweep, we looked near the bookshelf where officers had seen a naked drawing of Knoller with the two dogs, but that was gone."

Murphy and Celeya concentrated on the bedroom, and Becker and Daniele swept the living room, kitchen, and foyer. There were piles and piles of papers: junk mail, note pads, dozens of dog magazines, and so on. Then there were the letters—from Marjorie to Paul, from Robert to Paul—that the inspectors had extracted off the couple's computer.

When government experts were later able to retrieve everything Noel had *deleted* from his hard drive, the SFPD realized that the clock on the computer had been tampered with. It appeared Robert Noel had engaged in damage control, trying to come up with a "good doggy" campaign. He wrote letters to his mother in which he told her all about his "wonderful" loving pets. Though Noel tried to make the letters to his Mom look as if they were written weeks before the mauling, SFPD inspectors were 99 percent sure that Noel had predated the letters. The inspectors speculated Noel wrote them *after* Whipple's death, hoping to build a case to save Marjorie and Hera.

Of course, Inspectors Becker and Daniele had already seen the rancid apartment on the night of the crime, but Murphy and Celeya were quite shocked to find the place smelling like a dog barn. Up until then, Noel and Knoller were known to them only from TV reports, where the two managed to present themselves as persons of high caliber. In Murphy's opinion, the pair came off as quite successful attorneys living in a ritzy neighborhood.

During their sweep of apartment 604, the inspectors looked through every nook and cranny of the place, right down to the couple's socks and underwear, locating pieces of incriminating evidence in wastebaskets, bathroom medicine cabinets, and antique night tables. In one wastebasket was a crumpled handwritten love note from Marjorie to Paul Schneider, which later shocked even Robert Noel. In between the pages of a magazine was a photocopy of Hera's picture with the caption "Hera, Red Hot, One Fierce Bitch."

Each nightstand contained a Remington pistol and rounds of live ammunition. Under the queen-size bed, there was a shotgun as well as a "junk" pistol. In the kitchen were boxes of pet body-building supplements. Found in the bathroom were narcotics prescribed to Robert Noel and Bane Knoller.

Still, certain key pieces of evidence the police hoped to find—the incriminating drawings and the books about training guard dogs—were nowhere in sight. The inspectors knew that Noel and Knoller had left town and were seen with their hands loaded full of boxes. Those boxes, some of them locked in a storage unit by Knoller under an assumed name, were never to be recovered.

"I was looking for dog-training videos, harnesses, any letters, any photos—there was a laundry list of stuff," Murphy recalled. "I seized the computers because I wanted to see if there was anything on there to do with dog training, anything to do with the Aryan Brotherhood or the Mexican Mafia in regard to the dogs."

As it turned out, the computer and two floppy disks contained an incriminating letter from Robert to Paul Schneider that was entered into evidence in the criminal trial. Written at 11:40 P.M. on the day Diane Whipple was killed, Noel wrote, "There is no way to ease into this— *Bane is dead, as is one of our neighbors.* Marjorie, while bruised, cut and battered, is alive and more or less okay. I am sure that you have seen the news of the killing on either Channel 2 or 4 TV or picked it up on one of the radio stations. One report indicated that a decision would be made to put Hera down—that will not happen and we will not permit it."

"There were only five pictures of the dogs found in the apartment," Murphy remarked. "Noel and Knoller presented the grand jury with hundreds of pictures of the dogs, but those pictures were not in that apartment."

Noel and Knoller hadn't left any of the truly twisted evidence behind, but the many piles of papers they *had* left behind them posed a fire hazard. The inspectors found such interesting items as gun holsters, spiked dog collars, and harnesses. There were also medical records for Bane's lame leg, Hera's bad heart, and Noel's severed finger.

In the bedroom, there were various adult toys (vibrator and dildo type things) accompanied by more than 250 X-rated pictures of Marjorie in different stages of dress. Murphy and Celeya had to go through all of them, cringing at some of Knoller's brazen displays, sometimes performing a sex act on an unidentifiable male who had to pull his stomach back in order to take the snapshot.

"The first thing that was interesting," Celeya recalled, "was that the apartment manager told us Noel and Knoller refused to give her a key. Even in the case of an emergency, there was no way for anyone in the building to get into that apartment. That's why Murphy had to break down the door."

Celeya was told to look for things that related strictly to dogs and not to touch any official-looking documents. He spent his time looking through the bedroom closets, checking every shelf in every dresser for any weird props, checking the photo albums for evidence of bestiality, and looking through the pages of every book in the antique bookcase.

Celeya was very careful about his work, as were the other four men, and they took only what seemed absolutely pertinent to the case (for instance, generic dog magazines were left behind, as was the group of kinky photos). Of course, the inspectors hadn't yet compared notes with all the evidence that the District Attorney investigators were collecting up at Pelican Bay.

"In the nightstand, there were pictures of Marjorie in all different types of poses. I mean, every pose she could sort of yoga herself into was done," Celeya would later confide. "There were a lot of boudoir-type shots they had taken out in the hallway, which always struck me as kind of funny, because at that time they were telling the media about how police had embarrassed Knoller at the scene of the incident by telling her to pull up her shirt. But she couldn't be that embarrassed if she's taking these pictures out in the hallway."

Celeya wasn't in the least happy to be sorting through pornographic shots of the overweight Marjorie, and he quickly moved on to other matters, taking a few of Marjorie's perfume bottles, which they needed in order to dispute Noel and Knoller's claims that perfume could have provoked Bane. Nevertheless, as he continued his search, Inspector Celeya couldn't help wondering about the inordinate number of pornographic pictures that were there.

"Why would Noel leave them there for us?" Celeya would later wonder. "He left them there for a reason. He'd already taken out what he wanted to take out. But then there were these pictures of his wife, naked in her entirety, lying down, spreading her legs, with a lot of close-ups. Did he think we would take them and then somehow try to embarrass us because we took them?"

Murphy and Celeya later discussed it and decided that Noel most likely *did* leave the pictures there with the intention of causing a public ruckus over bad police protocol. It was one of Noel's typical stupid moves, and it would happen again.

The next time, however, Noel's "planted evidence" would backfire on him. Within days after the first search warrant was executed, Noel arrived back in San Francisco, claiming police had ransacked his apartment. To prove it, Noel invited a local TV news crew to take footage of the damage police did to his front door.

During the interview with reporter Christy O'Conner, Noel's eyes wandered over toward a book on his nightstand called *Manstopper!* It was a training guide for guard dogs with a photo of *Bane* superimposed on the cover. Even though he clearly led the reporter to the book, trying to insinuate that police were shoddy and that they hadn't done their job, it turned out that *Manstopper!* was later turned over to a judge. It became a key piece of evidence linking Noel and Knoller to the breeding of fighting guard dogs.

Since the book belonged to Dale Bretches, Noel had no idea that book would incriminate him. He was so sure of himself and so snide about his innocence that he had planted the book so he could publicly claim that the police were sloppy. Noel chuckled for the camera, wondering how SFPD could have been so stupid as to have missed such an interesting read.

As Robert Noel showed it to O'Conner, he explained that *Manstopper!* served as evidence that neither he nor his wife had any interest in training fight dogs at all. *Manstopper!* proved one thing, insisted Noel during the TV interview: that Noel and Knoller hadn't acted on any of the training techniques therein described.

"Later, when we got the stuff from Pelican Bay, there was a receipt proving that Noel received *Manstopper!* from Dale Bretches," Murphy reflected. "From what I read and saw in the apartment, I think Noel has a very huge ego. He's very controlling, and I truly believe he knew what kind of dogs he had, and he was proud of that. From what I saw of Marjorie's history, I would say she was a poster child for an emotionally abused woman. From the things we were reading, it seemed like she was his puppet."

After a second search warrant was executed, there were still no pictures or drawings of Knoller with either of her dogs. But rumors were flying all over town that bestiality was somehow involved in the mauling death, and the DA's office was being pressured by the public to get to the bottom of it.

Suddenly, when the DA's investigators sat down with the SF police to sift through 20 boxes of evidence, the whole picture started coming together. The weird man/beast drawings from Schneider's cell were placed into evidence, as were the letters from Noel and Knoller to Schneider, some of them glued back into place after being found shredded into bits and pieces.

Meanwhile, special agents were extracting a slew of letters from the hard drive of Noel and Knoller's computer. The experts found not only Marjorie's fantasy letters about the medieval king, queen, and prince, but letters that seemed to be actual reports about sexual experimentation with dogs. Some, written by Noel, described interaction between humans and animals in great detail.

"There were letters about the Aryan Brotherhood, and about relationships between dogs and humans, but that was all sealed by the judge," Murphy would later confide. But Steve Murphy wasn't the only one to read them: Terence Hallinan and his investigators, Carlos Sanchez and Dave Parenti, also viewed this bestiality evidence, as did officials from the California Department of Corrections, who later confirmed the existence of drawings and one snapshot.

When the four most damning letters made their way into the hands of Jim Hammer, the DA and the SFPD began toying with the idea of presenting them to the grand jury. Hammer was so riled about the blurring of the lines between man and animal, he was ready to file animal-cruelty charges.

In February, Russell and Brenda Storey claimed to DA Investigator Dave Parenti that they learned of an illegal dog business being run through Pelican Bay Prison from CDC Special Agent Devan Hawkes. The Storeys admitted to Parenti that they handled the exchange of moneys between attorneys Noel and Knoller and inmates Schneider and Bretches. They further confirmed that Schneider wanted the dogs removed from Hayfork because Janet Coumbs was "babying the dogs."

The Storeys also later told Inspectors Becker and Daniele that they were not the official owners of the dogs, that Noel and Knoller took ownership of Bane and Hera in January 2001. Becker and Daniele ran a check on Animal Care and Control records and discovered that Marjorie Knoller *had* in fact registered herself as the owner of Bane and Hera. Paying thirty-two dollars to get animal tags for the two dogs, she listed them as her "mastiffs" on January 3, 2001. At this time, Noel and Knoller were denying ownership of the dogs, claiming they were only "keepers" of the animals and that the animals' rightful owners were their *clients*. Noel and Knoller, as Hera's guardian, called the offices at Animal Care and Control to demand a meeting, hoping for the return of their beloved Presa. ACC Director Carl Friedman and his Deputy Director Kat Brown would speak with the attorneys to explain the protocol at the animal shelter.

On the night Whipple was mauled, before anyone knew whether she would live or die, Robert Noel telephoned the Animal Care and Control shelter. He told Deputy Director Kat Brown he had gotten Bane only a month before. Brown was surprised by Noel's tone. All he seemed to care about were *his dogs*. He never once asked about the status of Diane Whipple—he just wanted to know if Bane was dead.

When Brown told him that Bane had been put to sleep, offering Noel her sympathies, Noel didn't particularly care to hear that. Since it was too late for Bane, now he just wanted to focus on Hera.

Noel was playing dumb about his dogs, requesting special treatment, insisting that his dogs were good animals, and asking if they could meet with her right away. Kat Brown came in on her day off, on the Sunday after the mauling, to accommodate Noel and Knoller's upcoming travel schedule. Before the 1:00 P.M. meeting, ACC officers gave Brown the complete documentation on the rare breed. Many of the officers at the animal shelter, afraid Brown might let Hera go home with the attorneys, wanted to be sure that Kat Brown would make no mistake.

But by that time, Diane Whipple's death was front-page news throughout the Bay Area. People were terrified, the energy at the ACC shelter was pretty high. The ACC officers at the crime scene had been traumatized, so much so, that more than one of them needed post-trauma counseling. There was no way Kat Brown was going to release Hera. She was meeting with the lawyers just as a courtesy, mostly because Noel was being so insistent and pushy about his rights.

In a letter to Paul Schneider, written the day Whipple died, Noel wrote: "We have a meeting scheduled with the assistant director of Animal Control on Sunday. The Director opined that Hera should be put down as she 'is very dangerous.' What B.S. They move on Hera and they will have the fight of their lives on their hands. *Neighbors be damned— Hera did nothing and has not acted in a dangerous manner toward anyone. If they don't like living in the same building with her, they can move.*"

Noel and Knoller were dressed very casually that Sunday afternoon, Knoller in sweatpants and a sweatshirt, Noel in a Polo shirt and jeans. They wanted Kat Brown to be aware that Hera had nothing to do with the attack. They wanted their dog back and made it abundantly clear that they were prepared to fight for Hera, that they would go to every length to save her. Indeed, appellate records indicate that Noel and Knoller did just that. Voluminous paperwork was filed regarding Hera, for over a year after Whipple's mauling.

"I had no judgment about what was going on with Hera," Brown confided. "I told them that we would have to go through a vicious and dangerous dog hearing, and that, if there hadn't been problems with Hera in the past, they would have the right to get Hera back. But I suggested very strongly to them, that in the context of what happened, it might not be a good thing for Hera to go back into the environment of that building, that that environment might hurt her."

But Noel and Knoller wouldn't listen. Brown explained that Hera would be in danger if she would be allowed out on the streets in Pacific Heights. Because a woman had died, people were up in arms, and that might jeopardize the health and safety of the dog. But Brown's advice just seemed to get Noel and Knoller further agitated.

"I told them Hera couldn't go back into that environment and have a good quality of life, but they didn't get that at all," Brown recalled. "It was all about them, what they wanted, how they wanted to get their dog back because it was their dog, and the rest didn't matter."

As the meeting continued, Kat Brown was flabbergasted by the couple's audacity. She discovered that Marjorie Knoller had never owned a dog in her life; that the couple was aware that their dogs were fighting guard dogs; and that the couple had used Hera as protection when a stranger supposedly tried to "jackhammer" his way into their apartment.

In addition Noel and Knoller kept switching their stories. They had had Bane for four months, not thirty days. They talked about earlier incidents with other dogs, which Brown didn't need to hear. It wasn't her place to listen to stories about how Hera "woofed" at a few people or to decide about Hera's behavior. In fact, Kat Brown had no idea why all this information was coming to her.

Because it was so early on in the investigation, Kat Brown still thought she was dealing with a "terrible accident," that the fatal mauling was a "horrible tragedy." She was very polite to the two attorneys, explaining once again that the decision about Hera would fall into the hands of Captain Vicky Guldbech and Sergeant Bill Herndon, who would conduct a "vicious and dangerous animal hearing" that would be scheduled at a courtroom in City Hall as soon as possible.

"At one point in the meeting, Marjorie got very upset," Brown reflected. "She had been sort of shy and diffused and sort of let her husband do most of the talking, but then—I hate to say it—but there was a point where she got so aggressive, she was almost like a mad dog."

"You really should think about giving Hera up," Brown told Marjorie. "I can't imagine it would be good for her to go back into that apartment—it just would be very difficult for Hera."

"No! I won't have that, I love my dog," Knoller quipped. "*Hera has never done anything to hurt anyone.* There's never been any problem with that dog, and I'm going to get her back!"

CHAPTER TWENTY-FOUR

Diane Whipple's killer was "man's best friend." With 54 million dogs living in 30 million American households, a lot of people were interested in finding out about what would happen to the owners of the dogs that killed a beautiful young athlete. The death of Diane Alexis Whipple had spawned fear in the hearts of many. Dog owners worried about whether their happy pets could turn into monsters. People who knew little about dogs started to worry about dangerous canines getting out of control.

Robert Noel told the press that he had good, well-behaved animals. Bane and Hera were perfect animal specimens, but he also cautioned, "There is no control. If the dog decides to charge, there's no way to stop him."

When Noel and Knoller appeared on *Good Morning America* on February 8, 2001, Knoller said she did "everything humanly possible" to try to stop the fatal incident, insisting: "I wouldn't say it was an attack. Bane was just overly interested in Ms. Whipple."

"Miss Whipple came out into the hallway, which I didn't understand," Knoller told ABC's Elizabeth Vargas. "I thought she was just going to slam her door shut." Knoller quipped, *"I know I would have."*

But Vargas wouldn't let Knoller off the hook so easily. As much as Marjorie wanted to claim that what happened was just a "terrible accident," that any witnesses who had come forward to complain about her dogs were people who just wanted "their fifteen minutes of fame." But Vargas kept pushing Knoller with hard questions.

With a smirk, Marjorie Knoller asserted that everything her neighbors were saying about these dogs was "*total fabrication*." As Marjorie refuted her neighbor's reports, her husband, Robert Noel, sat next to her, visibly chuckling.

"Well, at what point did it go from your dog being just interested in Diane Whipple, to it being an attack?" Vargas wanted to know.

"I wouldn't say it was an attack," Knoller insisted.

"Well, Diane Whipple was mauled to death. The woman is *dead*," Vargas reminded her.

"She did strike me with her fist in my right eye," Knoller explained, "and that's when it went from Bane being overly interested in her—to him wanting to bite her."

That night, when the Whipple story aired on *Prime Time Live*, Sharon Smith would tell ABC's John Quinones that Diane Alexis was "scared to death" of the dogs. After Diane was bitten by Bane, Diane would put Sharon in front of her, for protection, just in case dogs might appear.

Smith told Quinones that Whipple had planned to make a little dinner for them that evening. Diane had gotten groceries and was going to make tacos. They were going to eat something quickly before catching a movie. Smith called her partner "a generous, loving, giving, and loyal wife." With tears in her eyes and her voice quivering, Smith talked about the night of the mauling, saying that her partner had been revived after twenty-three minutes of losing consciousness, but by then Diane was brain dead.

Lieutenant Henry Hunter told the reporter that Diane Whipple had "pieces of her missing." Some partial shots of the mauled victim were shown, but most footage focused on the bloody hallway, and the door to Whipple's apartment, 606, which, because of TV camera angles, looked like 666.

Of course, when Marjorie Knoller and Robert Noel appeared on the show, they had a different perspective.

"Bane just loved to have his belly rubbed," Noel confided. "Bane loved women. He was a really gentle dog."

"Bane was really friendly toward females," Knoller said, smiling.

When asked if they were ever warned about the possibility of the dogs being dangerous, Robert Noel paused and then emphatically said, "No."

But *Prime Time Live* also interviewed Donald Martin, the veterinarian who vaccinated the dogs at Janet Coumbs's in March 2000. He told ABC that he didn't think the dogs had been controlled or properly handled. They couldn't be properly examined, and he called them "a recipe for disaster." At the time Noel and Knoller came to retrieve the Presa Canarios from Hayfork, Dr. Martin had warned them that these dogs were like "ticking time bombs waiting to go off."

"It sounds like you ignored his warning," Quinones later remarked to Noel, "and had you listened, this woman might still be alive."

"No. We didn't ignore his warning," Noel told the newsman. "We heard what he said. Dr. Martin was paid to do a veterinary examination. He missed the level-six heart murmur of Hera."

"So you question his credentials?"

"I do."

This time, when Knoller was asked to describe the attack, she gave yet another rendition of the events. As she spoke to ABC, spliced into the program were shots of the bloody hallway and photos of Diane Whipple crossing the finish line of a marathon.

"She reached back, and hit me in my right eye," Knoller told Quinones, never looking straight into the camera. "I believe it was just because she was panicking. And that's when Bane became aggressive. It wasn't as though he locked on to her. It wasn't a continuous agitation biting."

"Why couldn't you control Bane?" Quinones wondered.

"He was never out of my control," Knoller said.

"He *killed* this woman. *How can he not be out of control?*"

"Being out of control, to me," she explained, "means letting the dog run wild."

"But *you couldn't physically take him off*," Quinones said. "You couldn't take him into your apartment."

"Actually, that's what I did. But it was too late."

People posted banners all over San Francisco:

"Kill Hera!"

"Save Hera!"

With animal activists writing letters to the San Francisco DA, to Mayor Willie Brown, and to Animal Care and Control, insisting that it was not Hera's fault, that the animal should be saved, with neighbors and Pacific Heights residents wanting the dog destroyed, it was becoming a battle. Whether Hera participated in the attack in any way was of no concern to the neighbors. They did not want that dog back out in public. But then all these activists had come forward, flooding the media and public officials with constant requests to be humane.

"It boggles my mind, how people treat animals compared to how they treat their own species," ACC Director Carl Friedman confided. "I once questioned one of the animal rights people on this, and they told me it was because animals can't take care of themselves, they're just helpless. Well, that may be true. But look at all the homeless and mentally disordered people out there. They're helpless too."

The Whipple mauling had brought the man-versus-animal issue to a whole new level. On the night of the incident, Friedman described Bane as being "one of the biggest, most powerful animals" he'd ever seen. The ACC Director hoped the public outrage and frenzy would die down after people learned that Bane had been humanely destroyed.

Friedman was overwhelmed with calls from folks who said Hera shouldn't die—she was another victim of the bizarre situation. Some people claimed they would blow up the shelter before seeing Hera unfairly put to death. There were so many death threats, the ACC put new security systems and video cameras in place.

"People were calling here saying we shouldn't hold Hera or kill her," Friedman reflected. "Many people offered to adopt her, but she wasn't our property, the matter was still in the courts."

Friedman would quietly note that the people who wished to adopt

Hera were not unusual. In his decades of experience working with animals, Friedman had often seen this phenomenon—people always wanted to adopt "special needs" animals: the cat with the eye missing, the dog with the leg missing.

"It's astounding to me, listening to all the people who got very angry at me because I wouldn't give Hera to them," Friedman confided. "I tried to explain to them that I had thirty-seven other dogs here—sweet, wonderful dogs, who haven't been involved in killing anybody, who needed homes desperately. I had good, healthy dogs that would fit in with families and would love kids, but I couldn't turn these people around. They wanted to come down for Hera."

Friedman hoped for the day when people would start to realize that they didn't need to go out and purchase "designer" dogs. He hoped people would realize that they didn't need to go to fancy breeders and pay up to $6,000 for a dog. He wondered if people were ever going to realize that purebred dogs, because of overbreeding, were often the dogs with the health problems, like hip dysplasia, and other kinds of genetic diseases. He couldn't understand why people would reject perfectly good mutts, crossbreeds who were overcrowded in shelters, who were being killed, unnecessarily, every day.

"I ask people all the time, *if you want love and want the best companionship you can ever find, go down to your local animal shelter*," Friedman said. "You look from cage to cage. You look through that door, and you look into the eyes of those animals, and one of them is going to get to you."

"What are you going to do with that dog?" an anonymous caller's voice boomed.

"We've scheduled a dangerous and vicious dog hearing," Vicky Guldbech responded. "I'm sorry, but I can't tell you anything more."

"You kill that dog, and you'll die!"

Then all Guldbech could hear was a dial tone.

"I remember I thought, Sheesh! What is this?" Guldbech reflected. "When I sent out a press release about the date for Hera's hearing, people started calling me with even more threats, and I thought, Oh, wow, here we go!"

Guldbech had many years of experience in dealing with distraught people and their animals. A tough cookie, she handled all kinds of problems—with strays, with pets belonging to the homeless, with illegal dog-fighting rings, with guard dogs working for drug dealers. She'd been threatened and yelled at by angry dog owners. Whenever there was a vicious animal situation, Guldbech was usually the first official on the scene, accompanied by SFPD Sergeant Bill Herndon or SFPD Officer John Denny.

Together with her fellow ACC officers, Guldbech had removed countless violent or threatening dogs from people's homes. Sometimes she responded to calls about dog bites; other times, she accompanied SFPD on drug busts. Either way, it was a dangerous job, but Guldbech always handled it. She was a sweetheart, but a whole different person in uniform.

"A lot of times, what will happen, if someone is into illegal activity, if they have pit bulls guarding their drugs and the cops are going in there to serve a warrant, we have to go in and get the animals," Guldbech explained. "We handle the dogs because we don't want a bloodbath."

In her many experiences with vicious animals, what Guldbech would notice most was that there always seemed to be strong correlation between people and their pets. The more dangerous the people, the more dangerous the pets. She would also take note that owners of aggressive male dogs wanted to keep their animals only if they could remain "intact." She would go into an area with a gang presence, for example, where crack houses were guarded by unneutered pit bulls, and after she removed the animals, the owners would come to the ACC building to put up a fight. The ACC officials would give the owner of an aggressive pit bull the option of having the dog returned *after* it had been neutered, but if the owner was a drug dealer or a gang member, he wasn't interested. One minute, he'd be fighting for his "pet" with all his might, the next, he'd sacrifice the dog, walking away in a huff.

But even with the many problems that pit bulls seemed to cause, Guldbech had also grown to love pit bulls. She felt the breed had gotten an unfair rap. When she first started working at Animal Care and Control, she was doing surveillance, busting people who were putting on pit bull fights, busting people who were using pit bulls to guard drug labs. But then, she got to thinking about it and realized it wasn't the breed's fault—it wasn't that a pit bull or a Rottweiler or a German shepherd was bad.

"These breeds are victims of society just like some people are," Guldbech insisted. "Yes, the large breeds are capable of hurting somebody, probably more than a Jack Russell terrier, but intelligent people who have experience in dealing with these animals can read them," she would say. "People can read a dog. Most people can see that pit bulls and Rottweilers are beautiful dogs. They have a place here. They shouldn't be banned."

In the first week after Whipple's death, reports started flying in about how spooky Bane and Hera were (some people claimed they sensed a supernatural fear surrounding the dogs, or that flocks of birds would fly away from the two Presas), so Guldbech decided to study Hera's behavior. As more people came forward to say they were afraid to be in the presence of Bane and Hera, she realized there was something very undoglike about Hera.

"If you've ever been around a wolf," Guldbech explained, "for instance, if you watch one in a zoo, when a wolf is eating his food, he never lifts his head up. He just looks at you with his eyes, and keeps eating. Wolves are confident, they don't need to warn you. They can just look at you. But a dog, most dogs, if they're eating, they'll stop and look up at you and then go back to their food.

"I mention this because it was something I noticed about Hera. She would stare over at me the way a wolf would, her eyes would move, but her head would stay in place. I thought it was kind of weird."

In dealing with a case where a human life had been lost, Guldbech couldn't believe that Noel and Knoller would even want to put themselves through a vicious and dangerous hearing. The ACC captain couldn't understand why the two attorneys wouldn't acknowledge the participation of their dogs in the fatal incident, especially since Knoller had already made a statement to police that Hera was tugging at Whipple's clothes. Then there was the blood seen on Hera by ACC officers that night, as well as the remnants of Whipple's garments seen in Hera's feces.

"During the whole hearing," Guldbech reflected, "I watched Marjorie holding her forehead, bowing her head down, you know, very theatrical. I just kept staring at her while she was rolling her eyes. We were presenting all these witnesses who had been attacked by Hera, and I didn't know what could be going through her head. She got up and testified and started crying. I think she was up there crying for *herself*, not for what happened to Diane Whipple."

To everyone in the packed courtroom, at Hera's hearing on February 13, 2001, it seemed that Ms. Knoller was busy feeling sorry for herself, crying so she could win her dog back. Between Knoller's dramatics, Noel's arrogance, and the two of them sitting there plotting, trying to discredit each witness who came forward to describe the incidents that occurred, no one could figure out what motivated these people. They contended that everyone who testified was a part of a conspiracy. Noel and Knoller each took the stand, and tried to make every witness out to be a liar.

"I have never been in a situation where somebody was crying for their dog after it killed a human being," Guldbech confided. "But if my dog killed somebody, or if my dog was even *present* when somebody was killed, I would think that dog would be scarred for life. I would want the dog put down. It would have been creepy to me to have a dog like that around."

"We were holding a hearing about Hera," Guldbech said. "When I was interviewing people who'd been bitten or lunged at by Hera, several of them wanted to remain anonymous. They wouldn't come to court. Some people were embarrassed because of their irresponsibility. I tried to tell them, nothing could have saved Diane's life."

The ACC held an administrative hearing. Unlike a criminal proceeding, no one could be subpoenaed and compelled to testify. But four victims did agree to appear: David Moser, who'd been bitten in the elevator of 2398 Pacific; John Watanabe, a mail carrier at whom both Presas had lunged; Neil Bardack, whose Shetland dog was attacked; and Ron Bosia, the dog walker whose client's dog, Bogie, was harmed. Beyond that, Guldbech would present written statements from two other victims, as well as the testimony from the ACC officers at the scene of the crime and the SFPD officers who had tried to comfort Diane Whipple.

Captain Guldbech wanted to present David Moser first. She felt his story was the most important in terms of prior incidents, but she could tell when she first interviewed him that he didn't want to come forward. He didn't want to relive the incident, he was respectful but reserved, but he finally agreed to tell his story, testifying that he'd been bitten by Hera, describing the bruise he'd gotten, the hematoma that appeared on his buttock.

"I watched David Moser's face when Robert Noel got up there to say what an idiot Moser was. Noel got on the stand and said Moser wasn't bitten by Hera, that Moser hit himself on the elevator door knob, and I thought, this is so wrong. When Moser first told me about the incident, it brought me chills. I thought about that night with Diane Whipple, and I could see that elevator. Then I realized, the same thing could've happened to him. It could have been him."

San Francisco Police Department Sergeant Bill Herndon, the person in charge of Hera's fate, was a man who took the job of holding ACC hearings very seriously. A quiet guy with a kind disposition, Herndon worked with the health department as well as the police and ACC. Over the course of his years of service, Herndon had made many tough decisions, literally taking hundreds of vicious animals off the streets as he enforced state code to protect the rights of innocent citizens.

"I had a lot of calls from people asking me to be nice to the dog," Herndon said. There were some people who just didn't think Hera was involved, or they believed Hera could be rehabilitated. I know they meant well.

"When I first got this job, the hardest thing about it was having animals destroyed," he explained. "It's hard to make that decision, because it's a touchy-feely thing, but you have to look at the way the code is written. It's a lot easier to say the dogs can go home, but that's the easy way out."

The same day the hearing began, Noel and Knoller filed a declaration asking to have Sergeant Herndon disqualified as the hearing officer. They contended that because Herndon was a member of SFPD, he couldn't possibly be fair in his assessment of Hera. But Herndon wasn't privy to the criminal investigation being conducted by Becker, Daniele, and Murphy. In fact, Herndon was so concerned about being fair and unbiased that he deliberately chose not to read the papers or listen to TV newscasts. Herndon knew that Hera had already been convicted in the court of public opinion. But if there was a possibility that Hera wasn't guilty—if the evidence presented had not been sufficient—in Herndon's way of thinking, he wanted to give Hera a chance.

"The evidence presented at the hearing from Marjorie, when she first started out, she said Hera wasn't involved, that Hera was just sitting there barking," Herndon reflected. "But, I mean, as the details came out that Diane Whipple's clothes were all stripped off her, and Bane couldn't have done all that damage to Whipple's body alone—I think Hera was a lot more involved. Marjorie was very vague about it."

On Tuesday, February 13, 2001, there were more than forty TV cameras in the courtroom, as well as many newspaper and magazine journalists. The paparazzi were in full force, with cameras flashing, cell phones ringing, and pagers going off. Animal activists, the Pacific Heights neighbors, and other concerned citizens filled up the rest of the seats in the small courtroom in City Hall where Hera's fate would be decided.

Among the first witnesses was John Watanabe, who gave testimony about a near attack in mid-January. The U.S. postman testified that as he was making his deliveries on Fillmore Street around noon, he heard loud barking and snarling. When he looked up, two huge dogs were charging at him full speed.

Everything happened so quickly, Watanabe said. The dogs were upon him in a flash, so he dropped his mail and used his metal mail cart to protect himself. The incident lasted for almost thirty seconds, Watanabe said, and he was moving his metal cart back and forth to keep the ferocious dogs, whom he recognized as Bane and Hera, from coming at him.

Then for some strange reason, out of the blue, both dogs suddenly quieted down and walked away. Watanabe thought it was very strange, the way the animals just stopped in their tracks "as if someone had pulled the plug."

As they were trying to attack, Watanabe testified, he noticed Marjorie Knoller out of the corner of his eye. She was standing next to a vehicle, not moving at all, and not yelling any commands. After the dogs ceased their frenzy, Watanabe picked his head up and noticed Robert Noel was standing right near his wife, also observing, without saying a word.

236

According to Watanabe, both dogs were off leash.

The postman told Herndon that when it was all over, he watched Bane and Hera go back toward their caretakers. The postman thought it was odd that the owners never came over to him to apologize or to see if he was okay. Instead, Noel and Knoller just walked off with their dogs, as if nothing had happened at all.

When Captain Guldbech finally summoned Robert Noel to the stand, he came forward with a very smug attitude. He smiled at Guldbech, bidding her "good morning." He was confident and cocky. And he was ready to politely blast the hell out of the credibility of everyone who had testified earlier.

Noel began his comments by addressing a list of incidents, which he ran through one by one, providing quite a different version of each and every event involving Hera. Noel explained that when David Moser claimed to have been bitten, Noel told him, "Bullshit! You hit your ass on the door." Noel went on to claim that Moser "assaulted" his wife when he banged into her in his rush to get out of the elevator—without even apologizing.

"Moser was having a race with this idiot that came running down the stairs," Noel testified. "He actually pushed Marjorie as he turned to slide by her, and he hit his butt cheek on the elevator door handle."

Noel went on record to say that David Moser never received a dog bite. He basically called Moser a liar in front of God, national TV, and everyone else. With respect to Neil Bardack, Noel had no problem believing that Bardack's dog had been attacked. But Bardack was mistaken about who the attack dog was. Bardack testified his dog, Meryl, had been attacked at dinnertime on September 11. Noel was in San Francisco General then, recovering from the dog bite that resulted in his severed finger, and he said he had proof that Marjorie was visiting with him at that precise hour. According to Noel, there was no way that either of his dogs could have been the culprit, since Bane and Hera were handled solely by Marjorie.

Regarding Ron Bosia's report of the incident between Hera and Bogie, it was factual and accurate. But Noel claimed, it was Bogie, not Hera, who had gotten aggressive. Noel said that after Bogie started it, it was impossible to see "who did what to whom." When he and Bosia got the animals separated, "the dogs were like two kids on a playground. They were fine."

Of course, Noel had a completely different story to tell about Post-man Watanabe. He testified that Hera's lead was attached to her, that she managed to bounce out of their vehicle and she went up to Mr. Wata-nabe's mail cart, standing there barking at the cart for a few seconds. Noel never said a word about Bane being with her. Noel further claimed that the postman was nowhere in sight, perhaps behind a bush. Hera was just barking at a cart.

Without being pressed, Noel added that there was another letter car-rier who was delivering mail across the street who happened to yell over to Watanabe, asking if everything was okay. Noel testified that he heard Watanabe respond that everything was fine.

"We've seen Mr. Watanabe in the neighborhood any number of times," Noel told Herndon. "Mr. Watanabe's drop box is right on our corner. He never complained to us. Ms. Knoller can address this because she encountered him after the incident and they exchanged pleasantries and he never had any complaint."

Bill Herndon asked Noel about the letter he had in evidence from Dr. Martin, wondering what the condition of the dogs had been in Hayfork and what the warnings were. Noel testified that the vet said the dogs were "a problem to get to, let alone vaccinate" because the Presas had been penned up behind chicken wire with a large piece of plywood cov-ering their pen. It was a logistics problem for Dr. Martin, Noel explained, nothing more.

Noel explained that when Janet Coumbs introduced the dogs to them, she said that Bane was "an absolute love, of real gentle character." Coumbs showed them Bane's repertoire of tricks—sitting, giving paw— and Noel testified that Bane proved to be everything Janet said he would be. "Bane loved to lick people," Noel testified. "He licked me all over, he licked Marjorie all over. He was very approachable—you could just walk right up to him."

Noel said that Hera was the same way, very approachable and friendly, even though she was tied up to a tree. "Hera was not, at this point, a licker," Noel said, "but there were no problems with strangers approaching her or handling her." Of the dogs at Hayfork, Fury was the only problem, Noel testified.

"Because Fury was chained on a twelve-foot chain, and had been for about a year," Noel stated, "she was lunging and barking and growling when we first approached her. But as soon as the chain came off, Fury's behavior changed 180 degrees. She was a lovable, docile dog."

SERGEANT HERNDON: Sir, Animal Control officers stated here today that Hera was barking ferociously, and banging into the glass door where she was being held in the bedroom. Why do you feel that her behavior was that way even before Animal Control officers entered the bedroom?

ROBERT NOEL: She had witnessed an attack in the hall where Ms. Whipple was mortally wounded. My experience with Hera is that Hera would very probably have stood against Bane to protect Marjorie. Indeed, her harness that was left behind by investigating officers was discarded, because it had been ripped, apparently by a tooth mark, so that's why when she was found in the bedroom: she didn't have a harness.

SERGEANT HERNDON: Sir, I believe you're saying then, that Bane somehow ripped the harness off Hera?

ROBERT NOEL: I was not there to see it, but that would be the only explanation.

SERGEANT HERNDON: Can you tell us, sir, about when you saw Hera being led out by Animal Control officers?

ROBERT NOEL: Sure. I watched Hera being led out on the day of the incident. It appeared to me that she did not have any blood on her. My speculation would be that since Ms. Knoller was the one who secured her and took her back to the apartment, any blood on Hera came from Marjorie. When I encountered Marjorie on the

239

sixth floor, she was entirely covered in blood. If you can picture one of the classic movies of Lady Macbeth, with her hands covered in blood, that was the picture that greeted me.

After a short break in the proceedings, Marjorie Knoller, who had paraded by paparazzi like a movie star, hiding behind her sunglasses and ever-present Hermès scarf, waltzed back into the courtroom and took the stand on Hera's behalf. She wanted to address some of the statements that she had made to police officers the night of the event. She wanted to clear up the issue of Hera tugging at Diane Whipple's clothing.

MARJORIE KNOLLER: When I was sitting in the hallway and talking to the officers, I had stated that Hera had tugged at Ms. Whipple's clothing. And Hera had also tugged at my clothing. This was during a period of time when the attack was still going on and Bane was acting the way he was acting. Hera was pulling at the bottom of my sweats and Ms. Whipple's pants leg, and she was barking.

SERGEANT HERNDON: Hera was pulling at the bottom of your sweats?

MARJORIE KNOLLER: And at Ms. Whipple's sweats. I believe that Hera was trying to protect me from Bane by whatever actions she did. She was never involved in the attack of Ms. Whipple. She was barking hysterically in the hallway.

SERGEANT HERNDON: Where were you when Hera was biting at your pant leg and at Ms. Whipple's?

MARJORIE KNOLLER: She wasn't biting, she was tugging. There is, to me, a big difference. She had got the sweats I was wearing—there are no tears or pull marks on the bottom of my sweats. Bane was shredding Ms. Whipple's clothing. Hera was in no way involved in the incident.

Herndon didn't quite understand. If Knoller felt pressure on her legs, and Bane was at Whipple's neck, since Hera was the only other animal in the hallway, then Hera had been involved. Knoller tried to sidestep the issue, talking instead about her battle with Bane up near Ms. Whipple's torso. But Herndon persisted.

SERGEANT HERNDON: How did you know, then, that Hera was pulling at Ms. Whipple's pants?

MARJORIE KNOLLER: Because she was right underneath me and I guess I could—It was a guess, is what it was. In other words, Hera was pulling on my pants leg, then she was pulling on Ms. Whipple's.

SERGEANT HERNDON: Okay. So you don't really know the extent of what Hera was or was not doing?

MARJORIE KNOLLER: Actually, I do know the extent, because she was nowhere near Ms. Whipple's torso.

SERGEANT HERNDON: But she was near Ms. Whipple's feet?

MARJORIE KNOLLER: Yes, because she was near my feet.

Knoller didn't know how far up the body Hera may have gone, but she insisted that Hera never got into her peripheral vision and that the dog wasn't anywhere near the areas on Whipple's body where there were injuries or bite marks.

Knoller also testified that she herself had bite wounds. They weren't puncture wounds, but she had bite wounds "in the same areas, more or less, that were on Ms. Whipple's body."

SERGEANT HERNDON: I understand that the clothes were completely shredded off Ms. Whipple?

MARJORIE KNOLLER: Yes. Bane was shredding her clothing.

SERGEANT HERNDON: If Hera was tugging at her pant leg, why do you believe that Hera hadn't pulled any clothing away from her body?

MARJORIE KNOLLER: Because I was the one dealing with Bane and backing him up and I saw what he was doing

	when I would pull him back. Every time I would pull him back, he would try to be tugging at something she was wearing.
SERGEANT HERNDON:	If Hera's harness was cut, and you believe it was cut by Bane's teeth? Then Bane would have tried to bite Hera?
MARJORIE KNOLLER:	Yes. Because Bane was going over Ms. Whipple's body and my body. He was crossing it, and that's how I got the blood on my back. He was covered in blood, and he was going back and forth across us. I believe one of those times he probably did—He and Hera had contact and that's how her harness was ripped.
SERGEANT HERNDON:	How did the dogs get back into the apartment?
MARJORIE KNOLLER:	I took them back into the apartment. I was the one who took Bane into the apartment. I told Hera to wait, and I came out and got her—No, actually, I got Hera to come with me and into the apartment when I was dragging Bane.

Herndon wanted to know if Hera had a lead on. Knoller answered no, because she had not been walked that day. Hera had been in the apartment, and she did have a harness on. Knoller usually grabbed her by her harness, she testified. However, on the day of Whipple's death, Knoller said she really didn't need to do that, asserting that Hera came back of her own accord.

SERGEANT HERNDON:	So you went into the apartment and the dogs were where?
MARJORIE KNOLLER:	Bane, I placed in the bathroom, and I put Hera's harness in the bathroom with Bane. And then I took Hera by the scruff of her neck and placed her in the bedroom, so any blood that's on Hera would be from me.
SERGEANT HERNDON:	What did you do then?

MARJORIE KNOLLER:	I went out into the hallway. The keys that were in my sweat suit were missing, so I went to check where the keys were—I knew Ms. Whipple was gravely injured—I went to check where my keys were. They were in Ms. Whipple's foyer. I picked them up and came back and met the officers before I had time to check to see whether or not Ms. Whipple had a pulse.
SERGEANT HERNDON:	Your feelings on Hera: do you feel Hera is a dog that would be a good pet to have back in your home?
MARJORIE KNOLLER:	She's a wonderful pet and I do believe she would be just fine. She's a wonderful animal. She's loving. She's caring. I began to nickname her a certified lick therapist, because when you're not feeling well, she knows it.

The last person to testify was Ana Aureoles. Legally blind, with limited vision, Ana had been mistreated by her family and many of her fellow humans; she felt a very special bond with dogs, and Hera in particular. Ana wanted the ACC to spare Hera. For much of Ana's life, she lived in a mind-set somewhat like Gulliver of *Gulliver's Travels*, who, when he voyaged to a land ruled by horses, began to believe that animals, and not humans, were the beings who really had hearts and souls. To Ana, animals were the only real perfection of nature.

It was because of her service dog, Henry Miller, that she felt she received any type of respect. She would later remark that if it weren't for her gentle service dog, strangers around her wouldn't be so kind. Being a bleeding-heart liberal, Ana believed that privileged people would step on her if she got in their way. Ana was familiar with powerful people knocking her down any chance they got. And she felt that Hera was in the same boat.

Because Ana spent a lifetime being taken care of by service animals, she wholeheartedly believed that dogs were more loyal than people, and more trustworthy. Ana felt sorry for Marjorie Knoller, watching her crying big crocodile tears, and she just couldn't sit by and let Hera, whom she considered innocent, be sentenced to death. She couldn't understand why Hera had to pay for something that was her owner's fault. Ana blamed Robert Noel, whom she viewed as the evil mind responsible for Bane's atrocious behavior. Ana begged Sergeant Herndon to spare Hera.

Herndon told Ana Aureoles that he appreciated her testimony—she was a regular at the vicious and dangerous animal hearings—but he politely explained that his job was to make things safe for the people of San Francisco.

The week after the hearing, Sergeant Herndon released his decision to have Hera destroyed. The DA's office asked that Hera be held as potential evidence at the ACC animal shelter until criminal charges were filed. Hallinan's office was about to present the case to a grand jury.

Ana Aureoles didn't want to accept the ruling, and neither did Noel and Knoller, who immediately filed a motion to appeal. While Noel and Knoller were holding news conferences and filing more cases against the California Department of Corrections, Ana visited Hera at the shelter. Sometimes she cooked bones for Hera as a way to connect with Hera's soul. At church, Ana prayed for Hera, kneeling with the Franciscan friars who fed the homeless, the sick, and the poor. More than anything, Ana was hoping that Hera's death sentence would somehow be reversed. And Noel and Knoller felt there was a strong possibility that they could get Herndon's decision thrown out.

CHAPTER TWENTY-FIVE

"You can't believe how goofy these two attorneys were throughout this whole case," Inspector Murphy confided. "Marjorie Knoller is nuts—that's my opinion. She and her husband should have known better, but they both felt they hadn't done anything wrong, that they would walk away unscathed."

Inspectors Becker, Daniele, and Murphy were in agreement about Noel and Knoller's culpability. They had done their jobs well, had collected all the evidence in support of their search warrants; thirteen warrants were pulled together. They had cooperated fully with Hallinan's office, with Hammer and Guilfoyle, with the DA Investigators Sanchez and Parenti, and with CDC officials.

Becker and Daniele had been to Sacramento to meet with Devan Hawkes on the Monday after the mauling. They had made the long trip up to Hayfork, interviewing Janet Coumbs and videotaping the pens Bane and Hera had been held in. While in Trinity County, Becker and Daniele interviewed retired police officer James O'Brien, who had assisted Noel and Knoller in picking up the eight Presa Canarios.

On tape, James O'Brien confirmed that Janet Coumbs did, in fact, warn the two lawyers about the vicious nature of the dogs, stating that he heard Coumbs single out Fury and Hera in particular, who had killed some of her livestock. Later at the criminal trial, O'Brien testified that Bane and Hera were placid, timid, and shy that day. However, on cross-examination, he admitted that he delivered *Bane* and five other Presas to a group of men with prison tattoos on their necks in the Los Angeles area.

During the ongoing investigation, media would confirm that Schneider and Bretches's dog-breeding operation was alive and well: the offspring of Bane and Isis were being raised by Carolyn Murphy in Los Angeles County. Murphy had little to say about the pups she had received. Only two of Bane's spawn were named—Menace and Roka. "I'm raising the dogs for me, they're mine," Murphy told the *San Francisco Chronicle*, refusing to say whether she planned to sell any of the rest of the litter.

Prosecutors later used documents seized from the Noel/Knoller apartment to show that the attorneys conspired with prison inmates to raise animals to "fight, attack, or kill." Noel & Knoller filed a motion to squelch any evidence that was attorney-client related, but San Francisco Superior Court Judge Leonard Louie agreed with prosecutors and found that the attorney-client privilege did not automatically apply, turning over four of the six packages of contested documents that had been sealed.

Jim Hammer would tell the press that there was "overwhelming evidence of a conspiracy between the attorneys and the inmates to circumvent prison rules and use intermediaries to raise and sell dogs for fighting purposes." Noel denied any such conspiring, remarking to a reporter at the *San Jose Mercury News*, "I'm also in a conspiracy to eat lunch."

After another round of hearings held before Judge Louie in camera, the judge ruled that four additional envelopes that contained sealed material—envelopes that had been challenged by Robert Noel—would be turned over to prosecutors as well. Of the eleven boxes seized from the apartment, the judge ruled that only the two envelopes were considered truthful "attorney-client privilege" and would be withheld.

To the media Hammer would also mention the book, *Manstopper!*, which was mysteriously missing. The book had a photo of Bane on the cover that Noel had shown on TV just days after the first search warrant was executed. Hammer said this "attack training manual," *Manstopper!*, was eventually handed over to Judge Louie by Marjorie Knoller during a hearing at Pelican Bay, and it contained "more warnings than a manual for owning a handgun."

The first warning is printed on the opening page of *Manstopper! Training a Canine Guardian*: author Joel McMains excuses himself and his publisher from any liabilities that might arise from the use of the manual, telling readers, "The training methods presented in this manual carry high potential for danger to owners, trainers, helpers, and dogs."

In the text, McMains writes, "Do you know what a good-sized dog can do to flesh? And how fast?" "Ponder words like 'ripped,' and 'fractured,' and 'hemorrhaging.' Imagine savaged meat and the coppery smell of congealing blood."

A chapter called "Faster, Harder, Tougher" opens with: "A manstopper does not prance up and daintily woof at or daintily nip a target. He overpowers. He becomes a tsunami with teeth."

Outside of court, Noel would tell reporters that the book was "insignificant," saying he was using it as a reference to read about dogs and the training involved. "The big thing about the book," Noel said, "was to find out what was involved in training the dogs, so if people wanted to go train them, they could go that way." Noel also mentioned that the book contained an entire chapter on keeping the guard dogs as family pets. However, Rob Morse of the *San Francisco Chronicle* would later report that he read the entire book, and it contained no such chapter.

Paul John Schneider, who granted an exclusive interview to the *San Francisco Chronicle* after Hera's death sentence, told reporters: "First and foremost, I want to express my deepest apologies . . . even though it's hard to apologize for a dog. . . . It's a horrible nightmare, a tragedy. It's an accident."

He went on to assert that he was in no way responsible for Whipple's death. Shifting the interview away from his culpability, Schneider preferred to talk about his deep fondness for his new adoptive parents, Noel and Knoller.

"I feel like I have a family. It's a good feeling to look them in the eye and feel that I can trust them," he said. "I can be open and honest—and there are not too many people I can trust in prison."

The inmate spoke articulately and authoritatively, expressing his belief that he and his lawyers had been "smeared by a bunch of prison lies." When journalists asked Schneider about the tattoos emblazoned on his left hand, the letters AB—along with a shamrock and the numbers 666—Schneider suddenly went off into a fit of rage. Bristling at the notion that he might be a racist, Schneider quipped, "I'm no Nazi. I'm in prison. Prison is made up of Blacks, Mexicans, Whites. The Whites are a minority. I've grown up around Black people. They don't relate to me and I don't relate to them.... Things are really racially divided in prison.... I'm not a White Supremacist.... I didn't start the Aryan Brotherhood, and I'm not going to end it. I'm just along for the ride."

Schneider criticized prison officials for seizing his legal papers and other materials not related to the dogs, including family photos and personal drawings. He told reporters that he and his cellmate Bretches used a $20,000 payment from a "prison abuse lawsuit" to purchase Bane, Hera, and two other Presas. Schneider admitted that he had read dozens of books on the topic.

Schneider told the *Chronicle* that he was offering people a chance to use his money to raise the dogs, with the understanding that, when the puppies were sold, any profits would be evenly split.

"We picked the Presas because it seemed like a really cool choice. They were a dog we could relate to. They weren't sissy dogs," Schneider told reporters. The inmate explained that he got Noel and Knoller involved because he suspected Janet Coumbs of animal abuse: "She kept the dogs chained up on a twenty-five-foot chain all the time. They were scarred around the neck, too. And I was worried. That is completely bad for dogs. It was definitely not good psychologically.

"I definitely didn't want the dogs chained up, because it makes them more aggressive. I don't want to send a dog to prison. I'm in prison. Why would I want to put a dog on a twenty-five-foot chain? That is prison. It's cruel and unusual punishment."

By the end of the interview, Schneider, speaking from behind a Plexiglas wall, stuck his right leg up on the table, looking for the reporters to feel sympathetic for him. He spoke about a claim Noel and Knoller had filed on his behalf over alleged prison negligence, maintaining that a sponge was left in his leg as part of a botched surgery.

As Schneider pulled up the pant leg of his mustard-colored jumpsuit, he exposed an oozing, raw puncture wound. Prison officials said that *Paul Schneider* was himself responsible for keeping the leg wound open for more than ten years—unlike other inmates who would hide weapons up their anal cavities, Schneider used his leg wound as a place to hide his handmade knives.

Marjorie Knoller showed up in Crescent City on March 7, just two days before she would appear before a grand jury in San Francisco. She was there to represent her adopted son, Paul. News cameras captured her in all her glory—wearing a miniskirt and go-go boots, completing her ensemble with rings on every finger, and long dark fingernails. In photos of the two of them at the defense table, Marjorie reviewed documents while Paul—in his CDC white jumpsuit, with leg and wrist shackles—beamed at the cameras. As Schneider flashed his steel-gray eyes, he smirked at the media, a dimple appearing in his cheek.

Knoller, who was there without Noel, was sitting very confidently at the makeshift defense table (the hearing was being held in a building just outside the prison's electrified fence). At issue was the legality of the seizure of materials from Paul Schneider and Dale Bretches's cell.

With Judge Leonard Louie presiding, Jim Hammer asked to be given a chance to review the eleven boxes taken from the cell. Hammer assured the judge that he and his team were interested only in the issues of dog ownership and training, promising he had "no interest whatsoever in getting irrelevant material."

Because Knoller was possibly about to face criminal charges herself, Judge Louie asked Schneider whether he was aware of the potential conflicts in having Marjorie Knoller represent him. Schneider said he didn't care. He waived the right to claim any conflict of interest. He wanted Marjorie.

Two armed prison guards stood beside each inmate—Schneider and Bretches—during the evidentiary hearing, which included a twenty-minute public session and then moved to a closed session in which special masters assisted in the review of the boxes of materials taken from Schneider's cell.

In Knoller's motion produced for Schneider's hearing, she faulted prosecutors for refusing to disclose affidavits in support of search warrants, stating: "In light of the absurdity of the District Attorney's position on conspiracy . . . shining the light of day on this question . . . would cause authorities to run from the light, as do carrion-feasting cockroaches when the curtains of night are parted to admit the light of day."

During a break in the session, Knoller made self-contradictory statements to the press, saying she didn't object to prosecutors using any of the relevant dog-related material but wanted anything marked "attorney-client" to remain sealed.

Down in San Francisco, minutes before their appearances before the grand jury, Robert Noel and Marjorie Knoller chatted it up with the maze of television reporters standing in the hallway outside the courtroom, having brought Marjorie's bloodstained sweat clothes along in a clear plastic bag. They were looking for TV cameras and reporters to project the image of Knoller as a hero. Knoller was contending that she had fought Bane with all her life—she had the bloodstained clothes to prove it. She wanted to set the record straight about the death of Diane Whipple.

However, Marjorie never helped Whipple after she got her dogs inside her apartment; she never called her husband; and she never dialed 911. Beyond that, Noel and Knoller had no business testifying at a grand jury on their own behalf. Any lawyer worth his or her salt would have forbidden it, since grand jury appearances do not allow for objections of defense counsel. Once a suspect places himself in that position, he becomes free game for the prosecutor and the grand jury foreman and thus must answer any and all questions posed.

Up until the very last minute, Hammer had no idea whether Noel and Knoller would actually show. He had subpoenaed them as a matter of course. He had an inkling that they might be brazen enough to testify, but in his heart of hearts, he thought they would bail at the last minute.

But that didn't happen. Noel and Knoller wanted to come forward. Noel testified first, while his wife was friendly with reporters outside the courtroom. Later, Knoller took her turn. Neither Noel nor Knoller had the faintest idea about what evidence the prosecutors had amassed. Even in the wake of the Hera hearing, and the Pelican Bay evidentiary hearing, they remained in denial about their culpability and the frightful actions of their dogs.

Noel and Knoller felt confident that they could dispute the claims of the few witnesses who had testified against Hera, and they relinquished their rights to have an attorney present at the grand jury. Each was eager to take the stand to talk about their wonderful Presa Canarios, and Noel had even come equipped with poster boards full of shots showing the two dogs playing and strolling around the streets of San Francisco.

Noel and Knoller hadn't ever considered that total strangers might have recognized them on TV newscasts. They had no idea that all these people had already come forward, testifying to the grand jury about scary run-ins and attacks caused by Bane and Hera.

The grand jury proceedings lasted for weeks, culminating on March 27, 2001. After explaining that the targets of the investigation were Marjorie Knoller and Robert Noel, Jim Hammer told the grand jury that the allegations would include various forms of homicide, from murder down to involuntary manslaughter, along with the violation of section 399 of the penal code, a mischievous dog statute.

Kimberly Guilfoyle had prepared the summary of the opening, which Hammer read aloud, describing the gruesome scene on January 26, 2001—the incident being partially witnessed by Esther Birkmaier, through her peephole. The prosecutor touched on the fatal wounds that Diane Whipple suffered, alleging that Noel and Knoller, due to previous instances of aggression exhibited by their dogs, knew that these dogs had a propensity to be vicious toward humans and other animals, and that they failed to keep the dogs within reasonable care, thereby placing anyone who came in contact with these dogs in danger of grave bodily harm.

Hammer explained the first count of the indictment—murder—stating that Robert Noel and Marjorie Knoller, on January 26, 2001, unlawfully killed a human being, Diane Alexis Whipple. It would be up to the grand jury to determine what degree should or would be charged: the grand jury could recommend that Noel and Knoller be charged with second-degree murder, which did not require a need to show malice or ill will, or they could decide, after being instructed on the definition of involuntary manslaughter, that Whipple's death was a result of some other unlawful act by either Noel or Knoller.

The prosecution opened with the testimony of Esther Birkmaier, followed by SFPD Officer Leslie Forrestal, ACC Officers Andrea Runge and Michael Scott, SFPD paramedic Alec Cardenas, and Whipple's domestic partner, Sharon Smith. The members of the grand jury were given all the gory details—from Whipple's screams to her cries for help; from the 911 calls made by Esther to the horror scene police discovered in the hallway, where Whipple was found crawling, lying facedown in her own pool of blood.

The grand jury heard about Knoller's bloody hands and Knoller's "excited utterance" admitting that Hera was tugging at Whipple's clothes. They heard about Bane, who was found soaked in blood and pacing in the bathroom, and about Hera, who was going absolutely wild, banging against the walls and doors of the bedroom.

The grand jury learned that Marjorie Knoller admitted that she was the "owner" of the dogs. They learned that Knoller had not been aware that she had a contusion over her right eye. They learned that Knoller was only too happy to remove her shirt to show Cardenas that she had no grave injuries whatsoever. All Knoller suffered were a few scratches and perhaps a bite mark on her hand. Or rather, *Knoller* claimed it was a bite mark, but a med tech would later testify that Knoller's hand injury looked more like something caused by her pulling on a nylon leash.

Sharon Smith testified that she and her partner, Diane Whipple, had lived in their Pacific Heights apartment from May 1999 until January 26, 2001. Sharon spoke very softly as she told the grand jury about how large the two Presa Canarios living in her building were, identifying photos of Noel and Knoller as her next-door neighbors who owned them. She told jurors that she would see Robert Noel and Marjorie Knoller with their dogs a few times a week, usually in the downstairs foyer of the building—and she described the beautiful lobby the building had, with its red carpet entrance and fireplace off to the left-hand side.

Smith testified that a typical interaction between herself, Diane, and the dogs would occur when they were getting their mail, or heading out to the garage; if Noel and Knoller came too close or if they were exiting the elevator with the dogs, she and Diane would stand back to let them pass. The lobby had a very narrow foyer and Smith stated that she herself was intimidated in the presence of the dogs.

Sharon described a phone call Diane made to her at work one day in early December 2000. It was in the middle of the afternoon, around lunch time. Sharon recalled that as Diane spoke, her speech was heightened—she was talking fast, and very loud. Diane told Sharon that she'd just been bitten by a dog. Whipple's tone of voice was unusual. Diane was quite anxious. She was almost out of breath as she was saying, "That dog just bit me!"

Smith told the grand jury that she knew Diane was referring to Bane or Hera, because even though they didn't know the dogs by name, the two of them had spent time talking about "those dogs." The dogs were a "problem," they felt, and shouldn't be living in an apartment. Diane had once even stated that she couldn't believe Marjorie was walking dogs of that size.

Smith told jurors that when she received the call from Whipple that afternoon, she asked Diane if she was okay, and Diane said she was fine, but said she was scared, and also angry at the dog owner.

"That was on my mind as I was driving home," Smith testified. "And so, when I walked into the apartment, the first thing I asked her was if I could see where she had gotten bit. And she showed me her left wrist, and she had, in this area of her wrist, about two or three deep indentations that were red."

Whipple told Smith that she was downstairs in the foyer when the incident happened. Whipple was getting ready to leave the building when Robert Noel walked in and his dog lunged at her, biting her on her wrist. Diane said that she had her sports watch on, *Thank God*, or she could have been bitten more seriously.

After the dog bite, according to Smith, in the subsequent interactions with Noel and Knoller and their dogs, Diane became more standoffish—she was outwardly frightened by the dogs. Smith explained to jurors that Whipple would use *Smith as a human shield* to stay further away from the animals, that, after the bite, Whipple would hurry out of the building just in case the dogs might appear.

"Several times when we would be at the elevator door up by our apartment at the sixth floor, if I were to open the door too quickly," Smith recalled, "she would grab my arm and tell me, '*don't do that*'—you know, worried that those dogs were going to be there."

Smith informed the grand jury that she had first encountered Robert Noel and one of his large dogs in September or October of 2000 and, being a dog lover, she had reached out to pet the dog, but Noel shouted, "No! Don't do that!" Smith jumped back, a bit frightened by Noel's reaction. Smith testified that Noel didn't want her to touch the dog, explaining that Bane had just been in a fight with another dog in the park, and in his words, Bane was "a little spooked."

Then, with her voice shaking, Sharon Smith recounted the horrible afternoon when she came home early from work on January 26, only to discover crime-scene tape all around her building, describing how she arrived at San Francisco General in time to see her partner alive for a few moments.

When Hammer asked if Whipple was wearing any perfume on that particular afternoon, Sharon Smith broke down in tears. After a five-minute break Smith said that Diane didn't usually wear perfume to work; furthermore, the only medication Whipple was using was Levoxyl, a synthetic thyroid, because she had thyroid cancer. As far as Smith knew, her partner did not ever take any kind of steroids, nutritional supplements, or vitamins.

Venus Azar, the forensic pathologist, was the next witness. She described her findings at Whipple's autopsy, including the graphic details of abrasions and deep lacerations and the gaping laceration on the right side of the neck.

Azar told horrified grand jurors about the 5½-inch wound that lacerated Whipple's external jugular vein, and about another life-threatening injury, a 2¼-inch laceration that transected Whipple's external carotid artery, also known as the thyroid artery.

The cause of Diane Whipple's death was the loss of blood from the lacerations to the jugular vein and thyroid artery, combined with injuries to the larynx—the Adam's apple area—which had been completely crushed.

Before the media throng became aware of the grand jury proceedings, among the witnesses to testify were Janet Coumbs, Dr. Donald Martin,

Ron Bosia, Hank Putek, Neil Bardack, John Watanabe, Alex de Laszlo, David Moser, Diana Curtis, and Jill Davis.

Stephen and Aimee West would also testify, as would their dog-trainer friend, Mario Montepeque, who informed jurors that Robert Noel and Marjorie Knoller refused to take any advice, and that they wouldn't even consider putting choke collars—much less muzzles—on their out-of-control dogs.

Also testifying on behalf of the People was John O'Connell, whose six-year-old son had had a run-in with the two Presa Canarios. The incident happened one morning in mid-December as O'Connell was walking his son, Timo, to elementary school.

O'Connell told the grand jury that because he was familiar with mastiffs, he encouraged Timo to take a close look at the dogs, telling the six-year-old that his aunt used to have a dog like that. O'Connell assumed Bane and Hera were mastiffs, and they looked like a friendly pair of dogs, at least from a distance of thirty feet.

However, as Timo got closer to Bane and Hera, one of the Presas lunged at the little boy and was barking and growling in a dramatic, frightening way. According to O'Connell, Robert Noel held on to the dog's leash, but the animal was able to lunge a few feet, its legs lifting completely off the ground, as if Timo was going to become its prey.

O'Connell testified that his little boy shrank back, going "kind of catatonic." The witness said his son was "clearly terrified," insisting the dog was baring its teeth and was definitely in "attack mode." It all happened very quickly—O'Connell was on his toes, ready to dive on the dog, trying to decide what to do, when suddenly Noel was able to pull the dog back.

Hammer asked if Noel apologized or even acknowledged his dog's actions; O'Connell said that Noel might have murmured the word "sorry." But Noel couldn't have said anything too loudly, because O'Connell could barely make out whatever perfunctory remark was said. Noel was soon halfway down the street, having pulled the dogs away, holding both dogs by their leashes in his one hand.

Another witness who saw the dogs lunge at children was Rhea Wertman-Tallent, a longtime resident of San Francisco. She told the grand jury that as she was walking to work one morning, heading down Fillmore Street surrounded by schoolkids, she began to hear very loud guttural sounds. The sounds were so loud, she could hear them from a block away.

As she approached the corner of Fillmore and Jackson, walking toward Pacific Avenue, she heard one little boy say, "Those dogs are rumbling again." The witness heard a yelp and then a high-pitched squeal, and as she turned the corner, the sounds of the dogs became so frightening that birds started flying in the sky, "just flying crazily."

"The dogs were reared up on their hind legs with their teeth showing," Wertman-Tallent testified. "They were on leashes, but they were lunging. They were lunging at me and the children that were walking with me, and they were still making the same type of sounds. The same guttural frightening, low-toned, not even growling, beyond-growling sounds.

"I was looking at their teeth and their eyes rolling around in their heads," she explained, "and their muscles lunging, with their really big heads, and it scared me. The dogs seemed bigger than me. The bigger dog, the chest was really wide. I'd never seen dogs like that before.

"The man had the leash with both hands pulling back, trying to pull the dog back—it looked like with all his strength—because the dog was lunging, and he was trying to control the dog," Wertman-Tallent testified. "The woman had both hands on the leash, pulling the dog back. The dogs were reared up on their hind legs and they were trying to get free.

"I have never been more scared in my life," the woman told jurors. "I thought the dogs were going to get free and bite my legs off. And I know about animals, so I didn't make eye contact; I just walked as fast as I could without running, and prayed they wouldn't get free. That's all I could do."

CHAPTER TWENTY-SIX

There were a lot of antics that accompanied Marjorie Knoller's many appearances in court on her own behalf. She said rude things at the pretrial hearings, once yelling over to Guilfoyle, calling her a liar in front of Judge Louie. In early hearings, Knoller appeared with a neck brace on, then the next time, the neck brace disappeared. On three or four occasions, she showed up being strolled in a wheelchair.

It was quite extraordinary, all the melodrama she could stir. She must have learned some of that from Noel, who had pulled similar stunts in Del Norte. For instance, he wore a black patch for weeks, moving it from the right eye to the left, amusing courtroom observers throughout the Garcia trial.

But none of those props seemed necessary the day Marjorie Knoller took the stand in front of the grand jury in San Francisco. She wasn't given time to confer with Noel, so she had no idea what Noel had or hadn't said. Still, Knoller was ready to put on her show, complete with tears and strange body language. She tried to exude confidence. In the end, Knoller had to be bodily removed from the courtroom. By the last of her testimony, she found herself having a panic attack, claiming she was unable to move.

"She was extremely rude, she was very angry, she was just really abrasive," Guilfoyle reflected. "Everything was a battle. You couldn't get her to say yes to anything. It was always a long, drawn-out answer, and everything was a fight."

Everyone later commented that Knoller's body language was off. She walked in wearing sunglasses, as if she was a movie star and couldn't be bothered with all the drama of the experience, as if she was above it all. But Jim Hammer would break her down. And he would break her down in stages.

Knoller knew that Robert had told grand jurors how intelligent the dogs were, offering the list of witnesses who adored Bane and Hera. She knew that Noel had walked in with poster boards to show the "happy dog" photos. In essence, she had heard his testimony at Hera's hearing and felt assured that she could convince the grand jury that anyone who claimed to have problems with Bane and Hera was confusing them with other brindled dogs.

That was the story that Robert and Marjorie believed; and they were sticking to it. But it didn't quite work that way. Noel and Knoller were mistaken about how integral Schneider's dog operation was to the criminal case. They never even imagined that prosecutors might file animal-cruelty charges, or that they might bring up bestiality. Knoller had no idea that her crazy fantasies and alleged deviant behavior would become public.

As it was, when Noel took the stand, he made matters worse by telling the grand jury that neither he nor his wife had any problems controlling the dogs. Noel testified under oath that his dogs *never* lunged at anyone, and that prior to Whipple's death his dogs *never* misbehaved toward any person in any way. Terence Hallinan would later comment, after witnessing Robert Noel's testimony: "The case was all over right then and there."

But Noel didn't understand the damage and self-sabotage his behavior caused. He repeatedly referred to himself and Knoller as the dogs' guardians, telling grand jurors that he and his wife had no legal responsibility regarding the actions of the animals. He wanted to be clear on that, that he and Knoller were not the legal owners—the dogs belonged to Paul John Schneider. But Hammer had already shown the grand jury proof that Knoller had registered Bane and Hera just weeks before Whipple's killing. The prosecutor just let Noel talk, without comment.

Then Hammer moved on to other things—things that would shake Noel up. For the first part of his testimony, Noel had been cocky. He was acting composed and relaxed. So Hammer decided he would have to get down and dirty. Hammer wouldn't allow Noel to place a shadow of a doubt in any juror's mind.

By then, the Whipple case had become very personal for Hammer. He had grown close with Sharon Smith, and Hammer wanted Noel and Knoller tried to the fullest extent of the law. Hammer was willing to go to the mat. With all that he knew, he wanted Knoller to be locked up for life, and he set things up perfectly, letting Noel tell one version of events, then letting Knoller hang herself in front of the grand jury immediately thereafter. Noel and Knoller were exactly where Hammer wanted them to be.

When Hammer asked about the existence of a "triad," Robert Noel's cool and calm mask started to crack. At the opening of his grand jury testimony, Noel had been very convincing, making the dogs seem like innocent victims who just *happened* to get wild one day, making himself look like a disinterested party.

Noel's act was really quite good, so the prosecutor decided to pull out all the ammunition, to wipe Noel's charming smile away. Hammer went on record with some of the letters that had been pulled from Noel and Knoller's hard drive, asking Noel to talk about his personal relationship with Paul Schneider, asking him to talk about the nature of his relationship with his dogs, and whether he had ever referred to his dogs as the guards of a medieval kingdom.

Noel had nothing to say about that. He just said nothing. When pressed by the prosecutor, Noel said that he didn't know what Hammer was talking about. Noel claimed that nothing like that ever existed.

HAMMER:	Okay, this is Grand Jury Exhibit 52, it's a letter dated on December 27 regarding Triad and various other matters. Do you recall that?
NOEL:	Yes, I recall it.
HAMMER:	And I showed you a passage that dealt with a sexual encounter, is that correct?

NOEL: Well, you showed me a paragraph. I don't know that I'll accept your characterization of a sexual encounter, but I remember the paragraph.

HAMMER: I'm trying not to be too specific, but as you put it yesterday, you and your wife were either involved or about to be involved sexually, and one of the dogs came up and got involved in some way? Is that correct?

NOEL: Yes. Basically came over and stuck its nose in to see what was going on, and we got up.

HAMMER: Again, if I have to, I'll mark the whole letter.

NOEL: Why don't you!

HAMMER: I'll decide that in a moment. Let me read from a letter dated Jaunary 11, 2001, a letter to Paul Schneider, regarding Triad and other matters. It begins, "Dear Paul." Then on page two:

> This morning's was an interesting walk. Getting used to the jailbreak approach the kids have. Break from the door like horses out of the starting gate. Stand next to the elevator shifting from one leg to another. The ferocity of the panting directly proportional to about how badly the mutt feels he or she has to go at that point. Elevator comes. Hopefully with no one in, otherwise they'll knock them down rushing in . . .

HAMMER: Now, let's just pause there for a moment. When you say, "Otherwise they will knock them down rushing in," what do you mean by that?

NOEL: That refers to them going out the door. They needed to go to the bathroom.

HAMMER: You had a fear they would knock someone down, didn't you?

NOEL:	No, I didn't.
HAMMER:	You just wrote that.
NOEL:	I just wrote it. It never happened and I would never let it happen.
HAMMER:	Okay, for the record, in this letter here, you write, "Sent the elevator back down so the dog walker can get the other mutts out of the lobby and home. As soon as the door opens at six, one of our newer female neighbors, a timorous little mousy blond, who weighs less than Hera, is met by the Dynamic Duo exiting, and almost has a coronary." Who is that?
NOEL:	That's Ms. Whipple.
HAMMER:	Are you concerned that she almost has a coronary at this time?
NOEL:	Not particularly, no.

Hammer would later reflect at how shocking Noel's response was. Here was Noel, speaking to a grand jury about a woman who was killed, and he was showing the utmost disrespect. Moreover, the prosecutor wondered what kind of lawyer Noel was, because any good attorney would have sidestepped the question about who the "little mousy blond" was. *That blond could have been anyone.* It could have been a visitor to the building. Noel didn't need to admit that he had been *mocking* Diane Whipple in his letter to Schneider just weeks before her demise.

Noel further admitted he didn't do anything to allay Diane Whipple's fear. He watched Diane get in the elevator, and that was all.

HAMMER:	Two weeks later, Diane died, correct?
NOEL:	As it turns out, yes.
HAMMER:	By your dogs?
NOEL:	As it turns out, yes.

Hammer was able to get Noel so riled up that the witness forgot to correct the prosecutor here. Noel had admitted that it was *both dogs,* thereby setting a very difficult stage for his wife, Marjorie, who throughout her grand jury testimony claimed Hera wasn't involved. Hera was still being held at the shelter, and Marjorie was obsessed with saving Hera's life. Clearly, Knoller didn't realize the serious nature of the charges that would be filed against her.

Throughout her slow-motion version of what happened that afternoon in the hallway on the sixth floor, Knoller would tell a very strange and ever changing tale.

Marjorie Knoller began her testimony with a sob story about Hera's bad heart and Bane's rotten treatment in L.A. As she told a convoluted version of how she and Robert came to be in possession of the dogs, she insisted that she and Noel were not the owners of the dogs. But Hammer got Knoller to admit that the two of them were indeed the keepers of the dogs. Then he pulled out a document, showing that in January 2001 Noel & Knoller prepared a document for Brenda Storey to sign in which Storey relinquished all rights to the eight Presa Canarios that were picked up in Hayfork.

Hammer wanted to make it known that the document he was presenting, Grand Jury Exhibit 41, in fact transferred the rights of ownership of the eight dogs to Noel and Knoller. But Knoller insisted that wasn't the case. She claimed that Paul Schneider and Dale Bretches had become the legal owners, even though their names did not appear on the document; the inmates were always the "beneficial owners" of the dogs.

HAMMER: Now, is it your testimony that Schneider and Bretches became the owners on January 2, 2001, or that they owned them all along?

KNOLLER: They have always been the beneficial owners of the dogs. Do you understand, are you familiar with real estate law?

Jim Hammer reminded Knoller that he was not the person on the stand. He was not there to answer questions, *she was.* Knoller still insisted on asking Hammer a question, but the prosecutor interrupted her, making sure that she understood she was talking to the grand jurors, not to him.

KNOLLER: I don't know if you are familiar with what is known as a purchase money mortgage. You have money and you want to purchase, let's say, a house or a car, but you don't want to do it for yourself, you want to do it for your friend. You're the one who's supplying the money so the title doesn't necessarily belong to you. Your friend will have the pink slip to the car, okay? And they will be, basically, the nominal owner of the car. But you supplied the money for the car, so *technically*, if anything comes up, you can also prove that you're the owner of the car, okay?

Knoller would go on and on, explaining her weird logic about car ownership and legal titles to vehicles, trying to get the grand jury to follow her train of thought. Hammer let her go off on her tangent talking about cars, then about property and mortgages, and then explaining about putting down payments on houses, telling the grand jury that if she supplied the down payment for a house, even if it was put in someone else's name, if the person defaulted on their mortgage, she could just keep the house because she would have been the one to supply the original funding. . . .

HAMMER: Ms. Knoller, I'm going to ask you some questions, okay? And my question is this: In January of 2001, you signed a document whereby Brenda Storey transferred all of her interests, again, to you as trustees, for undisclosed principals, correct?

KNOLLER: That's what the document stated. That's correct.

HAMMER: Did you ever state to anyone that you owned Bane or Hera?

KNOLLER: No.

263

HAMMER: I'm going to read you something and you tell me if it's true or not. This purports to narrate some of the events after the attack on Diane Whipple:

> One woman cop asked Marjorie how she had gotten so bloody and Marjorie told her that she had jumped on the woman to put herself in between Bane and the woman, to protect her. The cop got wide-eyed and asked, "Why did you do that? Weren't you afraid?" And Marjorie responds, "Why? It's my job. I owned him and it's up to me to protect her from him. I was just taking care of business."

Did you make those statements?

KNOLLER: I didn't say that I owned him, no.

HAMMER: So that's false?

KNOLLER: Yes, I said that he's my dog in terms of, I'm taking care of him; I have the responsibility to make sure he behaves himself. When you say something's mine, you don't necessarily mean that you're the owner. It's just like adopting somebody, or it's just like a foster kid. You're saying that "he's mine," or "she's mine," if that's the nature of the love relationship or whatever relationship you have with the dog or with the person.

Marjorie went on to describe her normal habits with Bane and Hera, admitting to jurors that she usually let Hera run loose in their hallway, and that Hera would "more often than not" be off lead when she was taking Hera out of the elevator at the sixth floor. Marjorie said it was her practice to allow Hera to walk through the lobby of the building off lead, explaining that if any neighbor appeared, she would just grab Hera by the harness for a minute. Marjorie called Hera an "off-lead dog," asserting that the dog was always under voice control. Hera was allowed to walk the streets of Pacific Heights without being on a leash.

Marjorie also talked about walking Bane, telling grand jurors that she walked Bane whenever Robert wasn't available—for instance, when Robert had been hospitalized. Marjorie insisted she never allowed Bane to walk off lead, but then she was forced to admit that on the day Robert came home from the hospital, the dogs got so excited to see him that they both went running free out into the sixth-floor hallway.

HAMMER:	Before January 26, 2001, did Hera ever do anything in your presence that gave you cause for concern that she might be a danger to another person or animal?
KNOLLER:	No.
HAMMER:	Never?
KNOLLER:	Never.
HAMMER:	Before January 26, 2001, did you ever see Bane bite another person?
KNOLLER:	No.
HAMMER:	Did you ever see, during that same period of time, Bane lunge at another person?
KNOLLER:	No.
HAMMER:	Did you ever see, during that period of time, Bane be aggressive to another person?
KNOLLER:	No.

When Hammer asked the same string of questions regarding Hera, he got the same string of answers. No. No. No. Marjorie said that Hera would perhaps bark at people, mentioning two occasions where someone was crowding her on the street and Hera "woofed" to keep the person from getting too close. There was also an occasion when Hera "woofed" at Mr. "Moran" in the hallway of their building.

Hammer asked Knoller if she might be referring to David Moser, who testified at the Animal Care and Control hearing, wondering if she might have had her neighbor's name wrong. Marjorie said she wasn't sure: "It was whoever that idiot was that hit his butt on the elevator door."

HAMMER:	So let's get right to it. Did your dog bite the idiot, Mr. Moran?
KNOLLER:	No. She did not.
HAMMER:	Were you watching well enough to see that happen?
KNOLLER:	I was between him and Hera, so yeah. I would say yes.
HAMMER:	So if he said that your dog bit him, he's lying?
KNOLLER:	Yes, he is.

Knoller decided to show the grand jury a diagram of the elevator and the hallway, explaining how narrow the space was, certain that jurors could see what little room there would have been for "Mr. Moran" to get around her and Noel. Hammer marked the diagram, pointing to the elevator gate, and asked Marjorie to go review the event, minute by minute. She explained that Noel was holding Hera by the harness, she marked the spot where David Moser slammed into her, demonstrating how Moser was backing out of the elevator door "when he hit himself."

Knoller didn't recall what Noel might have said to the neighbor, though she remembered that Robert was "pretty annoyed at the individual, for not being considerate enough to wait and see if there was anybody standing in the lobby."

Hammer marked Knoller's diagram of the Pacific Heights elevator and hallway as Grand Jury Exhibit 87. He also entered into the record a packet of color photocopies Knoller brought of her happy dogs, as well as Hera's blue and white chew toy, and then he closed the grand jury proceedings for the day.

Knoller would be called to resume her testimony the following Tuesday. And by then Hammer had Knoller by the short hairs.

CHAPTER TWENTY-SEVEN

AFFIDAVIT SF ASSISTANT BUREAU CHIEF, SAN FRANCISCO DISTRICT ATTORNEY'S OFFICE

My name is Carlos Sanchez, Star #7127, and I have been an Investigator for the San Francisco District Attorney's Office since May 1985. I have been involved in thousands of cases, both criminal and civil, and I am a graduate of the San Francisco Police Academy, the FBI National Academy. I possess Intermediate, Advanced, Supervisory, and Management Peace Officer's Standard of Training (POST) certificates.

I am currently working on the death of Diane Whipple who was attacked and killed by one, and possibly two dogs known as Bane and Hera as she entered her apartment located at _____ [*words redacted*].

We have learned in our investigation, through letters, dog license registration, and dog purchase contract, that the dogs were owned by Marjorie Knoller DOB 6-20-55, hereafter Knoller, and Robert Noel, DOB 6-22-41, hereafter Noel. It is our Belief that the subjects, Noel and Knoller, are a flight risk if indicted in the death of Diane Whipple. In the course of our investigation, we have learned that Noel and Knoller have connections with the Aryan Brotherhood prison gang, which is a notorious prison gang with affiliations in and out of prison. Noel and Knoller have adopted Paul Schneider, a leader of the Aryan Brotherhood gang as confirmed by CDC. Per Special Agent Devan Hawkes, Schneider has ties outside of prison, where he runs the business of the gang.

Currently, one witness in the Diane Whipple investigation is already in the Federal Witness Protection Program, due to the fact that she was stalked at her home, her vehicle was tampered with, and her daughter was also stalked and chased down by a white male in his car, after following her several times before. The white male suspect approached the daughter and told her he wanted to know where her loyalties lied. The daughter believed the man who followed her was affiliated with the Aryan Brotherhood gang, as described in Del Norte' County Sheriff's report (attached).

Per Lt. Wise of the CDC Gang Task Force, the Aryan Brotherhood has the capacity to place Noel and Knoller underground, and to assist them with funds. The gang is known to run drug labs and carry out illegal activity in and outside of prison. Noel and Knoller represent gang members at Pelican Bay State Prison, Susanville State Prison, and Deuel Vocational Institute. It should be noted that, per the Criminal Information System, Noel has purchased a semi-automatic Military-issued M-1 carbine rifle, purchased 1-5-2001. The weapon was not discovered during the execution of a search warrant on their home.

Noel and Knoller have not been staying at their home, according to reports from neighbors, the media, and surveillance teams. According to surveillance teams and CDC personnel, Noel and Knoller have been staying at different Motels throughout the State, renting vehicles, and have not demonstrated any other home or relatives in which they stay.

Per Associate Warden Teresa Schwartz of Pelican Bay State Prison, Noel and Knoller both indicated on their last visit on 3-16-01 to the Intake Correctional Officer that it was probably their last time visiting and they were "not coming back." Noel and Knoller were personally served with Grand Jury Subpoenas on 3-15-01, after their visit with inmate Schneider, whom they visited regularly in the past.

It should also be noted that during the course of our investigation, we have not been able to ascertain where Noel and Knoller maintain bank records. We have not discovered any checking or savings accounts. The money transactions that have occurred between Noel and Knoller and between inmate Schneider and Brenda Storey have all been through exchanges of money orders or cashier checks. Noel and Knoller have always sent money orders to inmate Schneider's CDC account, and have received payments by cashier's check from Brenda Storey, who was responsible for Schneider's trust account. These payments have been cashed, never by a bank account. Noel and Knoller have no personal checks or business checks, and their rent to their Pacific Ave apartment in San Francisco is paid by Noel's mother.

Carlos Sanchez's affidavit suggested that bail should be issued to assure Noel & Knoller's appearance, even as the grand jury proceedings had begun, given that Noel & Knoller had no ties to bank accounts, local family, or any stability in the State of California, given the history of intimidation of a key witness in the Whipple case, the connections to the Aryan Brotherhood, and Noel & Knoller's comments on not returning to see their adopted son.

Sanchez's affidavit, later released to the public, stated that within property taken from Scheider's cell, allowable by CDC regulations, were letters that indicated the dogs had bitten a blind woman and her guide dog on two separate occasions.

The affidavit would further report that correctional officials at Pelican Bay had discovered drawings of Noel and Knoller with fighting dogs in the foreground, in addition to daily planners filled with dog histories, birth dates, dog business monetary records, and advertisements of fighting dogs.

Among the more bizarre items found in Schneider and Bretches's cell, all of which had been seized by CDC personnel, were letters disguised as legal mail from Noel and Knoller to Schneider "regarding sexual activity between Noel, Knoller, and the dog, Bane."

The affidavit would confirm the existence of "numerous photos of Knoller posing nude with fighting dog drawings," as well as communications between Noel & Knoller to Schneider that described, "sexual activities between Knoller and Noel and included photos and drawings of dogs and fighting dogs and photos of the dog's penis."

CHAPTER TWENTY-EIGHT

When Marjorie Knoller retook the stand to give the grand jury her account of what happened to Diane Alexis Whipple, Hammer wanted to walk her through the entire day of January 26, 2001. Marjorie told the prosecutor she arose at her usual time, 6:00 A.M. She fixed herself and Robert some breakfast, and Robert left somewhere between 8:00 and 9:00 A.M. to attend a hearing for Russell Stanton in Martinez, over in the East Bay.

Nothing out of the ordinary happened for most of the day. Knoller left her apartment twice. The first time, at 11:00 A.M., was to take Bane quickly up to the roof so he could eliminate—Bane was on medication that gave him the runs—and she'd been up there with him for maybe fifteen minutes. The second outing occurred about 1:00 P.M., when she took Hera out for her usual walk. She had no idea when Robert might return home, he hadn't given her any estimate.

Then Hammer brought out a diagram of the sixth floor at 2398 Pacific Avenue. He entered it into evidence, asking Marjorie if it was a fair and accurate depiction of her place of residence.

As she looked at the diagram, Knoller started to get nervous. She was having trouble figuring out which apartment was 604 and she wanted a glass of water. Hammer was happy to accommodate Knoller. Once she was able to orient herself, Knoller pointed out that the stairwell to the roof was a bit off center in the diagram.

She told Hammer that when she had taken Bane up to the roof the first time that morning, she had him on a leash with a harness. Hammer wanted to know if Marjorie had Bane wear a muzzle, a question to which she responded: "Absolutely not!" But Hammer pursued the matter, wondering why, since she admitted that she owned a muzzle for Bane, she never bothered using it. Marjorie explained that she had little Velcro muzzles for both dogs; they were reserved for taking the Presas on the city's Muni buses.

HAMMER:	A muzzle prevents a dog from biting someone, is that correct?
KNOLLER:	I wouldn't say that necessarily. It does other things as well.
HAMMER:	Does it prevent a dog from biting someone?
KNOLLER:	I can't say that factually, no.
HAMMER:	Why can't you say that?
KNOLLER:	Because I've never had the experience, and muzzles are all . . . there are all different kinds of muzzles.

Marjorie just didn't want to respond to Hammer's questions. Throughout all of the various court proceedings, including Noel and Knoller's celebrated criminal trial, which was moved down to Los Angeles, the woman couldn't give a straight answer. She was always playing the part of a lawyer, and Noel was the same way. They never once acted human. They were robots who were going to use the letter of the law to save their skin.

The muzzle used on Bane for Muni buses wasn't available to be brought in for the grand jury to see. Marjorie couldn't remember where it was. As for Bane ever wearing the muzzle, Marjorie did not recall ever seeing it on him. When Hammer finally got her to admit that she had seen it on him, she claimed it was just once, when it was first bought and she tried it on him to see whether it would fit.

Knoller told the grand jury that she hadn't bought the muzzle with the idea of stopping Bane from biting anyone. She claimed that she didn't really care about buying a muzzle because she never had any fear that Bane would bite.

Hammer went back to the morning of January 26, asking if Knoller had Bane on a leash the entire time they were up on the roof. Knoller said she always had the leash on him, always. She said Bane was having loose-bowel problems, that she had bagged up what she could, had brought it downstairs to the trash chute, and on the diagram, she showed Hammer where the chute was.

Hammer put a mark on that particular place, asking Marjorie to confirm that he was being accurate. It was brilliant the way Hammer later used that diagram, having Knoller pinpoint every single thing that she claimed happened in the hallway, then afterward, going back to the diagram and showing her how her testimony seemed to contradict itself, that a lot of what had been marked and pinpointed didn't match up with other things she had said.

The moment Hammer saw Marjorie's agitation in reviewing the diagram, he moved back to "happy questions" about Hera, wondering where Marjorie had taken Hera for her walk that day, and how long they'd been gone. Knoller first mailed a letter, then walked Hera down to a middle school on Chestnut Street for some exercise. She said they'd been gone for over an hour and, as she recalled, Hera walked without a leash.

HAMMER: As you exited the elevator in the lobby, and walked through the lobby, best memory: On or off leash?

KNOLLER: Off leash. My general habit, when I took Hera out for a walk, she would be off leash until we got to a commercial area where there was a lot of traffic, then I would put her on lead. Then, when we would get to the park, I would take the leash off.

HAMMER: Again, focusing on January 26, 2001. Is that what you did that day?

KNOLLER:	Yeah.
HAMMER:	Why do you put the lead on her?
KNOLLER:	Traffic.
HAMMER:	Is that the only reason?
KNOLLER:	And people.

So, Knoller's consideration about people seemed to be an afterthought. She was more concerned about protecting Hera from traffic than anything else. She testified that before January 26, no one had ever told her they were uncomfortable around Hera. She insisted that she had never seen any person show fear of Hera, claiming she put the dog on a leash to protect her from foot traffic or anybody "coming up to her in a threatening manner."

Hammer asked whether it was possible that Hera might bite someone. After much argument, Knoller admitted that, of course, Hera was an animal, and any dog or cat could possibly bite someone.

HAMMER:	And as you put it, in your mind on January 26, it was your belief that if Hera felt threatened, she could bite someone, correct?
KNOLLER:	That's more likely than not with any animal. If an animal feels threatened, it's more likely than not they would probably bite someone, yes.
HAMMER:	I want to ask you about Hera. On January 26, did you feel it was a possibility that if Hera felt threatened, she would bite someone?
KNOLLER:	A possibility? Remote.

Hammer wondered, in the remote possibility that Hera bit someone, how badly could she hurt a person. Knoller claimed she didn't know. A puncture wound was a puncture wound, she claimed, and a bite from a Chihuahua could be serious. Hammer asked whether Knoller thought a Chihuahua could hurt someone as much as Hera could, and Knoller answered yes. Knoller thought a Chihuahua was just as dangerous as Hera.

Knoller went on to tell Hammer about the Presa Canario breed, explaining that from the literature she read, she had no indication that the breed could be dangerous. Hammer asked Knoller about her Internet research and how much knowledge she had amassed about the Presa Canario. Knoller talked about a few Web sites, one called Showstopper Kennels, and another from Spain. But when Hammer brought out a Grand Jury Exhibit that included a printout from a Web site entitled the "Perro de Presa Canario," asking Knoller if she recognized it, she claimed she did not.

Hammer mentioned that inmate Paul Schneider said he received that particular document from Knoller. But Knoller couldn't understand that. She admitted she sent Schneider Web site materials, but not that one in particular—not the one about how aggressive Presas could be. Knoller testified that she hadn't ever seen the exhibit before.

Then Hammer moved on to the afternoon in the hallway. Knoller recounted that she left the apartment at 3:45 P.M. because Bane needed to "eliminate quickly." She put him on lead and took him back up to the roof, since it would have taken too long for her to get Bane down the elevator and out onto the street, according to "the way Bane was expressing his need."

Marjorie was up on the roof with Bane for the second time, maybe for about fifteen minutes. Then she collected his waste product, came down the stairs with Bane on the lead, deposited his waste down the trash chute, and headed toward her apartment.

When Knoller turned around from the trash chute, she testified, she noticed Diane Whipple was down at the end of the hallway. Knoller wanted to rush through it, but Hammer slowed her down and had her retrace every step. Knoller then explained that Bane accompanied her into the trash room to deposit the debris. When she and Bane exited the trash room was the exact moment that she first saw Diane Whipple. Knoller was not glancing at Whipple from the side but was looking at her "full face." Then she put an X—marking the spot—on the diagram where Diane Whipple stood.

Knoller saw that Whipple had a bag of groceries on the floor behind her, that Whipple's front door was open at the time, and she thought she saw some light coming from Whipple's open doorway. She said Whipple was about a foot away from her threshold at the time, that she was looking over at them, not saying anything. According to Knoller's testimony,

Whipple stood watching as Marjorie reached for her keys in her pocket, putting her keys in the door.

Marjorie opened the door and started moving Bane in; she had gotten his shoulders into the apartment when Hera suddenly stuck her head out of the doorway and "woofed" toward Miss Whipple. Hammer thought it was odd that Hera would woof at someone standing all the way down at the end of the hall, the two apartments being yards apart, but Knoller insisted she knew Hera was woofing at Diane Whipple.

When Hera poked her head out, Knoller testified, Bane became "interested in what's down the hallway," perking his ears up and cocking his head in Whipple's direction. Bane wanted to go down the hall toward Whipple, and with Hera waiting in apartment 604, Bane began to pull Knoller in Whipple's direction.

Knoller testified that Bane picked up either a scent or something that he was interested in, and he started pulling her down the hall again, passing apartment 605 on their left, moving toward Miss Whipple. By then, Knoller claimed, Bane had managed to pull her down the hall, about six or eight feet. She told jurors that every time she pulled Bane back, he kept moving farther down the hall, admitting that Bane was winning at their "tug-of-war."

HAMMER:	So you're not able to control him, correct?
KNOLLER:	That's not accurate.
HAMMER:	So, you were able to stop him from going that six or eight feet?
KNOLLER:	It wasn't all at once. It was an incremental thing. I'm pulling on him. I'm battling him. He's not out of my control. He never was.
HAMMER:	But you were not able to stop him from going over to door 605, correct?
KNOLLER:	Correct.
HAMMER:	So he was more powerful than you were.
KNOLLER:	I don't agree with that statement, no.
HAMMER:	Well, he overpowered you and pulled you, didn't he?
KNOLLER:	That's not accurate.

Hammer finally got Knoller to admit that she had not willingly gone down the hallway with Bane. Marjorie claimed that before that date, she had never had a situation where Bane pulled her in a way that she was not able to completely stop him. Marjorie contended that before January 26, neither she nor her husband had ever lost control of Bane.

Knoller maintained that during this period of time, Hera stayed inside apartment 604 and both dogs were silent: that was Knoller's recollection. Knoller testified that although she had initially been able to pull Bane back, as they reached the elevator door, Bane pulled Knoller totally off her feet. She fell on her knees and was prone on the floor.

From then on, Bane was dragging her down the hall toward Whipple. Knoller was holding on to his lead with her left hand, but Bane was able to advance. Then Bane jumped up and put his paws on either side of Miss Whipple's head; and Marjorie, still on her knees, pulled him back down.

Knoller testified that when Bane jumped up, Miss Whipple said, "Your dog just jumped on me."

Then Hera suddenly appeared and started barking at all of them. Knoller recalled that while Hera was barking, Bane put his head into Miss Whipple's crotch, sniffing her. Knoller testified that everything started happening so quickly and that she didn't like what she was seeing.

HAMMER:	What did it look like Bane wanted to do?
KNOLLER:	I wasn't sure.
HAMMER:	Well, you started to say something.
KNOLLER:	He was sniffing, he was acting agitated. He was sniffing her and acting peculiar.
HAMMER:	Like what?
KNOLLER:	Agitated, as if there was something he was smelling that was getting him excited.
HAMMER:	How was he acting that was excited?
KNOLLER:	My terminology, like a bitch in heat. Like he was smelling something that was stimulating him.
HAMMER:	Like, sexually?
KNOLLER:	You know, maybe.

Hammer wanted her to describe the term "bitch in heat." He wanted to be sure he was hearing Knoller correctly, that Knoller was referring to Miss Whipple. Knoller went into an explanation about how male dogs act around female dogs in heat, explaining that male dogs can become agitated by the female scent.

HAMMER: When you use the term "bitch in heat" referring to Miss Whipple, is that how Bane was acting around Diane Whipple?

KNOLLER: Right. His demeanor, his behavior, there was something about her that was getting to him or stimulating him.

Marjorie thought it was odd, the way Bane was acting. She would later tell the media that perhaps Whipple was menstruating at the time of the attack, trying to explain it away somehow, but the autopsy report would prove otherwise. Knoller testified, without having been asked, that she herself was still menstruating once a month, that Bane had never reacted to *her* in that peculiar way, surmising, nonetheless, that menstruation could have been a physiological reason as to why Bane was so "interested" in Diane Whipple. Knoller had no other explanation as to why Miss Whipple was slaughtered.

According to the forensics, there was no way to prove or disprove that Whipple was attacked by both Presa Canarios. But most experts would agree, based on the canine "pack" mentality, that once the dogs entered the "red zone" of full-on attack, Hera was likely to have been involved to a great extent. Hera had parts of Diane's clothes in her feces, blue and white fibers, which Noel and Knoller later tried to claim were from Hera's chew toys. They had enlisted a string of "Save Hera" animal activists to plead Hera's case to the public. Activists would insist that it was unfair to condemn Hera just because she was tugging at Whipple's pants. But the fact still remained that Hera was at Whipple's feet, grabbing at Whipple's clothes, and, according to experts, grabbing at clothes would also entail grabbing at skin.

The mystery about Whipple's clothing having been ripped completely off her, that these two animals would strip Whipple down and leave bite marks in bizarre places, in places like Whipple's *inner thighs* gave grand jurors reason to pause. Many wondered whether *bestiality* could have played some kind of role. Those who saw photos of Whipple's naked body seemed to think that was a possibility. It wasn't out of the question that bestiality would have had an impact.

Experts and authorities speculated that the bites on Whipple's inner thighs had most probably come from Hera. This educated guess was based on numerous things: Bane was known to have focused primarily on Whipple's head and neck, leaving Hera to cover the lower body. And not only had Hera been pulling at Whipple's clothes, Hera had also been mentioned in a number of the sealed letters, letters from Noel to Schneider that suggested that Hera was being repeatedly "experimented" with.

There was further speculation among experts that the dogs had somehow become humanized; once Bane and Hera felt they could control humans, they were no longer afraid of humans, and the building they lived in had become "theirs." Authorities and experts agreed that in some strange way, Bane and Hera "possessed" the building. It wasn't Diane Whipple's scent they were after. Bane and Hera could have killed Sharon Smith, David Moser, or any one of the residents of 2398 Pacific Avenue. After much discussion between authorities and experts regarding what might have happened in the hallway with Diane Whipple, one thing everyone knew: in their dog minds, Bane and Hera controlled that building, and anyone in it was *fair game.*

As Knoller continued her testimony, her story becoming stranger and stranger, people wondered if Knoller actually believed her own lies; if she realized how many contradictions she made under oath. For instance, Knoller testified that when Hera had come down to the end of the hallway that afternoon, *she herself, Knoller*, had knocked Whipple down to the floor, trying to protect Whipple from Bane.

Knoller would tell jurors that Hera's barking wasn't aggressive toward Whipple, that it was "just a matter of dog barking." According to Knoller, Hera seemed like "she didn't know what was going on in the situation," and she was just giving "a warning bark." Knoller claimed it was "the same bark Hera would give if somebody was walking past our doorway or rang our apartment doorbell."

Hammer wanted to concentrate on what happened to Miss Whipple, asking questions about Diane's reactions and Diane's demeanor during the attack. With a straight face, Knoller told the grand jury that while being attacked, Whipple wasn't afraid, that she was perhaps "concerned." Knoller admitted she was worried about Miss Whipple's safety, which was why she pushed Whipple into her apartment. After Bane first sniffed Whipple, Knoller explained, she was able to pull Bane off Whipple. But when she pushed Whipple into her apartment, they both tripped and fell in the foyer, and Bane started sniffing again.

To her detriment, Knoller asserted that she was controlling Bane at that point, that she was still holding and restraining him with her left hand. Rather than let the grand jury hear that she couldn't control her animals, Knoller believed that by insisting she was always in control, she would be viewed as a responsible dog owner.

As Hammer began to drill Knoller about the issue of control, Knoller dug herself into a deeper grave, insisting that she *absolutely* had control of Bane, even though he had dragged her down that hallway.

HAMMER: If he's dragging you down the hallway and then knocking you to your knees and dragging you on your face, is that control, in your opinion?

KNOLLER: Yes.

HAMMER: That's *control*?

KNOLLER: Yes.

HAMMER: Did you ever once, as this dog was dragging you down the hall, say, "Miss Whipple, get in your apartment"?

KNOLLER: I had no idea who she was. She was a complete stranger to me.

HAMMER: Okay. This complete stranger, this woman, this poor woman, did you ever say to her, "Get inside your apartment, I can't keep my dog back"?

KNOLLER: No.

Knoller reiterated that Whipple stood watching as she and Bane battled down the hallway, the victim having no expression on her face. She further testified that Miss Whipple maintained a blank expression throughout the attack, that Whipple never acted scared, that she acted rather *casually*.

When the two women fell to the ground, when Bane followed them into Whipple's foyer, Knoller told Whipple, "Stay down." Knoller didn't want Whipple to move. She claimed she was still pulling Bane away with her left hand, and Whipple was lying facedown, not saying a word, not moving.

HAMMER: Are you worried about her safety at this point?

KNOLLER: No. I wanted her to stay where she was. I mean, I have a dog that's acting peculiar, and when I told her to *stay down*, and *don't move*, from what I've read in the literature, that's what you're supposed to do.

HAMMER: Were you worried about her safety at the point after you knocked her to the ground?

KNOLLER: I wouldn't say I was worried about her safety. I was concerned as to what was going on with my dog. I wanted her to stay down where she was, because he was acting rather peculiar.

As Knoller recounted her version of the events, Hammer continued to impeach her. It seemed every other word out of Knoller's mouth contradicted the other. One minute, she was claiming that Whipple came out into the hallway, crawling on her hands and knees. The next minute, Knoller would correct herself, saying that Whipple wasn't crawling— saying that she herself had to jump on top of Miss Whipple again, to insist that Whipple not move.

Knoller would testify that she believed Whipple was attempting to get her keys out of her door, that "Whipple was more or less on all fours," when Knoller needed to jump on Whipple a second time, actually getting on top of Whipple as the two of them were facing Esther Birkmaier's apartment. At that time, Knoller said, Bane was still not aggressive. Bane was just acting "interested" and "agitated."

HAMMER: Okay. My question is: Before you jumped on her the second time, why didn't you just bring Bane back into your apartment?

KNOLLER:	Because of the way he was behaving. He was really agitated.
HAMMER:	At that point were you able, in your mind, to bring Bane back into the apartment?
KNOLLER:	In all likelihood, yes.
HAMMER:	Why didn't you do that?
KNOLLER:	Because of the situation. Hera's out there in the hallway barking, and Bane's acting peculiar. I don't like the situation, so I wanted to make sure that Miss Whipple would be protected from whatever was going to transpire.

Knoller didn't think trying to drag Bane down the hallway was a good idea. Given the fact that he was acting so peculiar, given that Hera was barking, given the fact that Miss Whipple, for whatever reason, whether disorientation or what, came back out into the hallway, Knoller was "uncomfortable" with the idea of bringing Bane back to her apartment. Knoller felt the most logical thing would have been for Whipple to have gone back into her apartment, or to have just gone in and shut the door, rather than stay out in the hallway with her and Bane, and Hera barking there.

Knoller testified while they were in Whipple's foyer, before she jumped on Whipple the second time, Bane hadn't lunged at Whipple yet, that he had just pulled at her sweater and her torso with his teeth. He was just "grabbing into her."

With all the confidence in the world, Knoller continued to assert to the grand jury that Whipple had no reaction whatsoever to Bane's attack, that she wasn't crying or screaming for help.

HAMMER:	So we're clear. While Miss Whipple is down on all fours, after you've knocked her to the ground and Bane is, with his teeth, pulling at her clothes. That is not aggressive behavior, *is that correct*?
KNOLLER:	That's correct. Because what it is, in terms of a dog . . . If you've seen other dogs, dogs pull at your clothing. I mean, they do that.

HAMMER:	You call that maybe *playing* with her?
KNOLLER:	Yes.
HAMMER:	Like a chew toy?
KNOLLER:	Well, Bane wasn't into chew toys. Bane didn't know how to really play.

Knoller said she was always attempting to get Whipple to keep still, and had already pulled Bane off Whipple a couple of times. She kept "starting to bring Bane back" to apartment 604, but because Bane had six feet of slack on his lead, he kept going over toward Miss Whipple. Throughout the entire attack, Knoller testified, Hera never tried to get close to the scene. Hera was just barking in the background while the mauling was taking place.

Knoller would later tell the jury of twelve in the Los Angeles County courtroom where she was being tried for second-degree murder as well as involuntary manslaughter, that every time Diane Whipple would move, Bane would go for Whipple's clothing again. Knoller was a broken record regarding this point: Every time Whipple moved, Bane would bite again; as long as Whipple didn't move and as long as Knoller kept on top of Whipple, surrounding Whipple with her scent, Bane would not bite down. But, unfortunately, Miss Whipple just kept on moving, therefore Bane recommenced his attack.

HAMMER:	At this point, after you've jumped on her a couple times, she moves toward Esther's door, correct?
KNOLLER:	Yeah.
HAMMER:	At that point, has he bitten any flesh that you can see?
KNOLLER:	No.
HAMMER:	So, what happens next?
KNOLLER:	I tell her to *stay down* and *don't move* again. I don't know if it was this point in time or a little closer to Esther's when she got up and moved again toward Esther's doorway. I was getting up

on my knees. She was kind of flailing around, and struck me.

Knoller demonstrated the way Whipple hit her. For the record, for the grand jury to see clearly, the witness reenacted the way Whipple reached behind her head to strike at Knoller. Knoller pointed out the precise location of Whipple's body at the time this alleged strike occurred. Since Knoller had already testified that Whipple was on her stomach, lying facedown throughout the attack, it was very difficult for the grand jury to picture Whipple, with at least one very large dog attacking her, somehow reaching behind her head to strike Knoller in the eye.

Hammer helped make Knoller's explanation all the more implausible by having Knoller mark the diagram of the hallway. Marjorie placed an X where Whipple's head was, an X for the angle of Whipple's torso, and another X for the position of Whipple's feet.

HAMMER:	She hits you with one of her hands?
KNOLLER:	With her fist.
HAMMER:	Hard or soft?
KNOLLER:	I would say, very hard.
HAMMER:	What happened then?
KNOLLER:	That's when Bane bit her.
HAMMER:	Where did Bane bite her?
KNOLLER:	I believe he bit her on the neck.

Hammer wanted to know if Miss Whipple, up until the time Bane had bitten her on the neck, had ever said anything other than "Your dog jumped me." Whipple said nothing that Knoller could recall. Hammer wondered if she might recall Whipple screaming for help, but Knoller said it was *she* who screamed for help, not Whipple.

Knoller contended that Whipple never yelled at all, not even when Bane went for the jugular. Whipple was silent throughout the whole "confrontation."

However, the grand jury had already heard testimony from Esther Birkmaier, the neighbor who made the 911 calls. As a longtime resident of the building, Esther claimed she was familiar with Knoller's voice and Whipple's voice. It was Diane Whipple who was screaming, *"Help me!"* and *"Somebody help me!"*

According to Knoller, after Whipple punched her, Bane started going after *both* of them. She claimed that she herself had bite marks from Bane "all over" her upper arms and back. Marjorie showed the grand jury one mark on her wrist, and asserted that Bane had "shredded" her sweat suit.

Of course, the sweat suit she was wearing at the scene of the crime had been out of the "chain of custody" for many weeks, having remained in the possession of Noel and Knoller. Authorities would observe that Knoller's sweat suit looked to be slightly more ripped in certain places and appeared to have been tampered with. Not that it really mattered, because in either case, Knoller's sweat suit wasn't ripped much at all—it was pretty much fully intact. Diane Whipple's clothes were the ones torn into bits of unrecognizable shreds.

HAMMER: You tried to get Miss Whipple to the elevator, correct? And how did you do that?

KNOLLER: We were both moving toward the elevator, basically, on her stomach.

HAMMER: She crawled, or pulled herself, part of the way?

KNOLLER: Yeah.

HAMMER: Well, here's what I want to know: You saw her pull herself to the elevator, correct?

KNOLLER: Correct.

Hammer couldn't understand how Knoller managed to move Miss Whipple toward the elevator. Knoller said she used her body, that the two of them were moving together. But Hammer didn't see how Knoller could move someone that she was *lying on top of* toward the elevator.

KNOLLER: We are moving together.

HAMMER: But are you pulling her? Are you pushing her? Are you dragging her? How do you get her to move, for your part, toward the elevator?

KNOLLER: We're both *shimmying* on our stomachs.

As Hammer kept pounding away, Knoller's memory of the event began to fade. Knoller couldn't recall if Whipple was moving toward the elevator on her own. Knoller couldn't remember how the two of them made their way toward the elevator. Knoller couldn't remember where she last saw Diane Whipple. . . .

Hammer asked about Whipple's neck injuries, wondering if Knoller could remember those or if she could describe the way Bane went for Whipple's neck. But Knoller couldn't describe it. All Knoller could tell jurors was: "I put my fingers into Diane's neck to see if I could stop the bleeding."

Knoller said she kept her fingers on Whipple's neck for about a minute, but then as Bane calmed down, she left Miss Whipple in the hallway so she could get Bane secured in her apartment, calling to Hera to follow behind them. Hammer wondered why, if the dogs were calm and were "no problem" at that point, Knoller felt she had to lock Bane in the bathroom and lock Hera in the bedroom. But Knoller danced around the question.

Hammer also wanted to know why, after first trying to give Miss Whipple some type of first aid, Knoller went back out into the hallway, actually *stepping over Diane Whipple*, who was still alive, to go fetch her keys.

"Actually, I was kind of jogging back out in the hall to see where my keys were located," Marjorie testified. "I went all the way down the hallway and into Miss Whipple's apartment and found my keys on the floor."

CHAPTER TWENTY-NINE

Later that day, the grand jury indicted the two lawyers for the fatal dog mauling of Diane Alexis Whipple; both of them were charged with involuntary manslaughter and "vicious and dangerous dog" violations, and Knoller was also charged with second-degree murder. By then the attorneys had already high-tailed it out of town.

When the indictment was handed down, Noel and Knoller had already left the city. Moments after Knoller's emotional testimony concluded, they headed out of town in a rented Chevy Impala. Even as the grand jury began its deliberations, the couple was heading northwest, in the direction of Eureka, where they planned to stay with "friends."

The San Francisco police had Noel and Knoller under surveillance throughout the grand jury proceedings, and that afternoon they followed the Impala 170 miles north of the city. Noel was speeding, sometimes at more than 90 miles an hour. SFPD called for backup from the California Highway Patrol, ready to call in helicopters if necessary.

Because it had taken authorities almost nine weeks to find the couple criminally culpable, with nightly news reporting new tidbits every day, and Bay Area people following the dog mauling as though it was the O.J. Simpson case, no one wanted a freeway car chase. The police were not going to take any chances with Noel and Knoller, who they believed planned to cross the state line into Oregon where they could disappear, and possibly make their way to Canada.

At the time the lawyers were pulled over for speeding, the indictments had just come down, but the arrest warrants were not yet ready. So Robert Noel was cited for reckless driving and he and his wife were released by highway patrol.

Then, just a few hours later, with arrest warrants in hand, police took Noel and Knoller into custody. The pair were followed by plainclothes cops to a remote hideaway in the outskirts of Eureka.

At the time of the arrest, Marjorie Knoller complained of chest pains. She was treated at a local hospital, was examined, and then transported to the Tehema County Jail, in Red Bluff, joining Robert Noel behind bars.

As the two attorneys were being issued their jail garb, SFPD Inspector Becker was writing an affidavit asking for bail enhancement. Given their flight risk, a judge agreed, and bail was set at $1 million for Noel, and $2 million for Knoller. Neither had the money or wherewithal to afford it.

Within three days of their arrest, when Judge James Warren unsealed more boxes of evidence seized earlier in Noel and Knoller's apartment and Schneider and Bretches's cell, DAI search warrants and Noel and Knoller's personal correspondence were made public. As the news spread everywhere about the Aryan Brotherhood, the allegations of bestiality, and the twisted "love triangle" between the two attorneys and Schneider, Marjorie Knoller again complained of chest pains and was placed on "suicide watch." Meanwhile, reports of bestiality began hitting the airwaves and the print media worldwide:

From a newspaper in New Zealand:
    And then there's rumors surrounding the killer dog case presently before the courts in San Francisco. Pictures have allegedly been found featuring defendants Marjorie Knoller and Robert Noel . . . of Knoller posing nude with a fighting dog drawing and a letter from the couple that discusses sexual activity between Noel, Knoller, and the killer dog.
    Knoller and Noel are in good company. Tales of intimate human-animal contact can be found throughout ancient folklore

and mythology. After all, Zeus, in the form of a swan, had intercourse with Leda, the Queen of Sparta.

From a newspaper in India:
Attorneys for Noel and Knoller have denied any bestiality between the clients and their dogs. Both defendants maintain their innocence.

From a tabloid:
Judge James Warren also ruled that Robert Noel and Marjorie Knoller must face trial together . . . with bizarre accounts of bestiality, dog breeding rings, and . . .

From Gay News Items:
Knoller and Noel were caring for the dogs after the owner was sent . . . to jail, there is also considerable speculation the issue of bestiality will be raised.

From wwww.gaypeopleschronicle.com:
With speculation that Noel and Knoller had sex with one or both of their dogs, it was ruled that prosecution must present the evidence clearly and show how bestiality affected . . .

From www.ABCNEWS.com:
"Bestiality Charges were Barred at Dog Maul Trial. The dog mauling trial weighs blame on bestiality . . ."

From the LA Weekly:
"The State of California vs. Marjorie Knoller and Robert Noel is conversationally known to include Bay inmates and rumors of bestiality . . ."

From the Texas Triangle Online:
"Look at the contrast of the behavior of Knoller and Noel, whose comments and slovenly behavior cavalierly shrug off rumors of bestiality as if it were no big deal . . ."

The case even made the *Wall Street Journal.*

American newspapers ranging from the *New York Post* to the *Los Angeles Times*, from the New York *Daily News* to the *Sacramento Bee*, were discussing the bizarre allegations and rumors surrounding Noel and Knoller.

The media spotlight didn't diminish when the trial started in February 2002 in Los Angeles. The list of media covering the trial included the four broadcast networks, CBS, ABC, NBC, and FOX; cable networks CNN, MSNBC, Court TV, and CNBC; and prestigious newspapers, such as the *New York Times* and the *Washington Post;* then all the tabloid journalists were present, from shows like *Extra!* and *Inside Edition;* and that was just the national and international press.

San Francisco and Los Angeles reporters, who had been following the case all along, were finding themselves shut out of the media-packed courtroom. With hotshots swarming on the scene, many of them were forced to watch the trial from closed-circuit sets up on the twelfth floor of the Los Angeles County Courthouse. The floor, a "press only" area, became known to reporters as "camp canine." This was the same place the O.J. media held camp, and some of the same reporters and photographers would comment that they felt they were living that nightmare all over again.

As the media hype grew, talk of the dog mauling and the alleged bestiality would flood Internet chat rooms around the globe. People everywhere, from little known countries in far-away places to suburbs and villages across the United States, had something to say. People were mortified, they couldn't understand how Noel and Knoller would have allowed this horrible thing to happen. Large-dog owners around the world were being questioned about using muzzles; dog owners in general were being scrutinized unfairly. In places like Japan, England, and Australia, TV crews and documentary teams were being sent out to do interviews with the principals in the case, and Sharon Smith was already talking to people about selling her story to Hollywood.

Although the grand jury, after hearing from thirty-nine witnesses, thought second-degree murder was justified in the case of Marjorie Knoller, it would be a difficult charge for prosecutors to prove. It would require showing "implied malice" or a "reckless disregard" for Whipple's safety that led to her death. But Hallinan, Hammer, Guilfoyle, and the rest of the team were ready to do battle.

One of the nation's top trial consultants, Howard Varinsky, was brought on board to help with the trial strategy. Varinsky would help with the voir dire and jury selection. He also advised Hammer on his courtroom demeanor by insisting that the prosecutor put on a mock trial first. Varinsky was key in assuring the best possible juror selection and courtroom communication when it came to the real thing, down in Los Angeles.

Varinsky had worked on the high-profile trials of Dr. Jack Kevorkian, the New York subway vigilante Bernhard Goetz, and Oklahoma City bomber Timothy McVeigh. For Varinsky, to say the Whipple dog-mauling case was *hot* was an understatement. Varinsky knew that people wanted justice. Animal lovers around the world wanted to see those awful dog owners be put away for a very long time, and the jury expert was going to make sure that if it were humanly possible, Jim Hammer would get a murder conviction for Marjorie Knoller.

Howard Varinsky knew that jury selection would mean everything. He stressed to Hammer how hard it would be to have a jury understand that "implied malice" did not have to mean "intent to kill."

Meanwhile Noel and Knoller, who had been transferred to the San Francisco County Jail, were also strategizing. During the eleven months they awaited trial, they hired and fired several attorneys. They finally agreed that Noel, who was bankrupt, would be represented by Bruce Hotchkiss, a court-appointed counsel. Dave and Harriet Knoller gave their daughter money to hire little-known attorney Nedra Ruiz. A freedom fighter in the 1960s, Ruiz was one of the people who participated in marches and sit-ins; Ruiz liked to stir up controversy, and that suited Knoller's style entirely. During the Noel and Knoller case, Ruiz would throw out conspiracy theories in the court, and would make outrageous statements, trying to cast doubt on the prosecution.

Ruiz was over-the-top, to say the least, but she cared about her client. Bruce Hotchkiss, on the other hand, was a gentleman in the unfortunate position of having been drawn from a hat the day Robert Noel's case came up for appointment of counsel. Hotchkiss did his job, but he didn't seem too happy about it. Robert Noel made things especially difficult for the defense team by continually throwing in his two cents every other minute. Noel was trying to put the California Department of Corrections on trial, and threatening to take the stand, always fighting against his counsel's advice.

Their trial, which lasted from February into March 2002, included a dramatic opening statement by Nedra Ruiz. She got down on all fours to reenact her client's attempt to save Diane Whipple's life, at one point even hitting her hands on the jury box. Reporters were aghast when Nedra, looking like a barking dog, actually crawled on the floor of esteemed Judge James Warren's courtroom.

After that performance, for fifteen minutes, Nedra Ruiz became a media star. She told CNN, MSNBC, FOX, and every other news team who would listen that she had wanted to do something that would grab the jury's attention. And Nedra Ruiz had done just that, drawing ire from fellow attorneys, who had never seen anything like that kind of courtroom performance before. Ruiz also made inferences that Smith was involved in a conspiracy with DA Hammer, who happened to be gay, and made other references to Smith and her "gay posse" using the trial as a political forum, a way for lesbians to fight for gay rights.

Even after all the nasty press that she got, Nedra would maintain that her notorious reenactment was well intended. And it was true that Nedra believed wholeheartedly in Marjorie's depiction of herself as the "great hero" who risked her life and limb to save Diane Whipple.

But Ruiz was sometimes overzealous about defending Knoller. She went to great lengths to lay blame on others, including the victim as well as Sharon Smith. When Smith was on the stand, Ruiz asked whether she had ever considered the fact that *if she had made a complaint* to authorities regarding Whipple's first alleged bite from Bane, *Diane Whipple might still be alive*. There were gasps from the gallery, and the prosecution objected. Everyone was shocked by Nedra Ruiz's tactics. Later during a short break, Sharon Smith, surrounded by her circle of beautiful lesbian friends, would stand around in utter disbelief, furious at Ruiz, and hurt that Nedra could be so insensitive. Really, Nedra Ruiz had gone too far.

The trial was an emotional event on many levels. Sharon Smith hired a Los Angeles–based public relations man to handle her media requests; however, he was so calculating and pushy that he reduced more than one news anchor to tears. Smith's PR agent was so arrogant about the importance of himself and his client, even *Smith* couldn't take it, and she wound up firing the guy, letting her attorney, Michael Cardoza, handle "media control."

Penny Whipple-Kelly was attending the trial, Diane's mom, and she too had hired a PR agent to handle media requests. Perhaps because she was looking for paid interviews, Penny Whipple wasn't seen much on TV. She did appear once on *Geraldo, Live!*, but the media quickly realized that Penny Whipple-Kelly knew little to nothing about her daughter. Apparently, the two had been estranged for years. In any case, it seems the victim's closest relatives were too distraught to speak to the media without first having "clearance" from their handlers—such was life in a high-profile criminal case.

Animal activist Ana Aureoles had flown to L.A. to support Marjorie, along with her service dog, Henry Miller. Dave Knoller, a retired dentist on a fixed income; and his wife, Harriet, a former beauty queen (Miss Brooklyn 1935, as she let everyone know) came from Florida on their daughter's behalf. Perhaps not surprisingly, not one person from Robert Noel's family ever showed up in the courtroom. Not his mom, not his kids, not a soul . . .

Also attending daily was a tall blond, a stunning woman who looked like a Ralph Lauren model and seemed to keep herself in the background as much as possible. Many courtroom observers would remark that the impeccably dressed and mild-mannered blond looked like the spitting image of Diane Whipple.

In deference to Sharon Smith, reporters would not make comments about the woman, who they understood was Smith's new girlfriend, Michelle. But authorities were well aware that Sharon Smith, for all her tears and courtroom drama, had long before moved on with her life, having bought a house with her new girlfriend in an affluent section of Marin County, in Tiburon, where Smith lived with "happy pictures" covering the mantel of herself and her gorgeous new wife.

No one who visited the Tiburon home ever bothered to notice whether Diane Alexis Whipple's *green marble urn* was present . . . or if anyone *had noticed*, they certainly made no mention of it in the press.

Before it was all over, the trial would become the typical media circus, surpassed only by the O.J. case, with appearances by Marcia Clark, among other legal pundits, many of whom would make daily comments about the trial testimony and second-guess the controversial charges, speaking to reporters just outside the L.A. County Courthouse on makeshift sets—under tents, in parking lots, and on courthouse steps.

If she was pronounced guilty of second-degree murder, Marjorie Knoller would be looking at fifteen years to life. Robert Noel, however, was facing quite a different punishment. If found guilty of involuntary manslaughter, Noel could only be sentenced to about four years' prison time maximum. In the State of California, with the "good time" rule, and counting the year served while he was waiting for his trial, Robert Noel would be eligible for parole just one year after sentencing.

It was outrageous to Sharon Smith and other victims of Pacific Heights that Robert Noel would get off so easily. The man was a selfish, inconsiderate monster. He knew Bane was sick that day, he knew Marjorie couldn't control Bane, that she surely couldn't handle both dogs, yet he left his wife alone with them anyway. The whole city despised Noel, perhaps even more than they despised Knoller. Unlike his wife, Noel was going to walk away from the crime, without having to pay much at all for his wrongdoings, for the death of the innocent and beautiful Diane Alexis Whipple.

To add more fuel to the fire, legal pundits would tell media that prison could be more like a "rest camp" for Noel. He could use public money to move forward with his court cases, get three square meals a day, meet and greet fellow inmates, and continue his efforts to thwart the California Department of Corrections, even if disbarred, acting as a jailhouse lawyer.

As for Paul John Schneider, early on Mayor Willie Brown determined that if held in San Francisco, "Cornfed" would not be allowed to testify in any of the criminal proceedings regarding Noel and Knoller. Mayor Brown didn't want to waste any more taxpayer dollars on the high security that would have been necessary. Brown would tell the press that not only would Schneider's transport involve helicopter escorts, it would also entail closing down the Golden Gate Bridge. But as it happened, the trial had been moved to L.A.

Although Schneider continually tried to get involved in the case in some way, writing to the judge to insist that he and his pal Dale Bretches be allowed to testify at the sentencing proceedings in San Francisco as well as the trial in Los Angeles, Schneider's pleas were of no use. With most of the Aryan Brotherhood information being deemed too prejudicial by Judge Warren, Schneider had nothing to offer.

Of course Schneider wouldn't stop there. He needed to make use of all the publicity, he wanted to make some kind of deal, so he tried another tack. Schneider began chirping to CDC authorities about some of his AB associates, eventually getting himself a transfer to a federal facility in Minnesota, the infamous super-max prison that housed the likes of mob boss John Gotti. Schneider's willingness to talk was based on a RICO indictment he still faced; the U.S. government had accused Schneider, Brenda Moore, and six other inmates of attempted murder in aid of racketeering activity.

The day of the Noel and Knoller opening statements, Jim Hammer, with large evidence boards under his arm, flanked by Kimberly Guilfoyle-Newsom and Terence "Kayo" Hallinan, marched past the paparazzi into Division 53, the courtroom where Judge James Warren would preside in Los Angeles.

Before the trial, Guilfoyle's life had changed quite a bit. She had married Gavin Newsom, the young, handsome San Francisco Supervisor and partner to Billy Getty, and her attentions had been drawn elsewhere. Guilfoyle had been through so much drama in preparing for her wedding that her work in preparing for the trial seemed to pale by comparison.

But Guilfoyle had other issues going on. The media was hounding her, reporting every little thing they could—from the fact that she wore Armani designer suits to the minutiae about her black-tie wedding. However, there was actually good reason to focus a spotlight on Guilfoyle, because in the fall of 2000, as the bride was being fitted for her Vera Wang wedding gown, Paul John Schneider was rumored to have sent a death threat. In the midst of Guilfoyle's extravagant preparations, she therefore found herself under guard and felt compelled to wear a bulletproof vest to her own wedding rehearsal dinner.

Even though, according to CDC investigators, the information about Schneider's threat "was a bit thin," everyone was still taking it seriously. Special Agent Devan Hawkes, along with Dave Parenti of the District Attorney's office, immediately flew up to the prison in Seattle, where the threat had come from, only to find it boiled down to a comment made by an inmate who apparently didn't even know Schneider. The inmate, having seen the gorgeous Guilfoyle on TV, just wanted to be part of the mix.

Once the threat against Kimberly Guilfoyle was deemed invalid, Paul Schneider would tell media that he didn't care a thing about Guilfoyle, that *Hammer* would have been the logical person to threaten. He claimed that he would never order a hit on a woman anyway, it being against the Aryan Brotherhood code.

Nonetheless, there was all that drama that had happened in the months between the grand jury indictments and the actual trial. In the weeks leading up to her wedding in December of 2001, since law enforcement would no longer use taxpayers' money for Guilfoyle's round-the-clock protection, Kimberly was given protection by the Gettys. Even though the Gettys were aware that the threat was deemed baseless, with Guilfoyle's upcoming marriage to Newsom and Guilfoyle fast becoming a member of high society, the Gettys weren't about to take chances.

Ann and Gordon Getty threw the Guilfoyle-Newsom wedding at their elegant, showplace home. The event cost the Gettys about $250,000, as reported in economic disclosure forms, and everyone who was anyone in San Francisco was there—including Mayor Brown, former Governor Jerry Brown, Danielle Steele, who gave the couple $1,500 worth of plates and chargers, and Senator Barbara Boxer, who gave a beautiful "congressional plate." However, there was one person who was distinctly missing from the event—Billy Getty, son of Ann and Gordon, who had once been romantically involved with Kimberly.

Gavin Newsom, a co-owner with the Getty family of the Plump Jack Management Group, owned an interest in the Plump Jack Winery, the Plump Jack Squaw Valley Inn off Lake Tahoe, the top-notch Plump Jack Restaurant in Cow Hollow, the popular Balboa Café, and just across the street, a brand-new nightclub called Matrix, which was *the* hot spot for visiting celebrities and dignitaries in San Francisco. Guilfoyle and Newsom would hold fund-raisers at Matrix and Guilfoyle earned the crown of Queen of the Mardi Gras Ball for all the money she raised for one of the Little Jim Club's favorite charities.

Gavin Newsom had bought a five-bedroom house in Pacific Heights, where he and Guilfoyle planned to start their family. A few months after the dog-mauling trial ended, Guilfoyle-Newsom took a leave of absence from the DA's office. Gavin Newsom, meantime, would announce his plans to run for Mayor of San Francisco. Newsom had the backers; he had the public sentiment with him. People loved to love Gavin, and they loved to love Kimberly. Gavin and Kimberly were the Camelot couple, both genetically perfect for the role of mayor and first lady of San Francisco. Once married, the two seemed to climb to the top of the social heap. Because Newsom's famed dad was the lawyer to Gordon Getty, even Bobby Kennedy Jr. sent them words of congratulation. Together, Newsom and Guilfoyle had it made.

But down in Los Angeles, with the high-profile trial getting under way, Kimberly Guilfoyle would have to take a backseat. This had become Jim Hammer's show, and the California press would later dub him "Hollywood Hammer" because of all the national interviews he gave. Some people at the DA's office seemed a bit jealous of the attention Hammer was getting. But in fairness, the man had done his preparation, he had done the gritty hard work. *Hammer* was the one who sat and sifted through the boxes of revolting Pelican Bay evidence. Hammer was the one who worked closely, day and night, with Hallinan and Varinsky. Hammer was the one who ultimately coached the special graphics team about the charts and graphs that were needed to show prior incidents and warnings. Jim Hammer had put in the time, he had put his heart and soul into the case; he was the lead prosecutor, and like it or not, Jim Hammer handled the majority of the witnesses. Some people had underestimated Hammer. Sharon Smith's lawyer, Cardoza, had picked on him, thinking he wasn't up to the task. But after watching DA Hammer rip into Marjorie Knoller, tearing her to shreds under cross-examination, Cardoza went from calling him Velvet Hammer to *Sledge Hammer*.

A Muni driver's son who once studied to become a Jesuit priest, Hammer had a knack for detail and a mind that moved like the speed of light. Nothing could get by him, and he worked the jury like a pro. Hammer had won murder convictions before, but this case would require special instructions, and so the prosecutor, building his case on multiple prior incidents that led up to the fatal attack, put thirty people on the stand to testify about how Bane and Hera growled and lunged, *scaring everyone to death.*

As they continued to hear witness after witness, the jury's mouths hung open. People were shocked, for instance, to hear that one of the dogs almost bit the face of six-year-old Timo O'Connell.

On cross-examination, Nedra Ruiz would lunge at each of Hammer's witnesses, asking why they didn't bother reporting any incidents to Animal Care and Control. With a voice that mimicked the Wicked Witch from *The Wizard of Oz*, Ruiz grilled every victim, trying to make their stories sound implausible, overblown, or inaccurate. Nedra Ruiz was putting up a fight to save Marjorie Knoller. Ruiz sure put up her fists. But witnesses would testify that Noel and Knoller were intimidating, that they hadn't complained because they wanted to avoid confrontations with them.

"Why did this happen to me?" Marjorie Knoller would ask her parents at one point during the trial. "I lost everything in just a few moments."

When Jim Hammer showed the jury members the photos of Diane Whipple—blowups of her body scratched and clawed and a close-up of the back of her neck with a gaping open wound—many people in the courtroom could not bear it. Sharon Smith got up in tears and ran from her seat.

After the prosecution rested, the defense put a number of "good dog" witnesses on the stand: mostly service people who worked in the neighborhood, the dry cleaners, the waiters at local pubs, the owners of the Mayflower Market. Then, not a peep could be heard in the gallery when Marjorie F. Knoller took the stand. Marjorie seemed to be doing well at first as she explained her heroic attempt to save Diane Whipple, reenacting the dramatic event to the best of her recollection.

"Let me tell you," Robert Noel later reflected, "one of the problems with the trial was that Marjorie was so traumatized, her memory was spotty. She comes and goes."

RUIZ: Marjorie, how are you feeling today?

KNOLLER: I am feeling awful. It's just thinking about the horrible way Miss Whipple died in that hallway—it causes me great sorrow. And I am in pain for everybody who knew her, and my heart goes out to her family and friends. And she died so horribly. I couldn't—I couldn't stop him from doing what he was doing.

Knoller, with tears welling up, had directed her initial comments to Sharon Smith, who didn't show any reaction. Some people thought Knoller's opening remark was staged; others, including Judge James Warren, thought it was the only truthful comment Marjorie Knoller uttered throughout her entire testimony.

Led by Nedra Ruiz through the events of the fatal mauling, Knoller told the jury about how she banged on the Puteks' door with her leg, and how she lay on top of Whipple to protect her. She delineated all the bites she'd gotten from Bane in the greatest of detail. There was discussion about the Dog O' War kennel operation, about Paul Schneider stabbing the attorney Couzins, about the attack on Bane at Crissy Field beach when Noel's finger was severed—Knoller acknowledged that she had been aware of those particulars, insisting that she'd just "wound up" with Bane and Hera. But she assured the jury that she had *no* intention of keeping the two Presas.

Marjorie Knoller talked about her youth, her days at Brooklyn College, her move to California, her becoming a paralegal and then a lawyer. She explained that when she had been a lifeguard back in Brooklyn, she learned CPR and emergency medical response. This was an important issue for Ruiz to cover, because on the night of the mauling, Knoller told police that she was an EMT. When the press got hold of that, they had a field day, wondering why Knoller never bothered to administer any kind of first aid to Diane Whipple. But, as it turned out, Knoller wasn't an EMT—she was only a lifeguard. She contradicted herself even on this key point, first admitting that she was not a licensed EMT, then insisting that she was.

"Basically, I am an EMT," Knoller told the jury, "because of being a lifeguard."

When it came to dog ownership, Knoller had to admit that before she got Bane and Hera, she had never owned a dog herself. She had "shared" dogs with her cousins and had spent a lot of time with big dogs. Knoller testified that she had experience with large animals because she was an avid horseback rider, having begun that sport at age five. However, in terms of keeping a pet, she and Noel once owned a parakeet and she herself had goldfish, tropical fish, and "various types of birds." Knoller told the court that she learned about the Presa Canario breed through a Web site called Showstopper Kennels, that she understood the Presa to be quiet, gentle, loyal, and "somewhat wary of strangers."

Knoller would admit to jurors that she *knew* her dogs had a fighting history but explained that "all dogs who have fighting histories, are not necessarily aggressive," insisting "it just depends on your socialization and personality of the dog."

When Hammer was ready to cross-examine Marjorie Knoller, it was suddenly, as many dubbed it, *"Hammer time."*

With Hammer's eyes piercing at her, Knoller's demeanor utterly changed. Her voice stiffened, and her left eye began to shutter. Throughout her cross-examination, Knoller kept staring into the distance, avoiding Hammer's eye. Without realizing it, Knoller was giving the jury the same strange type of facial expressions that she had shown on *Good Morning America.*

During his pronouncement of Knoller's sentence, Judge James Warren would comment that he had studied the *GMA* tape. The judge said that he watched the tape five times and *never once* did Marjorie Knoller look straight into the camera. On the day of her sentencing, Judge Warren made it clear that he did not believe there was much truth at all—in anything Knoller described—not to the cameras, and not in his court.

And it was true that Marjorie Knoller, when she had appeared on *Good Morning America*, was always looking away, her one eye fluttering, often with a kind of shit-eating grin on her face. But now, in front of

DA Hammer, Judge James Warren, and a jury of twelve, Knoller's grin was gone. Knoller was testifying on her own behalf; she was fighting for her life. At one time, she was the would-be socialite. She saw herself as a maven; she saw herself as a high-class lady. The last thing Marjorie Knoller wanted was to be sent to some horrible, filthy, stinking dirty prison. The idea that she might be sentenced to life without parole was unthinkable.

Knoller was on the stand for two consecutive days, and, just as she had during the grand jury proceedings, she would continually insist that her dogs weren't dangerous. Acting the part of the consummate lawyer, Knoller would tell the prosecutor that "there was no intent" in her not placing a muzzle on Bane the day that Diane Whipple was killed.

HAMMER: You intentionally did not put [a muzzle] on Bane, is that correct?

KNOLLER: No, that's not correct.

HAMMER: You accidentally didn't put it on him?

KNOLLER: I had no reason to put it on him.

HAMMER: You didn't put it on Bane on purpose. You chose not to put it on Bane, is that correct?

KNOLLER: There was no reason to put it on Bane.

HAMMER: I didn't ask you about a reason. Did you choose not to put it on Bane?

KNOLLER: Yes, I chose not to.

THE VOICE OF JIM HAMMER

"The scariest part of the trial, by far, was when Marjorie testified. Because here I am, this big, tall, young white guy, going to attack this middle-aged woman. It was completely high-risk. You get one person—one woman on the jury—angry at me for thinking I'm too tough, and it's over.

"But I knew I had to do it, even if it was high-risk. I just had to walk the line between being aggressive and not being mean. You know, you have to build it up. You have to build credibility with the jury. You can't come out screaming right away. So my first question to her was the hot

button issue. I asked, 'If you care about Diane Whipple so much, and felt sorry for her friends, why didn't you ever call Sharon Smith to say you're sorry?' That was the $64,000 question.

"Again, for a tall, young guy to attack a crying woman is very risky. But I had to call her on it. And it could have backfired, big time. But I watched the jurors. They turned away from her. They wouldn't look at her. And then she would cry, and she looked at the jurors with this hang-dog face. She tried to get eye contact, but everyone looked away.

"That was the whole case right there. When she hit the stand. Because in every criminal case, you're wondering, Is the jury going to have sympathy for the defendant? Are they going to want to cut her a break? And who's going to vote on murder for the woman and not the man? Once we'd gotten the murder charge, that was my biggest fear: Are they going to compromise?

"One of the last questions I had, since an important element of murder is an intentional act, the natural consequences of which are dangerous to a human life, you have to show an intentional act. So I asked, 'Let's be clear, you intentionally took the dog out into the hallway that day, didn't you?' And she kept saying there was no intent. So I blew it up for the jury, and I asked them to look at what kind of woman she was. Because everyone knew that intent was part of the jury instructions, and here she was, just being a lawyer. It was wild, just absolutely wild.

"At the trial, there were some new things she said. All of a sudden she remembers she was kicking somebody's door for help. She was kicking for help, trying to get someone to call 911. She made that up at trial. Another thing she made up was going back into Diane's apartment to look for her keys. That's not true. The cops didn't let her into that apartment. And she wasn't there when they got there.

"At the grand jury, when Marjorie said something about a bitch in heat, it never occurred to me, this whole sexual thing. It was shocking when she said it, including nerves in the crotch area. She said the dog acted excited, and I asked what she meant. And when she said 'like a bitch in heat,' that so offended me.

"And when she said that about the bitch in heat, I talked to the experts, and it became clear that a lot of the sexual stuff was really the projection of the defendant on the dog. Our expert, Randall Lockwood,

said, 'Dogs sniff, dogs bite, dogs eat, they scratch, they nibble. But dogs don't have romantic feelings for people. They don't have sexual thoughts.' That was the projection of Noel and Knoller. What became really clear was their projection. They were sexualizing everything.

"Lockwood took the stand on rebuttal and pointed out that 'Ten licks on the face and one bite to the child do not equal out. That bite erases all the good dog behavior.' I thought that was one of the great observations. I put that into my closing argument, that forty "good dog" witnesses don't erase a single bite.

"The heart of this case was the history, what came before January 26, and if it was going to be a homicide, the only way to make it such was to really, in detail, uncover every piece of evidence about their knowledge. So prior bites, and also writings and things like that, that's where we got the pay dirt.

"There's a letter that came into evidence, where Noel talks to Paul about the adoption. He goes into considerable detail about the adoption being one form of legal action that could bind them together as a family unit. Now there's another paragraph that didn't go into evidence at trial, but it says, 'I wanted to thank you for the thought expressed about your feelings, about how comfortable you would feel about Marjorie and I inhabiting your body.'

"I was ready to put on Devan Hawkes and the gang guys. I've worked on gang stuff, and I was ready to do it all, to put on all the gang stuff. I wanted the jury to look at these boxes of Pelican Bay stuff, and ask if they could really believe Noel and Knoller were rescuing these dogs. But at the last minute, the judge threw out two boxes of evidence. I was furious, because we were counting on using it. Out of eleven boxes from Pelican Bay, we were down to three boxes, and then it went down to forty pages. It was drawings of fierce dogs and warrior women, you know, salacious stuff. All this evidence on fighting dogs, I mean, it was powerful evidence.

"There were two witnesses we called the laughing-dog witnesses, where Marjorie supposedly laughs after the dogs do something bad. She laughs at people for showing fear, and Terence and Kim wanted to keep them in. But my strategy was: don't bore your jury; don't get distracted. The bigger issue was control, not laughing. So those two witnesses were *nixed. I had people almost getting bitten in the butt, and laughing is interesting, but it had nothing to do with control.*

"We got a fair trial. You'll never get a fairer trial. So when the jury came in with murder, I was in awe. The buildup in the back of my mind until the day of the verdict, seeing Sharon have a sense of relief, was great. But I had talked to Sharon at lunch and I told her to find her own peace, to find victory out of justice, because if the jury came back with manslaughter, then it was manslaughter.

"Robert Noel is a maniac. I don't know what the root of that is, and I mean this clinically, he's a narcissist. I don't know if he's bipolar or not. I think he's an egomaniac. He's narcissistic. I don't know what's behind that. I mean, he's the kind of person who's so taken with himself.

"The height of their egomania was having all the TV cameras follow them around. When Marjorie was crying down the hallway, outside the grand jury, it was like, 'Wow! I am the center of the world. Look! They're following every word I speak.' And there was Noel with his threats, just spinning out of control.

"One of the reflections I have about the case is, if Diane Whipple hadn't been ripped to death in her hallway, no one in the world—except for a few close friends—would have known she had this loving relationship with Sharon Smith for seven years. And there's still so many grotesque and unfair stereotypes about what it is to be gay or lesbian, you know? So out of this tragedy, with the verdict, one justice came, because people look at a picture of Diane with Sharon Smith, and they think, she looks like our neighbor, or our daughter. They think, these are our sisters. They look just like us."

When the jury came back from their deliberations to read their verdict, people were holding their breath. Defense attorneys maintained that their clients were not warned about the dangers of their dogs because nobody complained to the police. When the prosecution had put expert witness Dr. Randall Lockwood on the stand, he testified that the markings on Marjorie Knoller's sweat suit and the minimal injuries to her hand indicated that she was at some distance throughout the attack.

"At one point," Lockwood testified, "she might have been close enough to get some blood on her." But the animal expert, the Vice President of the Humane Society of the United States, maintained that in all likelihood, Knoller had never gotten too near. Lockwood testified that Knoller certainly had not gotten *in between* the dogs and Diane Whipple.

Jim Hammer reminded the jury to look at the book *Manstopper!* and he read a passage in the introduction: "a canine outsider, either in perception or location, or one who lives on a chain, should not be protection trained. Guard trained, a dog trapped in such indifferent circumstances, is to construct a time bomb that can explode in someone's face."

Hammer asked the ladies and gentlemen of the jury to consider the fact that Noel's own finger had been bitten off as evidence that the man knew his dogs were dangerous. He also asked the jury to think about the dogs' teeth, both sets of which Hammer had made casts of, when considering whether Knoller would know, by the sheer size of the teeth and jaws alone, that these aggressive dogs could inflict serious damage on someone.

Hammer finished by reading from Noel and Knoller's grand jury testimony, reminding the panel of twelve that both defendants had read that these dogs were "meaner than pit bulls, tougher than pit bulls, that Presa Canarios were used to hunt down pit bulls."

"By January 26, 2001, it was not whether somebody was going to be mauled or killed by one of these dogs," Hammer told jurors in his close. "The only question on January 26 was *when* and *who* and *where*."

Hammer wanted justice. He wanted the jury to come back with second-degree murder on Knoller and involuntary manslaughter on Noel. And to everyone's astonishment, that's just what the Los Angeles jury did. To most of the onlookers in the courtroom, the verdicts came back as a shock. Of the prosecutors, only Terence Hallinan had faith that the jurors would come through. Everyone else had talked themselves out of the murder verdict. People did not want to be let down.

As the verdict was being read, Marjorie Knoller being found guilty of murder in the second degree, Knoller gasped, her face looking like she was sorry for herself. She sighed, then she huffed, her eyes opened wide, and then she started to cry. Knoller looked over at her parents in the gallery, and mouthed the words "help me." Nedra Ruiz, who had repeatedly kicked the jury box and had called Bane "a berserk beast," remained composed as she tried to comfort Marjorie behind the defense table.

Robert Noel sat very quietly; never having taken the stand, he was letting his wife take the fall. When he was pronounced guilty of involuntary manslaughter, Noel never said a word and just looked straight ahead as the verdict was announced.

As for Sharon Smith, the victory would be bittersweet. When Hammer looked over, he saw that Smith had her head in her hands and was crying. The verdict was the first time in California history that a dog owner was convicted of murder in a dog-mauling case. Both defendants were also found guilty of involuntary manslaughter and of keeping violent and dangerous dogs. Noel, the jury felt, was perhaps even more culpable than Knoller, but since he was only charged with manslaughter, they came back with the harshest possible verdict they could.

"There's no real joy in this, but certainly some real justice was done for Diane today," Smith later told a throng of reporters. "I was glad to see that the jury didn't buy some of the smoke screens that were put in front of them."

The spotlight had turned Smith into an activist for gay rights. Spending more time in the public eye than she ever thought she would, Smith helped gain passage of state legislation allowing same-sex partners to sue for wrongful death. She had become a goddess in the eyes of gay women in San Francisco.

Weeks later, Robert Noel was sentenced to serve four years for involuntary manslaughter and was shipped off to the Deuel Vocational Institute. Eventually, Noel would be transferred out of the state; California corrections officials were tired of him, and didn't want him stirring up any more trouble from behind prison walls. Noel remained in isolation for a few months, where he would argue that the California Department of Corrections was still engaging in a plot against him. When he was given word that Paul Schneider was moved to a federal facility for medical treatment and might have to have his leg amputated, Noel had no comment. He didn't believe anything prison officials said.

Los Angeles jurors would later tell the media that they were repulsed when they were shown the taped interview of the defendants on *Good Morning America* shortly after the attack. They mentioned that, in sharp contrast to her tearful testimony at the trial, Marjorie Knoller spoke calmly about the mauling to the TV camera.

The trial had cost taxpayers about one million dollars, and the impact the verdicts would have on dog owners in San Francisco would be huge. In a continuing controversy, people were insisting that large dogs be muzzled and that dogs should not be allowed off leash, even at dog runs.

When the day came for the sentencing of Marjorie Knoller, June 17, 2002, a courtroom full of people awaited the arrival of Judge James Warren. Reporters clamored in the Hall of Justice, wondering if the judge would sentence her to *life*. People were speculating, news teams were chatting it up, the victims were prepared to make their statements before the judge, asking for the greatest penalty to be given.

As Judge Warren sat down in the courtroom with a very severe look on his face, he made a few references to Noel and Knoller being "the most hated people in San Francisco," he called Knoller "a liar," and he berated her for denying responsibility, for her ugly callousness, telling the defendant:

"You knew the dogs were dangerous. You knew that you could not control them, yet you took them out anyway and at some point, it was clear, someone was going to get hurt by those dogs."

Before Judge Warren's court, Hammer had asked Knoller to give Sharon Smith an apology; but Knoller just sat silent. The minutes ticked in the courtroom. For an instant, it seemed like all time had stopped. The silence was so deafening, but the fact was, Diane Alexis Whipple was gone, and nothing anyone could say or do would ever change that.

In her victim's statement, Sharon Smith told Knoller, "Even as Diane lay dying in the hospital, you began your lies. This has been a game to you. It's been one big legal game. This has not been a game for me."

But then, after the victim's statements were over, Judge Warren's tone suddenly changed, and he went on to say something new. Even though the judge hadn't believed a word of Knoller's testimony, even though he called her "despicable," there was one thing Knoller said that rang true with Judge Warren: Marjorie Knoller did not know, with *absolute certainty*, that her dog Bane would go out into the hallway and kill a human being on January 26, 2001.

That being said, Judge Warren ruled that the evidence presented in the trial against Noel and Knoller did not support such a harsh and rare verdict against Knoller. Judge Warren threw out the second-degree murder conviction on the grounds that the evidence did not show Knoller had acted with "malice aforethought." Shocking the courtroom and stunning the nation, he reduced Knoller's conviction to involuntary manslaughter. It was a crime for which she would serve only four years maximum. And like Noel, with the "good time" rule and her time already served, Knoller would be eligible for parole in just *fourteen months*.

Jim Hammer called the ruling "a travesty" and vowed he would appeal the decision, but then, upon reflection, Hammer, Hallinan, and everyone else on the team realized it would be no use. Judge Warren had gotten the last word. Perhaps he was thinking of his grandfather Chief

Justice Earl Warren, perhaps he was thinking about the case historically, realizing the verdict would have been overturned on appeal.

Outside the court, Hallinan would tell the press that "although it's not everything we wanted, these are two people who said they would never be punished for their behavior, and now they will see punishment, and that's some sense of justice." Still, Terence Hallinan debated making a request for a new trial, which he hoped would result in Marjorie Knoller receiving a life sentence. And in April 2003 California prosecutors asked a state appeals court to reinstate the second-degree murder conviction against Knoller. The California Attorney General's office, at the State Court of Appeals, said the judge in the case had erred by throwing out the murder conviction against the dog owner.

Meanwhile Robert Noel is serving the remainder of his four-year sentence for involuntary manslaughter in a state prison in Salem, Oregon. With good time served, Noel will be eligible for parole in 2003.

Ironically, another decision came down in the same time frame of Knoller's sentencing. It stated that former prison guard Jose Garcia was entitled to a new trial in Del Norte County; the judge based that decision on the "ineptitude of his attorneys," Robert Noel and Marjorie Knoller.

As for the dog-breeding ring, Dale Bretches continued to run his Dog O' War operation under a new name, contacting associates across the country and trying to extend his business around the world, reaching out to Great Britain, North Africa, and South America.

In Southern California, Carolyn Murphy would be charged with keeping unlicensed dogs and with running an illegal pet shop. The Mexican Mafia associate would be released on bail and would later plead guilty to lesser counts. Murphy paid a $300 fine and was placed on probation for thirty-six months. The whereabouts of two of Bane's offspring remain unknown, although investigators have tracked at least one Presa Canario to a Mexican drug cartel family.

After her arrest, Carolyn Murphy would later sell two offspring of Bane's to members of a legitimate animal rescue organization in Los Angeles, charging $400 apiece. One of the pups, Rubia, is a beautiful tan-colored dog living happily with her responsible owner in the San Fernando Valley.

The only person who seemed to be pleased by the overturned murder verdict was animal activist Ana Aureoles. She had been visiting Marjorie in jail, and perhaps because of her belief in animals, or of her tunnel vision, she believed in Marjorie's version of the events entirely. Marjorie had done a lot of pro bono work for the homeless, Knoller and Noel had also done pro bono work for people with AIDS, thus Ana felt personally connected to Marjorie, and she wanted Marjorie to go free. Ana felt for Diane Whipple, but also felt that Marjorie, Bane, and Hera were victims of Robert Noel.

Ana was devastated when Hera was put to death, even filing a police complaint against Animal Care and Control for being inhumane. After much begging and pleading, and under the veil of secrecy, the ashes of Hera were given to Ana, who took them to a Franciscan friar to be blessed.

Hera rests in a lonely pet cemetery, but continues to visit Ana in her dreams, where she and Bane play together in unison. Diane comes to Ana in dreams as well, giving Ana and dog lovers around the globe a wink and a smile.

As I wrote this book, I kept one thing in mind: Diane's will. It was her spirit that guided me through the horror I recounted, through the troublesome issue that this book would not be about her. During the months of my research on location, I couldn't understand why Sharon Smith refused to talk to me, why she shut down every friend of Diane's, both straight and gay, and did not let anyone tell me one thing about Diane Alexis.

But then I realized that in order to record the horror of what happened to this beautiful woman, maybe it was good that none of her people talked to me, none of her friends, none of her family, even though I beseeched Sharon Smith. Maybe I wasn't meant to know too much about her; it would have made things even more painful for me. But in the end, I still discovered important things about Diane Whipple: she loved Godiva chocolate; she had funny little nicknames, she called herself a Queen; she was bawdy; she once told Marjorie Knoller, "You better get control of your dogs!"

As for Robert Noel, whom I met with more times than I care to count, I can only say that each time, I felt like I was sitting down with the devil. He has absolutely no remorse, not one care about Diane Whipple, and I felt he was negative energy *incarnate*, as was his wife, Marjorie Knoller, whom I also sat down with. Fortunately, Marjorie Knoller is reliving the horror of the mauling every day, in her dreams and her day-dreams—so there is *some* retribution on this earth, even if it isn't in the form of a second-degree murder conviction.

The trial for Noel and Knoller cost taxpayers almost $1 million, and for that we have the convicted murderer Marjorie Knoller now serving a manslaughter sentence in a women's prison, doing *half of a four-year term*, the jury verdict having been overturned by Judge James Warren. Whatever his reasons, certainly a judge has the authority to change a verdict, but the judge's reversal perplexes me. There was plenty of opportunity during the trial for Judge Warren—even after all the evidence was presented—to intervene and remove the second-degree murder charge *before* the jury was given the chance to deliberate. I myself sat through the trial, and watched the blood, sweat, and tears. I held the shredded clothing of Diane Whipple, bloodstained and sealed in a clear plastic bag, and I felt the *jury of twelve* did the right thing. In my view, Knoller should have been sentenced to life without parole.

Perhaps readers will feel I digress too much when I write chapters about Paul "Cornfed" Schneider, the Hannibal Lecter of this story, but Schneider is the man who brought those animals to California, who had them sent to San Francisco, who masterminded the dog-breeding scheme . . . who single-handedly created a new demand for fierce "killer" dogs among the drug lords and gangbangers throughout the world. That's why I wrote about him—I think we need to see the chain of events that led up to this horrible death, this state of Bane and Hera entering the "red zone."

In terms of my painstaking efforts to tell the truth, and nothing but the truth, I wrote this book, as I write all my books, as a means of social commentary. As a good reporter following leads, I went to great lengths to make sure that every event recorded herein is accurate; I've read every public document, having collected *15,000 pages* of court transcripts, police files, depositions, unsealed documents, as well as hundreds of newspaper and Internet accounts. For the purposes of news reporting, and I do consider myself a journalist, certain events and dialogue in this book were re-created. I do this to give the reader the opportunity to be "in the moment" while reading a real-life tale.

I have one last theory I'd like to talk about, which I call the "Death Zone." In dealing with so many murder victims over the years, and in telling their stories in such intricate detail, I've discovered that each of us gets a psychic signal about our own demise, even though we can't seem to read it. We see that on the news all the time, how a mom will say she "had a feeling" before learning that her child was killed. This "feeling" is something Diane Whipple was getting in the weeks leading to her death; she verbalized her fears to many. From the time Bane bit her on the wrist, in those six weeks of terror, Diane Whipple knew, on some strange level, that her death would be inextricably bound to "those dogs."

Her death makes me think about the relationship of man and animal, the fact that we coexist on the earth, that we depend on each other for survival. Perhaps the death of Diane Alexis Whipple will force humans to accept our role as caretakers of animals, both of domestic pets and of animals in the wild. That would be the best result of this horrible tragedy—that stray animals will no longer be orphans, and that animals roaming free on the planet will be safeguarded from human overpopulation.

ACKNOWLEDGMENTS

Thank you to the people of San Francisco and the Bay Area, for their love and support. Listed here are those persons *and* entities whose courage, inspiration, insight, and help guided me through this battle. In alphabetical order:

Actors and Others for Animals; David Adamson, Roy Alverado; Sergeant Hank Akin; American Bureau of Prisons; Roger Armstrong, Esq.; Christine Arrigale; the Associated Press; Ana Aureoles; Lynn Balthazor; Cate Baker; David Barry.

SFPD Inspector Michael Becker; Val Belben; Diane Benjamin; Paul Berman; Matthew Bialer; Lisa Bianco; Thomas Bianco; David Blatte, Esq.; Sally Matluck Boisseau; Melanie A. Bonvicino; Claire Booth; Gwyneth J. Borden; Senator Barbara Boxer; Bennett Braverman, Esq.; Joan Brelsford; Captain Jeff Briddle; Kat Brown; the Office of Mayor Willie Brown; Dr. Rick and Mrs. Lilliane Bruns; Buena Vista Television; Bureau of Alcohol, Tobacco & Firearms; Pamela Butler, Scott Butler.

California Department of Corrections, Special Service Unit; California Department of Justice, Bureau of Investigation; California Health Services Department; California Highway Patrol; Page Calvert; Sarah Campbell; Louis Caneles; Cheryl Capitani; Maria Caracciolo; Michael

Cardoza, Esq.; Carlos Castaneda; Kyran Cassidy, Esq.; Mario Careaga; SFPD Inspector Dominick Celeya; Paulette Chernoff; "Chicago"; Kyle Christopherson; Maria Cina; Marcia Clark, Esq.; Coalition for the Homeless; Assistant U.S. Attorney Jeff Cole; Contra Costa County Animal Services Department; P. J. Corkery; Maria Costantinou; Daisy Coumbs; Janet Coumbs; Creative Artists Agency.

Rob Cummings; Chief Assistant DA Paul Cummins; Heidi Dahmen; D.K. Dang; SFPD Inspector Rich Daniele; David At La Belle; Simone de Beauvoir; Special Agent Noaz Deshe; William Dehaven, Ph.D.; Jim Delaney; Del Norte County District Attorney's Office; Del Norte County Sheriff's Department; SFPD Officer John Denny; Chris DeRose; Elon Dershowitz.

Deuel Vocational Institute; Joan Didion; Bing Dilts, D.V.M.; Dog Lovers of the World; Dog Psychology Center of L.A.; SPCA's Jean Donaldson; Jack Donahue; Drug Enforcement Administration, U.S. Department of Justice; Brett Dunham; Earth Communications Office; Martha Escobar; Estrada Investigations; Esther.

Federal Bureau of Investigation; the Federal Bureau of Prisons; Senator Dianne Feinstein; Executive Editor Henry Ferris; Warden Claude Finn; Mary Karen Fippinger; Special Agent Everett Fischer; Senior Assistant Louis Flores; Fox News Network; Carl Friedman; Pat Friedman; Liz Frillici; the Fugitive Information Line; Ani Gafgafyan; Robert Gajraj, M.D.; Alison Garbutt; Ann Getty and Associates; "Emily" Getty; Give-a-Dog-a-Bone; Karen Glass; Golden Gate University School of Law; Stan Goldman; Lydia Gomez; Michael A. Gordon; Anna Gorman; the staff at Got U Productions.

The San Francisco Grand Jury; Greenpeace; Alan Grigoletto; ADA Kimberley Guilfoyle-Newsom; Captain Vicky Guldbech; June Guterman; CNN's Thelma Gutierrez; Joey H.; Assistant U.S. Attorney Melinda Haag; District Attorney Terence Hallinan; the Hall of Justice security staff, San Francisco.

ADA James O'Donnell Hammer; Amy Hammond; Joe Harrington; Special Agent Devan Hawkes; Al Hayes; CDC Spokesman Russ Heimerich; Ernest Hemingway; U.S. District Judge Thelton Henderson; Sheriff Mike Hennessy; Suzanne Herel; SFPD Sergeant Bill Herndon; Steve Heslov, M.D.; Julie Hill.

Bruce Hotchkiss, Esq.; Inglewood Deputy DA Lisa Houle, Pat Huffman; the Humane Society of the United States; SFPD Lieutenant Henry Hunter; Special Agent Supervisor David Ikeda; Inglewood Police Department.

Holly Jacobs; Rear Admiral Ashton Blair Jones Jr.; Janet Blair Jones; Mary K. Jones; Mary Nell Jones; Aphrodite K.; Anthony K.; Ianthe K.; Jodie K.; Thalia K.; Virginia K.; Dr. Eliot Katz; Lisa Katz; Dean Peter Keane; ADA Paul Kelly; KGO-TV; Steve Kindred; Gregory King; Janis Ellen King; Nancy Kohatsu; James Kolber; KPIX-TV; Matt Kresnousky; KRON-TV; KTTV-FOX.

Bailiff Joe Langill; Last Chance for Animals; Katherine Leighton; David LeMaster; Candace Levinson, M.D.; Meriwether Lewis; the legacy of Lewis and Clark.

David K. Li; Detective Mark Lillienfeld; Randall Lockwood, Ph.D.; Stephen Loffredo; Los Angeles County Sheriff's Department, Homicide Bureau; Los Angeles Police Department Arrest Information; Los Angeles Police Department Gang Hotline; Los Angeles Superior Court; Corey Lyons; Niccolo Machiavelli; Mark MacNamara; P.I. Manatt, Phelps & Phillips, LLP; David Mann; Robert Mann; Marshals Service, Central District of California; Chance Martin; Lieutenant Art Martinez; Special Agent Bob Martinez; Matier & Ross; Caroline McCarthy-Kunitz; Peggy McCarthy.

Detective Mike McCravey; Manny Medrano; Mary Melvin; Captain Frank Merriman; Thomas Mesereau, Esq.; the Meth Hotline; Assembly-woman Carole Midgin; "Dog Whisperer" Cesar Millan; Chris Miller; "Henry Miller"; Jim Miller; Gina Minion; Special Agent Robert Moore; Gery and Gloria Moret; Rob Morse; U.S. Attorney Robert Muller III; Sergeant Inspector Stephen Murphy; Special Agent Khalil Nammour.

National Audubon Society; National Center for Lesbian Rights; Emily Negley; Christiani Nevis; Gavin Newsom; Hillary Newsom; Nikka; Norma Jean.

Office of the District Attorney, Los Angeles County, Juvenile Criminal Cases; Office of the San Francisco District Attorney; Palm Beach County Sheriff's Office; DAI Dave Parenti; Thomas Patrick, Esq.; Allan Paul; Matthew B. Pavone, Esq.

Pelican Bay State Prison; P.I. Lynn Peterson; Prisons Bureau of

Washington, D.C.; Angelo Prongos; John Quinones; Julie Ramirez; ADA Murlene Randle; Reuters; Janet Rice; Cheryl Rich; Mary Anne Richter; ADA Mike Riese; Rocket Science Associates; Harriet Robinson; Sheila Rosenbaum; Sharyn Rosenblum; Bruce Ross; Rottweiler-Rescue; "Rubia," Nedra Ruiz, Esq.

Patricia Saad; St. Mary's College; Special Agent Roberto Salinas; DAI Carlos Sanchez; San Diego Imperial Regional Narcotic Information Network; San Francisco Chamber of Commerce; San Francisco Department of Animal Care and Control; San Francisco Police, General Works Department; Santa Rosa Police Department; Judy Scheer; Craige Schuldice, Esq.; Sandra Schulman; Daniel Schumaker.

Bonnie Seets; Doug Seets; Angela Shapiro; Gary Shapiro; Guy Shalem; Deputy Sheriff Mike Shine; the Sierra Club; Judith Silverman-Orr; Chris Sloane; Brad Small, Esq.; Special Agent Daniel L. Smith; former FBI Agent Richard W. Smith; Tonya Snow; Society for the Prevention of Cruelty to Animals; Thea Sommer; Andy Spingler; Steve Squire, Esq.

State Bar of California; State of California Court of Appeals, First Appellate District; Gertrude Stein; Rochelle Steinhaus; Investigator Robert Stemme; Dr. Boyd Stephens; Serene Sterba; Debbie Stier; Brett Stimely.

Bill Stottler; Chance "Moo" Stottler; Jim Stringer; Suzanne Stuart; Sully's Crew; Jonathan Swift; Lieutenant. Rawland Swift; David Tenzer; Valerie Testa; Trident Media Group; Lieutenant Robert Trujillo; Mel Tublin, Esq.; U.S. Department of Justice, Sacramento Intelligence Unit.

U.S. Lacrosse "The Creator's Game"; Lili Ungar; Jaxon Van Derbeken; Ron Vandor; Elizabeth Vargas; Howard Varinsky and Associates; Sergeant Rey Verdugo; Pamela Wallmann; Joseph Wambaugh; Laura Wander; Superior Court Judge James Lee Warren; Diane Watchinski; Sean Webby; Jef Wheeler.

Diane Alexis Whipple.

Wild Eyes Productions; The Wildlife Care Center; The Powers That Be at William Morrow; Oprah Winfrey; Andy Winston; Witnesses for the People; Senior Special Agent Steve Woldwend; Evan Wright; Linda Yee and Lieutenant Michael Yoell.

ENDNOTE

In California, there were two important laws passed as a direct result of the Diane Whipple mauling. Governor Gray Davis signed a bill that closes a loophole in a current law related to dog mauling. Assembly-woman Carole Midgen, D-San Francisco, passed a bill that holds any caretaker of an animal (not just the owner) to be criminally responsible for its actions. Midgen also passed legislation that gives gay partners the right to file a wrongful death suit.

Hopefully, more laws will be passed and bills will be presented throughout the nation for the safety of humans and animals alike. We all share this planet, but it's up to humans to protect our animals, both in our neighborhoods and out in the wild.

As a result of writing this book, I have established a trust for a non-profit organization called The Wildlife Care Center. The organization operates out of Fort Lauderdale, and the group does extensive work to protect the wildlife in the Everglades. I think of the Everglades as our own Amazon. I hope everyone will realize our protection of animals in the Everglades extends worldwide. If you would like to contribute in any way, contact them at www.wildcare.org.

And please, please, I beg you to report serious animal bites and/or suspiciously abused or "fighting" animals to your local SPCA or ACC offices, because often abused or vicious animals are a link to abused children, drug rings, and other criminal activities, and reports help our hardworking law enforcement people as well. If you don't know who to call, contact Last Chance for Animals at www.LCA.org.

We all need to do our part to make this world a safer, unified planet. Helping our animals and wildlife means a lot. I ask with a sincere heart, that you take me up on it. Everyone can do something. Anything, to save our animals.